BRIDGE

The Basic Elements of Play and Defence

G.C.H. Fox, former bridge correspondent to the *Daily Telegraph* for 34 years, and for many years Chief Training Officer of the English Bridge Union Teachers' Association and now Chief Consultant, writes with clarity and precision about the fundamentals of play and defence.

Virtually all the basic situations in play and defence are covered at length and illustrated with example hands where the correct line is explained in easy to follow detail.

As Rixi Markus said in the *Evening Standard* when reviewing an earlier book, 'Mr Fox is an experienced teacher who has quite clearly experienced at first hand hundreds of thousands of people who play a little bridge and would like to improve their game.' This is *the* book to achieve that objective.

G.C.H. Fox has also written

Modern Bidding Systems in Bridge
Bridge: Standard Bidding
Begin Bridge
The Daily Telegraph Book of Bridge
Master Play: The Best of International Bridge
The Daily Telegraph Bridge Quiz
The Second Daily Telegraph Bridge Quiz
Bridge: The Elements of Play
Bridge: The Elements of Defence
The Second Daily Telegraph Book of Bridge

G.C.H. FOX

BRIDGE:
The Basic Elements of
Play and Defence

ROBERT HALE • LONDON

© G.C.H. Fox 1980, 1984 and 1994
Originally published separately as
Bridge: The Elements of Play 1980,
and in paperback 1990, and
Bridge: The Elements of Defence 1984

This edition first published in Great Britain 1994

ISBN-0-7090-5466-1

Robert Hale Limited
Clerkenwell House
Clerkenwell Green
London EC1R 0HT

2 4 6 8 10 9 7 5 3 1

Printed and bound in Malta by
Interprint Limited

CONTENTS

PLAY

Preface

Contents

DEFENCE

Contents

PREFACE

The first part of this book is concerned wih declarer play. It is divided into three sections. The first is introductory and covers the basic principles, the second deals with play in no-trumps and the third suit contracts. I have given more than one example of each subject. This is important as with more than one hand containing a similar point it is much easier to recognize the situation when it occurs in play.

The book is confined to standard basic situations and the type of hand which occurs several times in a session. There are no squeezes or exotic end-plays. There are plenty of books describing all these types of play but these situations do not occur very often, and are only of interest to the expert player or keen analyst.

Most players can make contracts when they hold all the high cards and all that is needed is to play off winners. The difference between the winning player and the loser is the ability to make the contracts that are not lay-down but require careful timing and planning. It is most important to know why a certain line of play is correct; you cannot achieve success by merely following certain rules. For example, beginners are told when playing no-trumps to go for the longest suit first. That is sound advice, but only if you add 'providing the suit is long enough'. It is sometimes advantageous to play a short suit before tackling the long one. It is important to recognize the situations when this is necessary. In other words, the reason. If you can learn how to play the borderline contracts then you can afford to bid more boldly and will get more enjoyment from the game.

The second part is devoted to defence. It is generally accepted that defence is the most difficult part of the game. Declarer has the advantage of being able to play both hands, his own and dummy's. The defenders are not so privileged and it is essential that they co-operate hence the need for standard types of leads and signals. Another factor that contributes to the difficulty in defence is the effect of holding bad hands with a dearth of aces and kings. Some players get bored and despondent and lose concentration. Their attitude is 'let's get it over quickly and maybe one day I will pick up a decent hand'. But much can be done with poor cards correctly handled, and this part of the book aims at showing how defence can become both successful and a pleasure.

The first chapter deals with the fundamental basics. Most books and some teachers lay down rules such as Third Player Plays High, Second Player Plays Low, Lead Through Strength up to Weakness, Cover an Honour with an Honour, etc. These so-called rules are presented as if they were government regulations. No explanation is given and whilst there is a certain amount of logic behind them they are useless unless you understand the reasoning. I personally prefer to refer to them as guiding principles. Rules to me apply to the rules of the game such as following suit when able, etc. When discussing these guiding principles I have endeavoured to explain the reason in every case. This I consider to be most important for if you are an ambulating parrot you will never be a good bridge player.

The final chapter deals with more advanced subjects such as Counting Declarer's Points, Distribution, Suit Preference Signals, Deception and Timing. The matters discussed and explained in this part of the book should be easily understood if the earlier chapters are assimilated.

G.C.H. Fox
1994

PART ONE

Introductory

When you are declarer and the dummy hand has been put down it is essential that you make a plan. After all, if you have contracted to make a certain number of tricks, either with a suit as trumps or in no-trumps, it is common sense that you should take stock of your resources and see whether the number of tricks required are readily available or whether some measures may be needed to find some more. It is logical that this should be done at the outset, as soon as dummy is exposed, as this is the only time that you have a full complement of cards in each hand. As play proceeds the number of cards you hold diminishes and if you have a bright scheme half way through the hand it may well be that you do not have the wherewithal to carry it out owing to some hasty play earlier.

1. Top Tricks

The first thing you should do is to count your Top Tricks. That is to say, count up the number of tricks you can win without losing the lead. Remember that when you play a card from one hand you have to follow suit from the other. This may appear an unnecessarily obvious piece of advice but beginners often miscount tricks with a combination such as:

A Q 3   opposite   K J 10

Having all the top cards they are apt to count on making

four or five tricks, whereas the maximum you can hope for is 'three. It must be stressed that top tricks refer to those tricks that can be won without giving up the lead.

Consider these two hands:

♠ A Q 4	♠ K J 2
♡ K J 10 9	♡ Q 8 5
◇ A 7 2	◇ K Q J 4
♣ 8 7 6	♣ A 3 2

There are eight top tricks: three in spades, four in diamonds and one in clubs. Admittedly it is possible to make tricks in hearts but not until the ace has been forced out. This involves losing the lead and, as will be explained later, you cannot always afford to lose the lead, especially when playing in no-trumps.

It frequently happens that the total of top tricks is short of the number you require and it is necessary to devise means of finding more. In no-trumps particularly the answer will be to establish additional tricks in a long suit. This will involve forcing out one or more top cards and, in so doing, giving away the lead.

2. Playing Tricks

To ascertain how many Playing Tricks you can expect from a suit the simple way is to take the hand with the greater number of cards in a suit and deduct one trick for each major card that is missing. For example:

(a) (You) ◇ K Q J 10 6   opposite   (Dummy) ◇ 9 5 2

The maximum number of tricks that you could expect to make is five. As the ace is missing, but no other high card, you do expect to win four.

(b) (You) ◇ Q J 10 8 6   opposite   (Dummy) ◇ K 4 3

Here you are missing two top cards (ace and king) but dummy has the king so, again, you should take four tricks.

(c) (You) ◊ Q J 10 8 6   opposite   (Dummy) ◊ 9 7 4

Here you are missing both ace and king. Therefore you must deduct two tricks and reckon to make three tricks.

Establishing tricks often involves taking a finesse.

3. Establishing Tricks: The Finesse

A finesse is an attempt to win a trick with a card that is not the highest and not necessarily certain to win, in the hope that the card or cards that are higher are favourably placed.

Consider this simple example:

	North	
	A Q	
West		*East*
	South	
	4 3	

To try and win two tricks in the suit you lead a low card towards the ace – queen. Assuming West plays low you play the queen. If West holds the king, your queen will win the trick. But if East holds the king you will lose. The finesse is an even money chance. Of course, you could have made certain of the trick by playing the ace, but it is highly unlikely that the king would have fallen on it and you would have lost the second round. By playing the queen you had a 50–50 chance of winning two tricks.

Here are some further examples of a finesse:

(a)	(b)	(c)
A Q 10	A J 10	K J 10
6 4 3	7 3 2	6 3 2

In (a) you lead a low card and, assuming West plays low, you play the ten. If you are lucky and West has king and jack it will be possible to make all three tricks. After the ten wins and providing you can get the lead back to your hand you can play another low card and finesse the queen. The opposing honours may well be divided and the ten may be taken with the king, leaving the ace and queen as winners. Or the ten may lose to the jack, in which case you can finesse the queen the next time.

In (b) you cannot expect to take all three tricks, but providing the missing honours are divided you will take two. You first lead a low card and, assuming West plays low, you play the ten. This will probably be taken by the king or queen. Later you lead again from your hand and play the jack, a simple finesse against the remaining honour.

In (c) if you hope to make two tricks you regard the queen as the important card. The ace is always going to win, but the queen can be captured providing it is on your left. So you lead a low card and if West plays low you put on the ten. If West has the queen your ten will either win or draw the ace from your right.

Often you may lead a high card from your hand to trap an opposing honour. For example:

(Dummy)　　A 10 9 7 6

(You)　　　Q J 8

Aiming to make all five tricks you lead the queen, hoping the king is on your left. If the king is played you take it with your ace and make all the tricks. If the queen wins you continue by leading the jack.

(Dummy)　　K 10 9 8 3

(You)　　　J 4 2

To make four tricks you must hope to capture the queen. Lead the jack and if West plays the queen cover with the king, but otherwise play low from dummy.

(Dummy)   A 10 9 6 2

(You)   Q 8 3

Here you are missing two honours (king and jack). Your best chance is to hope they are in different hands. Lead the eight and if West plays low, play low from dummy. If East wins with the jack you later lead the queen and finesse against the king.

It is essential that you have supporting cards. For example:

(Dummy)   A 6 3

(You)   Q 8 5

It is pointless to lead the queen towards the ace. Assume West covers with the king, what have you left? The correct play is to lead a low card towards the queen, hoping that the king is on your right. You should not lead a high card, intending to finesse, unless you are prepared for it to be covered.

PART TWO

The Play of the Hand in No-Trumps

Many players find the play of a hand in no-trumps more difficult than in suit contracts. This is very understandable as you have less control over the hand. There are also fewer ways in which you can win tricks.

4. Playing out with a Solid Suit: High Cards from Short Hand

The easiest hands are those where you have a nice solid suit to play and it is merely a question of playing out winners. The only point that requires a little care is not to get the lead into the wrong hand.

Here is a simple example:

Dealer South. North-South vulnerable.

```
                    ♠ Q 10 9
                    ♡ K Q 2
                    ◊ 8 2
                    ♣ K Q J 9 8
    ♠ A 7 6                         ♠ 8 5 3 2
    ♡ 8 3                           ♡ J 9 6 4
    ◊ K Q J 10 9                    ◊ 7 6 5
    ♣ 5 4 2                         ♣ 6 3
                    ♠ K J 4
                    ♡ A 10 7 5
                    ◊ A 4 3
                    ♣ A 10 7
```

South	West	North	East
1 NT	Pass	3 NT	Pass
(16-18 Points)			
Pass	Pass		

West led ◊ K, the top of his sequence, with the object of setting up his longest suit and hoping to regain the lead with his ace of spades. It does not matter whether South takes the trick now or later as he is in the fortunate position of having enough top tricks to make his contract. There are five sure winners in clubs and three more in hearts. After winning with the ace of diamonds South should play ♣ A and follow with ♣ 10 and ♣ 7.

The lead is now in dummy and the remaining two high clubs are played off. On these South discards ◊ 4 and ◊ 3. He next plays ♡ K, ♡ Q and ♡ 2. It is important to play the high cards from the table, for if the jack of hearts were to appear on these three leads an extra trick would be made with the ten of hearts. This could happen if East, possibly disinterested with his poor hand, discarded a heart on the clubs. As it is, providing East does not part with a heart, South is likely to make only nine tricks.

When playing out a solid suit a simple way of ensuring that you do not get the lead in the wrong hand is to play first the high card from the short hand.

One further point about this hand. When explaining top tricks in the introductory chapter it was pointed out that these are only tricks that you could win without losing the lead. It might be thought that tricks might be won in spades, but this would involve giving up the lead and the defenders would then lead out a number of winning diamonds.

In the following South has not a completely solid suit but the basic principles set out in the previous example hold good.

Dealer South. Love all.

```
                    ♠ A K 8 4
                    ♡ 9 6 5
                    ◊ A 9 5
                    ♣ Q 10 6
    ♠ 6 5 3                          ♠ J 10 7 2
    ♡ Q J 7 4 2                      ♡ K 3
    ◊ 4 2                            ◊ J 10 6
    ♣ A 7 2                          ♣ 8 5 4 3
                    ♠ Q 9
                    ♡ A 10 8
                    ◊ K Q 8 7 3
                    ♣ K J 9
```

South	West	North	East
1 ◊	Pass	1 ♠	Pass
1 NT	Pass	3 NT	Pass
Pass	Pass		

Playing a strong opening no-trump (16-18 points) South's rebid showed about 13-15 points.

West leads his fourth highest heart, the four, on which East plays the king. South decides to keep his ace a little longer and plays ♡ 8. East returns ♡ 3 and South eventually wins with ♡ A on the third round.

It might seem puzzling that South was so reluctant to part with his ace, but, as will be explained later, this is often advisable when playing in no-trumps.

Counting the top tricks there are only seven which means that two have to be found. It is too dangerous to play a club as West may hold the ace and be able to play out more hearts. But there is a good chance of making extra tricks from diamonds. With eight cards between the two hands there are only five left for the opponents. If these are divided three and two South would be able to make two more tricks with low cards as there would be no more outstanding.

To trick four South leads ◊ 3 to ◊ A and returns ◊ 5 to ◊ Q. He next plays ◊ K on which West discards ♣ 7. Eleven diamonds have been played so the remaining two in South's hand are winners. This brings the total to six and three tricks can be made from spades. However, care is needed, and ♠ Q must be led, followed by ♠ 9 over to dummy's ♠ K and ♠ A. Again, playing the high card from the short hand.

I am often asked whether it is necessary to remember every card that has been played and to count every suit. An expert probably does, but it is only really necessary to count suits that are important to you. In this case the diamonds were important, but you do not always need to remember all the cards. Once each opponent has followed suit to the first two rounds, the rest must be winners when you play the queen.

5. Counting Top Tricks: Establishing Extra Tricks

More often than not the number of top tricks will be insufficient and it will be necessary to establish additional tricks. This will involve giving up the lead and you can afford to lose the lead if you are certain of being able to get it back. This depends largely upon the amount of control you have over the opponents' suit. In other words, the possession of 'stoppers', cards that will prevent them from playing off numerous winners.

Here is a simple example:

Dealer South. Love all.

```
              ♠ K 4
              ♡ 9 7 6
              ◇ J 6 3
              ♣ K J 10 8 4
♠ Q J 10 8 5 3                    ♠ 9 7 2
♡ J 5                             ♡ Q 10 4 2
◇ 8 7                             ◇ K Q 10 2
♣ A 7 6                          ♣ 5 3
              ♠ A 6
              ♡ A K 8 3
              ◇ A 9 5 4
              ♣ Q 9 2
```

South	West	North	East
1 ♡	1 ♠	2 ♣	Pass
3 NT	Pass	Pass	Pass

West leads ♠ Q, top of his sequence, and South can count only five top tricks, two in spades, two in hearts and one in diamonds. Beginners are often tempted to play off their sure winners and say "Where do we go from here?" To do so is bad play and might be likened to the entry one sometimes sees in a horse racing form book – "Fast for five furlongs – faded". Needing to find four more tricks you should look for your long suit, in this case clubs. Between you you hold all the top cards except for the ace, so out of a possible five tricks you should expect to take four.

You win the opening lead in your hand with ♠ A and play ♣ Q. If the ace does not appear you continue the suit until the ace is out. You have given away the lead but you still have stoppers in each suit and whatever the opponents play you can regain the lead. They are likely to lead a spade to clear their best suit. This you take with ♠ K and play the remaining clubs and complete your nine tricks with ♡ A K and ◊ A.

You may have noticed that it was possible to win the first trick either in dummy with ♠ K or your own hand with ♠ A. It was important to take in the closed hand. Otherwise if ♣ A were held up until the third round you would be unable to get the lead over to dummy to enjoy the remaining clubs. The high spade is what is termed an entry card, that is to say, a card capable of winning a trick to enable you to play from the dummy hand. More about entries will be explained later.

The next example is less straightforward because there is a choice between two suits to establish.

Dealer South. Game all.

```
              ♠ K 4
              ♡ Q 6 2
              ◊ 7 4 3
              ♣ A K J 4 2
♠ Q 10 8 7 6                    ♠ J 9 5 2
♡ A 7 3                         ♡ 8 5 4
◊ J 8 5                         ◊ Q 10 9
♣ 8 7                          ♣ Q 6 3
              ♠ A 3
              ♡ K J 10 9
              ◊ A K 6 2
              ♣ 10 9 5
```

South	West	North	East
1 ♡	Pass	2 ♣	Pass
2 NT	Pass	3 ♡	Pass
3 NT	Pass	Pass	Pass

South's rebid of Two No-Trump showed 15-16 points and North's Three Hearts was forcing and offered the

(repeated for convenience)

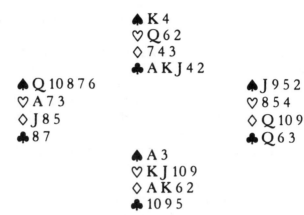

```
              ♠ K 4
              ♡ Q 6 2
              ◊ 7 4 3
              ♣ A K J 4 2
♠ Q 10 8 7 6                    ♠ J 9 5 2
♡ A 7 3                         ♡ 8 5 4
◊ J 8 5                         ◊ Q 10 9
♣ 8 7                          ♣ Q 6 3
              ♠ A 3
              ♡ K J 10 9
              ◊ A K 6 2
              ♣ 10 9 5
```

choice between Four Hearts and Three No-Trump, depending upon whether the opening bid was based on a four or five card suit.

West leads ♠ 7. There are exactly six top tricks (♠ A K, ◊ A K, ♣ A K) and three or more are needed. You can afford to lose the lead once as there will still be one high spade after the first trick. Beginners are usually told to go for their longest suit and such advice is basically sound. But it might cause you to seek your extra tricks in clubs.

Suppose you take the first trick in your hand and lead ♣ 10, playing low from dummy, and thus finessing against the queen. East wins and returns a spade. You now have four tricks in clubs, two diamonds and two spades (taken), a total of eight. Needing one more you play a heart but West wins with ♡ A and has three more winning spades.

When you chose to establish clubs you forgot that you had counted the ace and king among your top winners. Therefore, to make three more from that suit meant that you had to capture the queen. When that did not happen you had only two extra tricks and the spade return removed your last stopper. The correct play is to attack hearts at trick two. You have a solid combination apart from the ace and must win three tricks which is what you require.

The problem on the next hand is, again, to select the suit that will produce the required number of extra tricks.

Dealer North. East-West vulnerable.

```
                    ♠ K 7
                    ♡ A 2
                    ◇ Q J 10 9 7
                    ♣ K Q 10 7
♠ Q J 10 9 8                        ♠ 6 5 4 3
♡ 9 8 7                             ♡ J 10 4 3
◇ A 4                               ◇ 6 3 2
♣ A 5 2                             ♣ 6 3
                    ♠ A 2
                    ♡ K Q 6 5
                    ◇ K 8 5
                    ♣ J 9 8 4
```

South	West	North	East
		1 ◇	Pass
1 ♡	1 ♠	2 ♣	Pass
3 NT	Pass	Pass	Pass

West leads ♠ Q which you can win in either hand. It does not matter. You have five top tricks and need four more. You have two suits with a combined total of eight cards in each, missing only the ace. But the diamonds will provide you with four tricks and the clubs with only three. Therefore, immediately set out to drive out ◇ A. West wins and returns a spade, knocking out your last stopper. You play off your remaining diamonds and, needing three tricks from hearts, play first ♡ A and follow with ♡ 2 to your ♡ K and ♡ Q, the high card first from the short hand. You have now made your contract. You will not make any trick in clubs for as soon as you play the suit West regains the lead and makes the rest of his spades.

6. Simple 'Hold Up' Plays: Keeping Control

There are two things which, quite understandably, "go against the grain" for beginners. One is playing a card that is certain to be taken by the other side. The other is to decline to take a trick when you hold a card that could win. Examples of the former were given in Section 5.

The necessity for refusing to take a trick arises when you are likely to concede the lead when you establish your long suit but no longer have any stopper or control in the enemy suit.

Consider this example:

Dealer South. East-West vul.

```
                    ♠ 10 4
                    ♡ A K 3
                    ◇ K 8 2
                    ♣ Q J 10 8 6
   ♠ K Q J 9 8                      ♠ 7 5 2
   ♡ J 10 8                         ♡ 7 6 4 2
   ◇ 9 3                            ◇ J 10 7 4
   ♣ 7 5 4                          ♣ A 3
                    ♠ A 6 3
                    ♡ Q 9 5
                    ◇ A Q 6 5
                    ♣ K 9 2
```

South	West	North	East
1 ◇	Pass	2 ♣	Pass
2 NT	Pass	3 NT	Pass
Pass	Pass	–	–

West leads ♠ K. Counting your top tricks you can see seven (♠ A, ♡ A K Q, ◇ A K Q). If the diamonds are evenly divided your fourth one would win, but that would still leave you a trick short. To make your contract it will be necessary to give up the lead and if you no longer hold the ace of spades you may lose several tricks in that suit.

You must hold up your ace as long as possible which means that you must allow your opponent to win the first two tricks with the king and queen. When you finally part with your ace you must attack the clubs. East takes the second round with his ace but it unable to return his partner's suit. If he held a spade at this point it would mean that each defender held four cards and you would only lose three. As it is, whatever East returns you can win and the rest of the tricks are yours. Had you taken the first or second round with the ace, East, when in with club ace, would have returned a spade and you would have lost four tricks in spades plus a club.

Suppose that West held the ace of clubs. In that case if he also started with five spades you would go down through no fault of yours. Just bad luck. But there was good reason to think that the ace of clubs was with East. With a five card spade suit headed by king, queen, jack plus the ace of clubs West would probably have overcalled with One Spade.

In the next example you can be reasonably sure which opponent will get in and the contract is almost certain to succeed.

Dealer South. Love all.

```
                    ♠ A 9 3
                    ♡ Q 9 7
                    ◊ 8 5
                    ♣ A Q 10 8 2
    ♠ J 6 5 2                       ♠ Q 10 8 4
    ♡ 5 4                           ♡ J 10 8 2
    ◊ K Q 10 9 3                    ◊ J 4 2
    ♣ 7 6                           ♣ K 3
                    ♠ K 7
                    ♡ A K 6 3
                    ◊ A 7 6
                    ♣ J 9 5 4
```

(repeated for convenience)

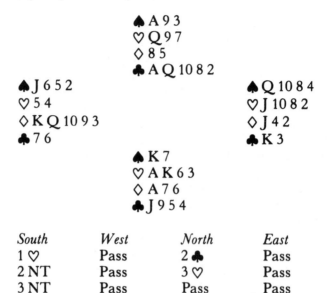

South	West	North	East
1 ♡	Pass	2 ♣	Pass
2 NT	Pass	3 ♡	Pass
3 NT	Pass	Pass	Pass

West led ◊ K on which East correctly played ◊ J. The opening lead was likely to be from a suit headed by K, Q, 10 and the play of the jack clarified the situation for his partner, who could safely continue if he remained on lead.

Again, South can see seven top tricks with a possible eighth in hearts, but to make the contract it will be necessary to establish the clubs. Once he has parted with his ace of diamonds, South no longer has control over the suit. Therefore, as in the previous hand, the ace of diamonds must be kept back until the third round. In all probability the remaining two diamonds are with West and he can only play them if he gets the lead by winning a trick. In the present case he has no chance, for if he holds the king of clubs it will be captured by the ace.

After winning with ◊ A South leads ♣ J and finesses, playing ♣ 2 from dummy when West plays low. East wins with ♣ K but due to the hold up of the ace of diamonds is unable to return his partner's original lead, and declarer takes all the remaining tricks, making his contract with one overtrick.

The last two examples have illustrated the need to hold up when you only possess one stopper in the opponents' suit. It might appear unnecessary if you have two sure tricks in the suit led, but this is not the case, especially if it is going to involve losing the lead twice before your own best suit is established.

Consider this hand:

Dealer South. North-South vul.

```
                    ♠ Q 9 8
                    ♡ A 8 7
                    ◇ K 9 4
                    ♣ Q 10 9 4
♠ 10 4                              ♠ J 7 6 5 3
♡ Q 10 6 5 4                        ♡ J 2
◇ 10 5 2                            ◇ J 7 6 3
♣ K 3 2                            ♣ A 5
                    ♠ A K 2
                    ♡ K 9 3
                    ◇ A Q 8
                    ♣ J 8 7 6
```

South	*West*	*North*	*East*
1 NT	Pass	3 NT	Pass
(16-18)			
Pass	Pass		

West leads ♡ 5. There are eight top tricks and at least one more can be obtained from clubs after the ace and king have been forced out. This will involve losing the lead twice and there is a danger that the opponents will set up their hearts before you can set up your clubs.

Suppose you play low from the table and take ♡ J with ♡ K. You lead ♣ 6, West plays ♣ 2, dummy ♣ 9 and East ♣ A. East returns ♡ 2 and West plays ♡ 10. Feeling a trifle

(*repeated for convenience*)

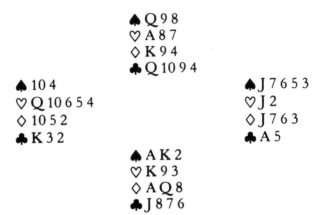

worried you hold up. But it is too late. West clears his suit and later regains the lead with the king of clubs and you lose in all three hearts and two clubs.

Consider the position more carefully. You are only in danger if West started with a five card suit, in which case East will hold only two. If you allow his ♡ J to win the first trick he will duly return ♡ 2 which you win with ♡ K. If East wins the first lead of clubs he cannot return a heart. He can only return another suit and you are now in control. You lead another club, won by West who clears his suit but you take the rest for an overtrick.

West could have taken the first club lead and cleared his suit but then he would not have had any card of entry for his hearts. Had West held both ace and king of clubs together with his five hearts you would be down, but that would be unavoidable.

In the next hand South might have got away with his mistake had his right hand opponent not played well.

Dealer South. Game all.

```
                    ♠ 8 6 3
                    ♡ A 6 2
                    ◇ J 10 9 8 3
                    ♣ A K
♠ J 10 5 4                          ♠ 9 7 2
♡ Q 10 9 8 5                        ♡ J 7
◇ K 5                              ◇ A 4 2
♣ 7 6                              ♣ J 10 8 5 2
                    ♠ A K Q
                    ♡ K 4 3
                    ◇ Q 7 6
                    ♣ Q 9 4 3
```

South	West	North	East
1 NT	Pass	3 NT	Pass
(16-18)			
Pass	Pass		

Wets led ♡ 10, the top of his inside sequence and South played ♡ A from the table, East unblocking with ♡ J. Needing to set up extra tricks in diamonds South led ◇ 3 from dummy and East put up ◇ A and returned ♡ 7. Although South held up his king, West was able to establish his suit and regain the lead with ◇ K. Had East followed the precept that second player plays low the contract would have succeeded. West wins with ◇ K and clears his hearts but when East gets in with ◇ A he has no heart left and West has no entry.

Although we are mainly concerned with the play of the hand as declarer it may be helpful to point out defensive opportunities and in the event East followed the principle of using his own entry card to establish his partner's suit, thus preserving his partner's entry card. But East would not have had the opportunity to display his defensive acumen had South played low from both hands on the opening lead.

It is mortifying to be dealt twenty-seven high card points and end up with a minus score. That was the sad fate befalling South on the hand below.

Dealer South. Love all.

```
                    ♠ 10 6 3 2
                    ♡ 7 5 4 3
                    ◇ J 10
                    ♣ 7 4 2
    ♠ 9 8                              ♠ J 7 5 4
    ♡ Q J 8 6 2                        ♡ 10
    ◇ A 9                              ◇ 8 7 6 5 2
    ♣ A 10 9 3                         ♣ 8 6 5
                    ♠ A K Q
                    ♡ A K 9
                    ◇ K Q 4 3
                    ♣ K Q J
```

After opening with a conventional game forcing bid of Two Clubs, South became declarer in Three No-Trumps. West led ♡ 6, fourth best of his longest suit, and South took East's ♡ 10 with ♡ K. He had five top tricks (♠ A, K, Q and ♡ A K) and needed four more. He started by leading ◇ 3 to dummy's ◇ 10 but West put up his ace and returned ♡ Q, knocking out South's last stopper. There were now eight tricks available with the addition of the three diamonds, but still one to find. South led to ◇ J, returned to hand with ♠ Q and cashed ◇ K and Q on which West discarded clubs.

As soon as South led a club, West regained the lead with ♣ A and defeated the contract with three good hearts. As the lead needed to be given away twice, two aces having to be driven out, it would have been wiser to allow East to take the first trick with ♡ 10. If he were able to return the suit

West would only have held four to begin with and these would be no danger. As it was, East would have had to switch and South would now have had ample time to develop his suits since both his heart stoppers would have been intact.

It may be necessary to hold up in two suits. Consider this hand:

Dealer South. Game all.

```
                    ♠ K 7 2
                    ♡ K 7 3
                    ◊ 10 9 3 2
                    ♣ K Q J
     ♠ 9 6                              ♠ Q J 10 8 3
     ♡ Q 10 8 5 2                       ♡ J 9
     ◊ K 8 7                            ◊ A 6
     ♣ 8 5 2                            ♣ 9 7 6 4
                    ♠ A 5 4
                    ♡ A 6 4
                    ◊ Q J 5 4
                    ♣ A 10 3
```

Playing a 15-17 range no-trumps when vulnerable, South opened One No-Trump and was raised to three.

West leads ♡ 5 and East plays ♡ J on dummy's ♡ 3. South must play low for, as we have seen earlier, the lead will have to be lost twice in diamonds. The contract is in danger if West started with a five card suit. Assume East returns ♡ 9, South wins in either hand and immediately plays diamonds making nine tricks.

Suppose, however, East were to switch to ♠ Q at trick two. It would be necessary to allow this to win for much the same reason. If ♠ Q is taken on the first round and West wins the first round of diamonds, returning a spade, East's suit will become established while he still holds the ace of diamonds as an entry.

7. When Not to Hold Up

From the foregoing it might appear that it was always correct to hold up an ace in no-trumps unless you were lucky enough to see nine tricks without giving away the lead. This is not the case. One instance where it is wrong to hold up is where, by winning the first trick, you will esablish a second. Here is an example:

Dealer South. North-South vul.

```
                    ♠ J 4
                    ♡ Q 8 6 3
                    ◇ K J 9 5 2
                    ♣ A 2
    ♠ K 9 7 6 2                      ♠ Q 8 5
    ♡ 10 9 4                         ♡ J 7 5
    ◇ A 7                            ◇ 8 6
    ♣ J 4 3                          ♣ Q 10 9 7 6
                    ♠ A 10 3
                    ♡ A K 2
                    ◇ Q 10 4 3
                    ♣ K 8 5
```

South	West	North	East
1 NT	Pass	2 ♣	Pass
2 ◇	Pass	3 NT	Pass
Pass	Pass		

South opened with a strong no-trump (16-18 points) and North made a conventional response of Two Clubs to enquire whether South had a four-card major suit. When South denied holding either four hearts or four spades North bid the game in no-trumps.

West leads ♠ 6 and ♠ 4 is played from the table. There is no point whatever in playing the jack "to bring out the queen or king from East". South's ten is just as good a card as dummy's jack and if the four is played East must put up either the queen or king to prevent South winning cheaply.

Suppose South decides to hold up his ace and allow the queen to win. East returns ♠8 and West's spades are established. South cannot make nine tricks without using the diamonds and as soon as he plays one, West will win and play off his remaining winning spades to defeat the contract.

South should take East's queen with his ace and immediately attack diamonds. West wins and can play ♠K, but South will take the third round with his ten which will by then be the highest remaining spade.

Here is a similar example:

Dealer South. Love all.

```
              ♠ J 10 3
              ♡ J 2
              ◇ K 10 4
              ♣ K J 10 9 4
♠ K 7 2                      ♠ 8 6 5
♡ K 9 7 5 3                  ♡ Q 8 6
◇ 8 5 2                      ◇ Q J 7 6
♣ 3 2                        ♣ A 6 5
              ♠ A Q 9 4
              ♡ A 10 4
              ◇ A 9 3
              ♣ Q 8 7
```

South	West	North	East
1 ♠	Pass	2 ♣	Pass
2 NT	Pass	3 ♠	Pass
3 NT	Pass	Pass	Pass

West leads ♡5 and, again, South plays low from dummy. To play the jack and take the queen with the ace would be fatal, for East when on lead with ace of clubs, would return a heart and West would take four tricks, holding ♡K 9 over South's ♡10 4.

(repeated for convenience)

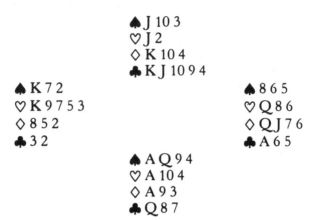

♠ J 10 3
♥ J 2
♦ K 10 4
♣ K J 10 9 4

♠ K 7 2   ♠ 8 6 5
♥ K 9 7 5 3   ♥ Q 8 6
♦ 8 5 2   ♦ Q J 7 6
♣ 3 2   ♣ A 6 5

♠ A Q 9 4
♥ A 10 4
♦ A 9 3
♣ Q 8 7

East covers ♥ 2 with ♥ Q, taken by ♥ A. South immediately plays clubs to establish the extra tricks he needs for his contract. East gets in with the ace and returns ♥ 8, but South still has a second stopper with his ten.

If the ace of clubs had been held up by the defence it would be possible to enter dummy with the king of diamonds to play off the remaining clubs on which South would discard ♦ 9 and ♠ 4.

It might be tempting to lead ♠ J and finesse, hoping that East held ♠ K and overtricks might be made. But this would be bad play, for if West held the king of spades and regained the lead he might be able to defeat the contract so undue risks should not be taken merely to score overtricks.

Another common situation where a second stopper will develop if an honour is captured on the first round is where one hand holds four cards headed by the ten. e.g.

(a)   (b)

10 9 x x   x x

A x   A 10 9 x

If West leads the king and South wins with the ace, the ten will be promoted to a winner on the fourth round. Failure to appreciate this fact led to the defeat of South's no-trump contract on this hand.

Dealer South. Love all.

```
                    ♠ 9 3
                    ♡ K 7 5
                    ◊ Q J 10 7 3
                    ♣ A Q 5
   ♠ K Q 7 4                        ♠ J 6 5
   ♡ Q 6 4                          ♡ 10 9 8 3
   ◊ A 5                            ◊ K 6 2
   ♣ J 10 7 3                       ♣ 9 8 4
                    ♠ A 10 8 2
                    ♡ A J 2
                    ◊ 9 8 4
                    ♣ K 6 2
```

South	West	North	East
1 NT	Pass	3 NT	Pass
Pass	Pass		

South opened with a weak no-trump (12-14 points) being not vulnerable and North raised to game. West led ♠ 4, not always a good lead from a suit headed by king and queen, but East held the jack and South decided to hold up his ace. East returned ♠ 6, South played ♠ 8 and West won with ♠ Q. As South evidently still had ♠ A 10, West did not continue the suit and switched to ♣ 3. South won and led ◊ 9, taken with ◊ K by East who led back ♠ 5. The defence finally made three tricks in spades together with two diamonds to defeat the contract.

South should have taken the first trick with ♠ A and immediately started on the diamonds. The defenders could make two tricks only in spades with the king and queen and then South's ten would have been promoted to a winner.

Another situation when it is wrong to hold up is where you fear a switch to another suit. Consider this example:

Dealer North. Love all.

```
                    ♠ J 3
                    ♡ 10 7
                    ◇ A 5 3
                    ♣ K Q J 9 6 3
    ♠ K 9 7 2                       ♠ Q 10 6 4
    ♡ Q 8 5 3                       ♡ J 6 2
    ◇ 8 7 6 4                       ◇ K Q J 10
    ♣ 7                             ♣ A 5
                    ♠ A 8 5
                    ♡ A K 9 4
                    ◇ 9 2
                    ♣ 10 8 4 2
```

South	West	North	East
		1 ♣	Pass
1 ♡	Pass	2 ♣	Pass
2 NT	Pass	3 NT	Pass
Pass	Pass		

Bold bidding resulted in an optimistic contract of Three No-Trumps. South was certainly entitled to bid a second time but a raise to three clubs would have probably been better than Two No-Trumps with weak diamonds. North's raise to game was made in the hope that his partner held the ace of clubs. West leads ♠ 2 and South can see four top tricks and can make five more in clubs. He has only a single stopper in spades, but if he allows East to win the first trick a diamond switch will leave him with three losers in the suit. South must therefore take the opening lead and play clubs at once. There is, in fact, very little risk as the two of spades, if a true card, should indicate a four card suit.

In the next example South again had a strong reason not to hold up his ace.

Dealer South. Love all.

```
                    ♠ 5 4 3
                    ♡ A
                    ◇ K Q J 10 7 5
                    ♣ 9 4 2
♠ Q J 10 6                          ♠ K 9 7
♡ K 8 6 4                           ♡ J 7 5 3 2
◇ 2                                 ◇ A 8 4 3
♣ Q 10 8 7                          ♣ 6
                    ♠ A 8 2
                    ♡ Q 10 9
                    ◇ 9 6
                    ♣ A K J 5 3
```

South	West	North	East
1 ♣	Pass	1 ◇	Pass
1 NT	Pass	3 NT	Pass
Pass	Pass		

The bidding is not unreasonable although the contract has virtually no chance on a heart lead.

Luckily for declarer West had an automatic spade lead and when East encouraged by playing ♠ 9 it might have seemed prudent to hold up. But a moment's thought should make it evident that dummy's only entry, the ace of hearts, will be removed at trick two and the good diamonds all be wasted.

To win with the ace of spades at trick one is not risky. East holds the king of spades and if West held five East would hold a doubleton king. In that event he should play his king on the opening lead to avoid blocking the suit. But, of course, whatever the risks, South had no sensible alternative but to win at once, thankful that his ace of hearts is still on the table.

If you decide it is necessary to hold up your stopper it does not mean that you should always hold up as long as possible. The object of retaining your control card is to save yourself from losing too many tricks in the opponent's suit. You only need hold up long enough to achieve this and to hold up too long may prove dangerous as in this example:

Dealer South. North-South vul.

```
                    ♠ 9 6 2
                    ♡ 6 5
                    ◇ A J 10 9 2
                    ♣ K Q 4
 ♠ K Q J 10 8                         ♠ 7 5
 ♡ J 10 2                             ♡ K Q 8 7
 ◇ 8 5                                ◇ K 4 3
 ♣ 7 6 3                              ♣ 10 8 5 2
                    ♠ A 4 3
                    ♡ A 9 4 3
                    ◇ Q 7 6
                    ♣ A J 9
```

South	West	North	East
1 NT	Pass	3 NT	Pass
(15-17)			
Pass	Pass		

West led ♠ K which was allowed to win and continued with ♠ Q. South decided to hold up again and now West, having no entry for his spades, switched to ♡ J. South held back this ace also but was two down, losing two spades, three hearts and one diamond.

South should have reckoned that he had six top tricks (♠ A, ♡ A, ◇ A and ♣ A K Q) and that the extra tricks could be made from diamonds. There was only any danger from the spades if West had a five card suit, for otherwise the defenders could only take three tricks in spades and possibly the king of diamonds. If West had five spades East could only hold two so that taking the second round of spades would safeguard against the loss of too many, as West was never likely to regain the lead. The only high card of any consequence held by the defenders was the king of diamonds and if West held this card he would not be able to take a trick with it as the ace was over him on his left.

It is of course true that West could defeat the contract by switching to a heart at trick two and had he done so there was nothing South could have done. He could not afford to win the first spade lead as East would still have one to return to his partner when he got in with the king of diamonds. But West would be likely to play a second round of spades as South might have had only two and been compelled to win the second, leaving East with a third.

8. When to Play Second Hand High from Dummy

A popular precept is "second player plays low". This applies more to the defending side as it is logical for the second player to play low, leaving it to his partner, who will be fourth, to win the trick if he can and considers it best.

The situation is slightly different for declarer as he can see both his and his partner's cards. Broadly speaking, if dummy has a doubleton honour and declarer has no good intermediate card to support his honour, it is correct to play high from dummy. It is essential that one trick from the combined holding should be certain.

Consider the following example:

Dealer South. Love all.

```
                    ♠ K 8 7 6
                    ♡ Q 5
                    ◇ K 5 3
                    ♣ Q 9 4 2
♠ 10 2                                    ♠ Q J 9 4
♡ A J 9 7 4                               ♡ 10 6 2
◇ J 8 6 2                                 ◇ Q 10 7 4
♣ K 6                                     ♣ 8 3
                    ♠ A 5 3
                    ♡ K 8 3
                    ◇ A 9
                    ♣ A J 10 7 5
```

South	West	North	East
1 ♣	1 ♡	1 ♠	Pass
1 NT	Pass	3 NT	Pass
Pass	Pass		

Not Vulnerable North – South were using a weak no-trump (12-14 points) so that South's rebid would indicate a balanced hand outside that range and consequently 15-16.

West leads ♡ 7 and South has to decide which card to play from the table. If he plays low, East's ten will force out South's king and the queen will be unprotected. Even if South holds up the king he will win only one trick in the suit. His correct play is to put up the queen at once and hope that it takes the trick. Indeed there is every likelihood that it will. For one thing, West overcalled in hearts and is more likely to hold the ace. For another, application of the Rule of Eleven would indicate that West must surely hold the ace.

Before proceeding with the play of this hand it may be as well to explain the Rule of Eleven. Assuming that the card led is the fourth highest of the suit, if you subtract the value of the card led from eleven, the balance will represent the number of cards higher than the card led which are divided between the other three hands.

To understand the Rule of Eleven, take a simple example. The lead here was the seven of hearts. Subtracting seven from eleven leaves four. There are in fact a total of seven cards in the pack higher than the seven, i.e. A K Q J 10 9 8, and of these the player who led must hold three for his lead to be the fourth highest and it follows that he does not possess four.

In the present hand South can see three cards higher than the seven, the queen in dummy and the king and eight in his hand, which means that East has one card higher than the seven. If it were the ace, West would hold ♡ J 10 9 7 and his correct lead would have been the jack, top of his sequence. Now we can revert to the hand we were discussing. South has played the queen of hearts from the table and it has held the trick. South still holds the king and the eight so that he is still protected in the suit provided that a heart is not returned by East through his king. If hearts are returned from West and South is the last player, he is safe.

More about the importance of being the fourth to play to a trick will be explained in a later chapter. South next leads ♣ Q from the table and finesses when East plays low. West wins with the king but cannot safely continue hearts without giving South an extra trick with his king. If he switches to any other suit, South is safe and makes two spades, two diamonds, one heart and four clubs.

Overleaf is another example:

Dealer South. Game all.

```
                    ♠ Q 10 8 5 2
                    ♡ Q 9
                    ♢ A J 6
                    ♣ 8 7 6
♠ J 7                                   ♠ K 6 4 3
♡ K 10 8 7 4 3                          ♡ J 6
♢ 7 4 3 2                               ♢ 10 9 8
♣ 3                                     ♣ K 9 4 2
                    ♠ A 9
                    ♡ A 5 2
                    ♢ K Q 5
                    ♣ A Q J 10 5
```

South	West	North	East
2 NT	Pass	3 ♠	Pass
3 NT	Pass	Pass	Pass

West leads ♡ 7. Having no card in support of his ace, South plays ♡ Q from dummy as being the best chance of taking a trick with it. The Rule of Eleven would also support the probability of the king being with West. There are three cards higher than the seven visible. If East holds the king West has ♡ J 10 8 7 and the jack would be the more normal lead.

When the queen wins the contract is in no danger. Even if the king of clubs is in West's hand, South still has the hearts stopped. To trick three he leads ♣ 6 and finesses ♣ 10. When this holds he re-enters dummy by playing ♢ 5 to ♢ J and leads ♣ 7, finessing ♣ J, West discarding a diamond. Crossing to dummy again by leading ♢ Q to ♢ A he leads ♣ 8 and finesses ♣ Q, leaving East's ♣ K bare to fall on ♣ A. South next cashes ♣ 5, ♢ K, ♡ A and ♠ A and finally leads ♠ 9. As it happens East wins with ♠ K and has to return ♠ 6 to dummy's ♠ 10 and declarer ends up with twelve tricks. A lucky hand which might have gone very differently if the queen of hearts had not been played and won the first trick.

When explaining the principle of playing high from dummy second hand, holding a doubleton honour it was emphasised:

(1)   there was no good supporting card in the partner's hand. Two examples have been given where the combined holdings were:

(a)	(b)
Q 5	Q 9
K 8 3	A 5 2

It would also be correct to play high from dummy with J x opposite A x x in the slight hope that the lead was from a suit headed by king – queen.

(2)   There must be a sure winner between the two hands. For example –

Dealer South. Love all.

```
                    ♠ J 3
                    ♡ K 10 9 5
                    ◇ J 10 8 6
                    ♣ K 10 5
  ♠ K 10 8 7 6                       ♠ A 9 5
  ♡ J 8 3                            ♡ Q 6 4 2
  ◇ K 7                             ◇ Q 4 3 2
  ♣ 8 7 6                            ♣ 3 2
                    ♠ Q 4 2
                    ♡ A 7
                    ◇ A 9 5
                    ♣ A Q J 9 4
```

South	West	North	East
1 ♣	Pass	1 ♡	Pass
2 NT	Pass	3 NT	Pass
Pass	Pass		

West leads ♠ 7. Although South has no good supporting card for his queen it would be quite wrong to play the jack from dummy. East would win with ♠ A and return the suit and West would make all his sapdes. A trick in spades can only be assured if a low card is played from the table second in hand.

East must play either ace or king to prevent your queen from winning. Therefore a high honour has been drawn out without using any of your high cards.

This is a convenient moment to mention two honour combinations that have one thing in common:

(a)	(b)
Q 4 3	K 2
J 6 2	J 6 3

Both combinations are reasonably certain to make a trick providing the suit is led initially by the opponents and a low card is played second in hand. We have discussed (a). In (b), if West leads a low card and the two is played from the table, even if East wins with the queen and the king later falls to the ace, the jack will be a winner.

If however you attempt to play either combination yourself you may well lose all the tricks. There is a better chance with (b) as the ace may be on your left, but it is preferable, if possible, to leave the suit alone.

9. Ducking

To duck is to play a small card and surrender a trick that could have been won, in order to preserve an entry. The term is also used when playing low when the suit has been led by an opponent. This is similar to a hold up play to retain control and has been explained earlier.

The most common situation where it is necessary to duck is where you aim to make a number of tricks in a long suit where one trick at least must be lost and the hand

containing the long suit has no outside entry.
Consider this example.

Dealer South. Love all.

```
                    ♠ J 5 3
                    ♡ 7 4
                    ◊ 8 4
                    ♣ A K 7 6 4 3
    ♠ 7 6 4                         ♠ Q 10 9 8
    ♡ K 10 8 5 3                    ♡ J 9 2
    ◊ K 7                           ◊ Q J 9 2
    ♣ Q 10 2                        ♣ J 9
                    ♠ A K 2
                    ♡ A Q 6
                    ◊ A 10 6 5 3
                    ♣ 8 5
```

South	West	North	East
1 ◊	Pass	2 ♣	Pass
3 NT	Pass	Pass	Pass

West leads ♡ 5 and South takes ♡ J with ♡ Q. There are
seven top tricks and the best chance to make more lies in
clubs. With eight cards between the two hands, leaving five
with the opponents, there is every prospect that the suit
would be cleared in three rounds. Suppose then, you play
off the ace and king and give away the third, you will have
three winners in dummy but it is not possible to reach them
as there is no high card on the table that can take a trick.

The answer is to duck a round of clubs. That is to say,
you play a low club from your hand and play a low card
from dummy. You are making no attempt to win the trick,
but you have drawn two cards from the opponents. When
you regain the lead, as you must, and lead your remaining
club to dummy's ace and king, the opposing clubs fall and
you take five tricks in the suit.

If the clubs are badly divided, four with one defender and one with the other, you will not make your contract, but it will be bad luck and not bad play.

Here is a further example:

Dealer South. North-South vul.

```
                    ♠ J 4 2
                    ♡ 9 7
                    ◊ 10 8 2
                    ♣ A 7 6 5 4
   ♠ 7 6 5                          ♠ Q 10 9 8
   ♡ 10 8 6 3 2                     ♡ A 5 4
   ◊ K J                            ◊ Q 6 5 3
   ♣ K 10 3                         ♣ 9 8
                    ♠ A K 3
                    ♡ K Q J
                    ◊ A 9 7 4
                    ♣ Q J 2
```

South	West	North	East
2 NT	Pass	3 NT	Pass
Pass	Pass		

West leads ♡ 3, won by East, who returns ♡ 5, taken by South. There are six top tricks and it is necessary to establish clubs. At trick three your lead ♣ Q to which West plays ♣ 3 and dummy ♣ 4. You continue with ♣ J and West covers this with ♣ K. It is tempting to capture his king with your ace but this would be a mistake. The third round would be won by West with his ten and the two good clubs in dummy would be wasted. You must allow the king to win, in other words, duck. Now, when you are in again and play your last club the ten falls to the ace and you are on the table to make the other two.

It may be necessary to duck twice or give two tricks away. Suppose the combined holding between your hand and dummy is:

```
            A 9 7 6 4
Q 10 8                    K J
            5 3 2
```

You will need to play low from each hand twice. When you finally lead your last card over to the ace you will make the remaining two. If you have to give up the lead twice you will need to have adequate stoppers in the other suits.

In this hand declarer was lucky in that the suit was divided evenly against him, but his failure to duck cost him the contract:

Dealer South. Game all.

```
                    ♠ 6 5
                    ♡ K 3 2
                    ◇ A 8 7 6 4 3
                    ♣ 4 3
♠ K 10 8 4 3                          ♠ J 9 2
♡ 8 7 5                              ♡ A J 10 9
◇ Q 2                               ◇ J 5
♣ J 8 5                             ♣ Q 10 9 7
                    ♠ A Q 7
                    ♡ Q 6 4
                    ◇ K 10 9
                    ♣ A K 6 2
```

South	West	North	East
1 ♣	Pass	1 ◇	Pass
2 NT	Pass	3 NT	Pass

(repeated for convenience)

<pre>
                          ♠ 6 5
                          ♡ K 3 2
                          ◊ A 8 7 6 4 3
                          ♣ 4 3
      ♠ K 10 8 4 3   ♠ J 9 2
      ♡ 8 7 5   ♡ A J 10 9
      ◊ Q 2   ◊ J 5
      ♣ J 8 5   ♣ Q 10 9 7
                          ♠ A Q 7
                          ♡ Q 6 4
                          ◊ K 10 9
                          ♣ A K 6 2
</pre>

North made a bold decision to raise to Three No-Trumps. His partner's rebid showed 17-18 points and should contain some fit with the diamonds in which case the suit might well provide several tricks. There was also a good chance that the king of hearts would be an entry card. So, rather than bid Three Diamonds which would be a sign off discouraging any idea of playing in no-trumps, North raised to Three No-Trumps.

West led ♠ 4 covered by ♠ 5, ♠ J and ♠ Q. Needing to establish dummy's long suit South played off ◊ K, followed by ◊ 10 to ◊ A. When each opponent followed suit he was quite pleased – but only temporarily. For the next round of diamonds was won in his hand with the nine. He tried to re-enter dummy by playing a low heart to the king but East held the ace and the contract ended one down, South taking two spades, one heart, three diamonds and two clubs.

He should have given up either the first or second round of diamonds. This would have enabled him to make five tricks if the suit were divided 3–1 between the opponents, and avoided being blocked if the division were 2–2, as it was.

10. Entries: Unblocking

It is most disappointing to have a number of winners in one hand but to be unable to make any use of them due to lack of entry. We have seen that one way of avoiding this type of calamity is by giving up one or more early tricks by ducking. Situations where you need to be careful to see that there is an entry card to the hand with a long suit are –

(a) Where the suit is blocked. That is to say, the cards in the shorter hand are higher than those in the longer. For example:

J 10 9 8 7 6

A K Q

After playing off your top honours you must have some means of getting to the hand with the six card suit.

(b) Where you are lacking the ace of the suit you aim to establish. Remember that the player holding the ace is likely to hold it up to break your communications.

This is a similar move to your hold up as described earlier. Two ways in which valuable entries can be provided are by unblocking and overtaking.

Here is a simple example of a blocked suit.

Dealer South. Love all.

```
                    ♠ Q J
                    ♡ 8 7 6
                    ◇ K Q J 8 7 4
                    ♣ 9 3
  ♠ 10 9 8 7 6                        ♠ 5 4 3
  ♡ K J 4                             ♡ Q 10 9
  ◇ 9 3                               ◇ 10 6 5 2
  ♣ A Q 10                            ♣ 8 7 5
                    ♠ A K 2
                    ♡ A 5 3 2
                    ◇ A
                    ♣ K J 6 4 2
```

(repeated for convenience)

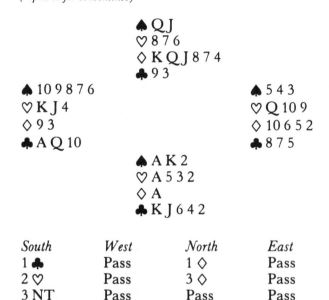

♠ Q J			
♡ 8 7 6			
◊ K Q J 8 7 4			
♣ 9 3			

```
              ♠ Q J
              ♡ 8 7 6
              ◊ K Q J 8 7 4
              ♣ 9 3
♠ 10 9 8 7 6                    ♠ 5 4 3
♡ K J 4                        ♡ Q 10 9
◊ 9 3                          ◊ 10 6 5 2
♣ A Q 10                       ♣ 8 7 5
              ♠ A K 2
              ♡ A 5 3 2
              ◊ A
              ♣ K J 6 4 2
```

South	West	North	East
1 ♣	Pass	1 ◊	Pass
2 ♡	Pass	3 ◊	Pass
3 NT	Pass	Pass	Pass

West leads ♠ 10 and you appear to have ten certain winners with three spades, one heart, and six diamonds. But you should have noticed that you hold a single ace of diamonds which blocks the suit and therefore an entry is needed to dummy. So you overtake ♠ J with ♠ K, lay down ◊ A and lead ♠ 2 to ♠ Q. You are now on the table to play off your diamonds.

The next example is less easy.

Dealer South. Game all.

```
                  ♠ Q 6
                  ♡ 8 5 3
                  ◇ Q J 7 6 3
                  ♣ Q 5 2
  ♠ 8 5 2                          ♠ K J 10 4
  ♡ K 9 4                          ♡ J 10 7
  ◇ 10 5                           ◇ 9 8 4 2
  ♣ A J 7 6 3                      ♣ 8 4
                  ♠ A 9 7 3
                  ♡ A Q 6 2
                  ◇ A K
                  ♣ K 10 9
```

South	*West*	*North*	*East*
2 NT	Pass	3 NT	Pass
Pass	Pass		

West leads ♣ 6 to which dummy plays ♣ 2 and East ♣ 8. This appears to be a lucky lead for you and if you have not taken a good look at dummy it is likely that you have taken the trick with ♣ 9.

It would be easy if you had a low diamond, but you haven't and after playing off ace and king you have to find a way to reach dummy. You may try playing ♣ K but West will not help you by playing the ace. You may, alternatively, lead a low spade towards the queen, hoping West has the king. But luck is against you.

To create an entry to dummy you needed to take the first lead in your hand with ♣ K. This might appear to be risky but if West led his fourth best, which appears to be the case, the Rule of Eleven should help you. There are five cards higher than the six of clubs missing from West's hand. You hold three, dummy one and East has played the eight. West's suit must, therefore, be ♣ A J 7 6 with, maybe, one or two more (♣ 4 and ♣ 3). After cashing ◇ A K you lead a low club and must force your way to dummy.

In the next example you are missing the ace of your long suit.

Dealer South. East-West vul.

```
                    ♠ Q J 10
                    ♡ 9 8 7
                    ◇ 10 7
                    ♣ K Q J 10 9
♠ K 9 8 7 2                          ♠ 5 3
♡ Q 5 3                              ♡ J 10 4 2
◇ K J 9                              ◇ 8 5 3 2
♣ 8 3                               ♣ A 7 5
                    ♠ A 6 4
                    ♡ A K 6
                    ◇ A Q 6 4
                    ♣ 6 4 2
```

South	West	North	East
1 ◇	Pass	2 ♣	Pass
3 NT	Pass	Pass	Pass

West leads ♠ 7, dummy plays ♠ 10 and East ♠ 5. Providing you can take four tricks from clubs you have nine. But you are missing the ace of clubs and if this is held up to the third round you will have no means of getting into dummy except with a spade. Therefore you must play ♠ A on the first round, leaving yourself two low cards opposite the queen and jack.

The next example is similar.

Dealer South. Love all.

```
                    ♠ Q 4
                    ♡ Q J 8
                    ◊ J 10 7 4 3 2
                    ♣ 8 4
  ♠ J 7 6 3                        ♠ A 8 5 2
  ♡ 7 6 3                          ♡ K 9 4 2
  ◊ A 9 5                          ◊ 8
  ♣ Q 7 2                          ♣ J 10 9 3
                    ♠ K 10 9
                    ♡ A 10 5
                    ◊ K Q 6
                    ♣ A K 6 5
```

South	West	North	East
1 ♣	Pass	1 ◊	Pass
3 NT	Pass	Pass	Pass

West was not keen to lead from his poor spade suit and preferred the top of nothing seven of hearts. South put on dummy's ♡ Q but East correctly played low, keeping his king over dummy's jack. South started on his diamonds but West kept his ace until the third round and it proved impossible to get across to make use of the long suit.

South should have played ♡ 8 from the table to the first trick and taken with his ♡ A to ensure an entry to the diamonds.

Greater care with entries would have saved declarer the disappointment of not making game on this powerful hand with twenty-six high card points.

Dealer South. North-South vul.

```
                    ♠ 7 4 2
                    ♡ 7 6 3
                    ◇ J 10 5
                    ♣ Q 8 5 4
   ♠ Q 9 5                        ♠ J 10 8 3
   ♡ K 5                          ♡ Q 10 9 4
   ◇ Q 9 8 3                      ◇ 6 2
   ♣ J 9 3 2                      ♣ 10 7 6
                    ♠ A K 6
                    ♡ A J 8 2
                    ◇ A K 7 4
                    ♣ A K
```

South	West	North	East
2 ♣	Pass	2 ◇	Pass
3 NT	Pass	Pass	Pass

West led ◇ 3 which appeared to be helpful to South who put up ◇ 10 from the table, playing ◇ 4 from his hand. He had now eight top tricks and the queen of clubs would be the ninth. But there was no entry to dummy.

Had declarer realized earlier that he needed an entry to dummy he could have ensured one by playing ◇ 5 on the opening lead, winning with ◇ K. After cashing ♣ A K a low diamond would guarantee an entry to the table for the queen of clubs.

Opening leads that appear to give you a cheap trick are often 'Greek Gifts'. Before accepting your gift look carefully at the hand and remember the advice given earlier. *If you are missing the ace of the suit that you depend on for your extra tricks, be certain you have an entry into the hand with the long suit.*

Here are two further examples where a lucky opening lead is a snare and a delusion.

Dealer South. Game all.

```
              ♠ K 9 3
              ♡ 7 5
              ◇ Q 5
              ♣ K J 10 8 6 2
♠ Q 10 5 4 2                    ♠ 8 7 6
♡ K 10 3                        ♡ J 8 6 2
◇ J 8 6 4                       ◇ K 9 2
♣ 9                             ♣ A 7 3
              ♠ A J
              ♡ A Q 9 4
              ◇ A 10 7 3
              ♣ Q 5 4
```

South opened with a strong no-trump (16-18) and North raised direct to Three No-Trumps. It would be pointless to bid clubs.

West leads ♠ 4, dummy plays ♠ 3 and East ♠ 6. If you unthinkingly play ♠ J you will regret it. East will hold up the ace of clubs until the third round and the rest of dummy's clubs will be "out of work". As you do not have the ace of your vital suit (clubs) you need a sure entry to dummy and that is the king of spades. Therefore take the first trick with the ace.

This is the second example.

Dealer North. East-West vul.

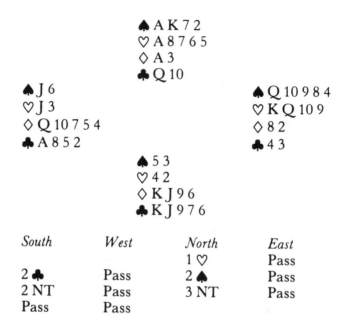

	♠ A K 7 2	
	♡ A 8 7 6 5	
	◇ A 3	
	♣ Q 10	

♠ J 6		♠ Q 10 9 8 4
♡ J 3		♡ K Q 10 9
◇ Q 10 7 5 4		◇ 8 2
♣ A 8 5 2		♣ 4 3

	♠ 5 3	
	♡ 4 2	
	◇ K J 9 6	
	♣ K J 9 7 6	

South	West	North	East
		1 ♡	Pass
2 ♣	Pass	2 ♠	Pass
2 NT	Pass	3 NT	Pass
Pass	Pass		

South's two level response may appear light by some standards that require 9 or 10 points, but if he responds One No-Trump the same contract is likely to be reached.

West leads ◇ 5 which, again, seems to present you with a cheap trick. But stop and think before playing to the first trick. You have five sure winners with ♠ A K, ♡ A, ◇ A K and if you can make four tricks from clubs you are home. As you do not have the ace of clubs you need an entry to your hand, which must be the king of diamonds. Therefore play ◇ A at trick one.

Next lead ♣ Q, which is likely to be allowed to win. Continue with ♣ 10 and overtake with ♣ J. Your clubs are sequential except for the ace. If you do not overtake and the ace is not played you are still in dummy and you cannot afford to use the king of diamonds to get back to establish your clubs as you need it to get in to cash the winners. If West does not take ♣ J you continue with ♣ K and your contract is safe.

In the last hand it was necessary to overtake in order to make sure of being able to establish your suit. Here is another example.

Dealer South. Love all.

```
                    ♠ 6 5 3
                    ♡ A 7
                    ◇ 5 3
                    ♣ A J 10 9 8 3
    ♠ K 10 8 4                        ♠ Q 9
    ♡ Q J 10 9 8                      ♡ 4 3 2
    ◇ 9 8                            ◇ Q J 10 6
    ♣ 4 2                           ♣ Q 7 6 5
                    ♠ A J 7 2
                    ♡ K 6 5
                    ◇ A K 7 4 2
                    ♣ K
```

South	West	North	East
1 ◇	1 ♡	2 ♣	Pass
2 ♠	Pass	3 ♣	Pass
3 NT	Pass	Pass	Pass

West leads ♡ Q and you can see seven top tricks. The best chance of making the extra two is in clubs rather than diamonds as they are more solid. The only problem is with entries as, apart from clubs, there is only the ace of hearts. You win the first trick in hand with ♡ K and lead ♣ K and overtake with ♣ A. You continue with ♣ J and, if necessary, ♣ 10 and ♣ 9 to force out ♣ Q. Now you make five tricks in clubs, one spade, two hearts and two diamonds.

In the next example the need to overtake is made a little clearer by the fall of the nine on the second round.

Dealer South. Love all.

```
                      ♠ 6 5 2
                      ♡ K 9
                      ◇ A 10 8 6 3
                      ♣ 7 4 2
  ♠ K Q 9 7                              ♠ J 4
  ♡ Q J 10 4 2                           ♡ 8 6 5
  ◇ 9 2                                  ◇ J 7 5 4
  ♣ 10 8                                 ♣ Q J 9 6
                      ♠ A 10 8 3
                      ♡ A 7 3
                      ◇ K Q
                      ♣ A K 5 3
```

South	West	North	East
2 NT	Pass	3 NT	Pass
Pass	Pass		

West leads ♡ Q and you can see eight top tricks with one spade, two hearts, three diamonds and two clubs. There are two possible ways to make the ninth, either in clubs or diamonds, each holding a combined seven cards. The diamonds represent the better chance as one hand (dummy) holds five and the intermediate cards are better.

The opening lead must be won in the closed hand to leave the king of hearts in dummy as an entry. At trick two you lead ◇ K, covered by ◇ 2, ◇ 3 and ◇ 4. You continue with ◇ Q on which West plays ◇ 9. The significance of this card can be appreciated if you look at the intermediate cards, the ten and eight of diamonds on the table.

You may be tempted to play low from dummy, then lead a low heart over to the king and lay down ◇ A, hoping that the jack will fall. But when it doesn't you are defeated as your hopes of extra tricks in diamonds are gone. You must overtake ◊ Q with ◊ A as the ten and eight of diamonds are now sequential and the lead of either card will force out the jack, leaving two winners in dummy with the king of hearts as entry.

Suppose that West had contributed a low card on the second diamond lead. It would still be correct to overtake with the ace, for if the diamonds are divided three in each hand, a third round will establish the suit. While, if East held originally jack and another or nine and another you would still be able to establish extra tricks.

In the final example of overtaking care is also needed to resist the temptation of a cheap trick.

Dealer South. East-West vul.

```
                ♠ A Q J 4
                ♡ K J 3
                ◊ K 5 4 3 2
                ♣ Q
  ♠ 9 7 6 3                      ♠ K 10 8 5
  ♡ 9 7 6 2                      ♡ Q 8 4
  ◊ 8                            ◊ Q J 10 9
  ♣ A J 5 2                      ♣ 4 3
                ♠ 3
                ♡ A 10 5
                ◊ A 7 6
                ♣ K 10 9 8 7 6
```

South	West	North	East
1 ♣	Pass	1 ◊	Pass
2 ♣	Pass	2 ♠	Pass
2 NT	Pass	Pass	Pass

North might have bid Three No-Trumps on the second round as South was unlikely to hold a four card spade suit, having failed to rebid One Spade over One Diamond.

However, we are more concerned with the play and West led ♡ 2 which South considered to be a friendly lead.

(*repeated for convenience*)

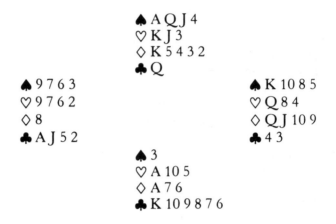

Without giving the matter too much thought he played low in dummy and took East's queen with his ace. He next led ♣ 6 to ♣ Q, West playing low. This gave him two tricks and he still had two in hearts, two in diamonds and one in spades. One extra trick in spades would not be enough and he lacked the entries to set up the clubs. So he did the next best thing and attacked diamonds. With eight cards in the combined hands there was a good chance of making four tricks. But luck was not on his side and the contract failed.

Reconsider the hand from the start with West leading ♡ 2. The lead gives South three tricks and in addition he has two in diamonds and one in spades, a total of six. The clubs are solid apart from the ace and jack. If these two can be forced out and providing South has the necessary entries to his hand his contract is safe.

To the first trick he must play the jack of hearts. If this wins, South has his two aces for entries. If East, as here, covers the jack with the queen, South wins and still has his ten for an entry. With the lead in his hand he must lay down ♣ K. It does not matter whether West plays his ace or not. Assume he holds up, South continues with ♣ 10. Whatever West decides to do South will be able to establish his club suit and have the entries needed to enjoy the winners.

Small cards can often provide important entries as can be seen from this example.

Dealer South. North-South vul.

```
                ♠ J 10 9 8 5
                ♡ 6
                ◊ K Q 4 3
                ♣ Q 9 4
♠ K 7 6                          ♠ A 4 3 2
♡ Q J 10 9                       ♡ 8 5 3
◊ 10 8                           ◊ 9 7 5
♣ J 6 5 2                        ♣ K 10 8
                ♠ Q
                ♡ A K 7 4 2
                ◊ A J 6 2
                ♣ A 7 3
```

South	West	North	East
1 ♡	Pass	1 ♠	Pass
2 ◊	Pass	3 ◊	Pass
3 NT	Pass	Pass	Pass

West leads ♡ Q which South wins. To duck might result in difficulty with a club switch. South has seven top tricks and his best prospects lie in spades where only the two top honours are missing. Again, the problem is one of entries, for when South leads ♠ Q neither defender is likely to cooperate and play an honour. He needs three entries to dummy, two to drive out the ace and king of spades and a third to play off the established winners. There are two entries with the top diamonds and the queen of clubs might provide a third if West held the king, but there is a better chance. To trick three he plays ◊ A and follows with ◊ 6 to ◊ Q. He next leads ♠ J, taken by West with ♠ K. South wins the heart continuation and plays ◊ J to ◊ K and ♠ 10 forces out East's ♠ A. The defence cash two heart tricks but South regains the lead with his ace of clubs and is able to get back to dummy by leading ◇ 2 to ◇ 4. Had West switched to a low club when in with the king of spades, South would have played low from dummy and won in hand with the ace.

The point to remember is that if you hold a combined eight cards in a suit, four in each hand, and the opposing five cards are divided normally 3–2, after three rounds you will have the two remaining cards, one in each hand.

It is always possible to make an entry into either hand with the fourth card. A further example will make the position more clear.

Dealer South. Love all.

```
              ♠ 8 7 3
              ♡ 7 5 4
              ◇ A Q J 4
              ♣ K Q 2
♠ J 10 9 5                      ♠ K 6 4 2
♡ A Q 6 2                       ♡ 10 9 3
◇ 10 9 6                        ◇ 8 7
♣ A 8                          ♣ 10 9 7 6
              ♠ A Q
              ♡ K J 8
              ◇ K 5 3 2
              ♣ J 5 4 3
```

Being not vulnerable South opened with a weak no-trump (12-14 points) and North raised to Three No-Trumps.

West leads ♠ J, East plays ♠ 6 and South ♠ Q. There are six top winners and the best chance of making three more is in clubs. If the opposing cards are divided 3–3 there will be no problem, or if the ace can be brought out without using a club honour all will be well.

To trick two South leads a low club towards dummy. The correct technique with this type of combination is to lead twice towards the hand with the double honour. When

♣ Q wins, South needs to get back to his hand to lead another low club. Suppose he plays ◇ 4 to ◇ K and continues with ♣ 4. West puts up his ace and continues spades to South's ace. South can lead to ♣ K but there is no sure entry back to the closed hand to make ♣ J. He may try hearts but the honours are badly placed.

Following the principle stated earlier, an additional entry can be found with the fourth diamond. After winning with ♣ Q declarer cashes ◇ A Q, following with ◇ 3 2. When each opponent follows suit he lead ◇ J and overtakes with ◇ K, leaving ◇ 4 in dummy and ◇ 5 in his hand. He plays a low club from hand, West putting up the ace. South wins the next spade lead with the ace, leads over to ♣ K, returns to hand with ◇ 5 and cashes ♣ J for his ninth trick. Had dummy been short of entries it would have been necessary to employ ◇ 5 early, leaving dummy with ◇ 4 and South with ◇ 2 or ◇ 3.

11. Simple Avoidance Plays: Safe Hand and Danger Hand

As we have seen, it is not so often that you have nine top winners in a contract of Three No-Trumps. More often than not you will need to establish extra tricks in a suit and this will involve losing the lead. If you no longer have a stopper in the opponents' strong suit you must be careful to ensure, if possible, that the player with the winning cards is not given the opportunity of playing them off.

One counter measure available to the declarer is the hold-up described earlier. By holding up a stopper such as an ace it may be possible to cut communications between the two defenders so that if a trick is lost to one opponent he may not be able to return his partner's lead.

Here is a simple example.

Dealer South. North-South vul.

```
                    ♠ 6 3
                    ♡ Q 7 6
                    ◇ A 10 7 5
                    ♣ K Q 5 4
♠ K J 9 7 2                         ♠ Q 10 4
♡ K 8 3                             ♡ 10 5 4 2
◇ Q 4 2                             ◇ 8
♣ 7 6                              ♣ J 10 9 3 2
                    ♠ A 8 5
                    ♡ A J 9
                    ◇ K J 9 6 3
                    ♣ A 8
```

South	West	North	East
1 NT	Pass	3 NT	Pass
Pass	Pass		

West leads ♠ 7 and East plays ♠ Q. South can see seven top tricks and the extra tricks can be made in diamonds.

Missing the queen, there is no guarantee that a trick will not be lost and there is danger from the spades.

South must hold up his ace of spades until the third round, discarding a low heart from the table. He must next tackle the diamonds. With nine cards between the two hands, missing the queen, the normal play is to lay down the ace and king and hope that the queen falls.

But here the situation is different. If West started with a five card suit as is quite likely, he now has two good spades to play. But he can only lead them out if he wins a trick and gains the lead. Therefore it is essential that South makes sure that West does not take a trick in diamonds.

At the fourth trick South lays down ◊ K in case the queen falls. He next leads ◊ 3 and when West follows with ◊ 4, finesses ◊ 10 in dummy. This ensures that West will not take a trick with the queen if he holds it. It may be that East wins with ◊ Q but that will not matter. If he still has a spade West can only have one, but if West started with five East will not have one. No doubt he will return a heart up to dummy's weakness, hoping his partner can win a trick, but South must take no chances and must play his ace. He will now win one spade, one heart, four diamonds and three clubs.

As it is, the finesse of the ◊ 10 succeeds and South makes all his diamonds and the contract with one overtrick, West making his king of hearts at the end. The situation is similar on the next hand.

Dealer South. Game all.

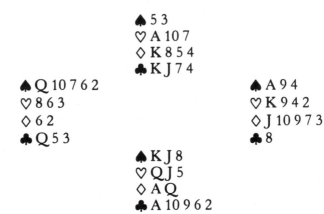

South opened a strong no-trump which North raised to Three No-Trumps. West leads ♠ 6 taken by East with ♠ A and ♠ 9 is returned. Again, South must not part with his stopper (♠ K) but must hold up to exhaust East of the suit.

After winning the third round with the king South needs to establish the clubs to make the additional tricks required for the contract. Despite the combined holding of nine cards it is necessary to ensure that West does not get a chance to play off his other two spades. Therefore ♣ A is laid down, followed by ♣ 2, ♣ J being finessed when West follows low. When the finesse wins South makes ten tricks in all, losing a trick at the end to East's ♡ K. If East had held the queen of clubs the contract would have been safe as he did not have a spade to return.

The foregoing examples have shown the necessity of keeping the lead away from the opponent with winners to play, often referred to as the "danger hand". This was achieved by finessing into the hand that could not do any harm referred to as the "safe hand".

There is another common situation where care is needed about which opponent is permitted to win a trick. You may have a weak suit which is vulnerable if attacked from one side but not from the other. Suppose your holding in a suit is something like this:

5 4 2   (dummy)

K 7   (declarer)

If East leads the suit and you as declarer have to play second in hand, your king may be captured by West. On the other hand if West leads the suit you are last to play and your king is safe. By the time it gets round to you, you have seen what everybody has played.

The principle can be stated as follows –

If you hold a king in either hand, with no ace nor queen to support it, always ensure if possible that the hand containing the king plays last.

A few examples may prove helpful.

Dealer South. Love all.

```
                  ♠ 8 5 4
                  ♡ 10 5 4
                  ◇ A 10 7 2
                  ♣ K J 9
♠ J 10 9 7 6                      ♠ 3 2
♡ A Q 8                           ♡ J 9 7 6 3
◇ 6 5                             ◇ Q 8 4
♣ 7 3 2                           ♣ Q 6 4
                  ♠ A K Q
                  ♡ K 2
                  ◇ K J 9 3
                  ♣ A 10 8 5
```

South	West	North	East
2 NT	Pass	3 NT	Pass
Pass	Pass		

(repeated for convenience)

```
             ♠ 8 5 4
             ♡ 10 5 4
             ◊ A 10 7 2
             ♣ K J 9
♠ J 10 9 7 6              ♠ 3 2
♡ A Q 8                   ♡ J 9 7 6 3
◊ 6 5                     ◊ Q 8 4
♣ 7 3 2                   ♣ Q 6 4
             ♠ A K Q
             ♡ K 2
             ◊ K J 9 3
             ♣ A 10 8 5
```

West leads ♠ J, won in hand with ♠ Q. There are seven
top tricks and the remaining two will come from either
diamonds or clubs or both. In each case the queen is
missing and it is possible to finesse either way. That is to say
that you could lead a low diamond to the ten, hoping West
holds the queen, or you could play from dummy and finesse
the jack. The vital point is, what happens if the finesse
loses?

Remembering the important principle set out above you
will note that your hearts are weak. In fact, if East were to
lead a heart there is no certainty that you would make a
trick at all. So East is the danger hand. Therefore start by
leading ◊ 3 to ◊ A and return ◊ 2. When East follows
with ◊ 8, cover with ◊ J. The trick will either be yours or
West's, certainly not East's. Let us suppose West holds the
queen and wins. If he switches to hearts you will make a
trick with your king as you will be the last to play, in which
case you will make three spades, one heart, three diamonds
and at least two clubs.

If West continues with spades you will only have eight
sure tricks. In this event you will need to establish clubs and
you play the suit in a similar manner to that in which you
played the diamonds. Start by leading ♣ 5 to ♣ K and
return ♣ J. If East does not cover with ♣ Q, play low as,

again, it will not matter if West gets in. Remember you still hold king and another heart with the lead in the safe hand.
Second example:

Dealer South. North-South vul.

```
                    ♠ 7 5
                    ♡ A J 6
                    ◇ A J 9 4 2
                    ♣ Q J 5
♠ A Q 9 6 3                           ♠ 10 4 2
♡ 9 8 7                               ♡ K 4 3 2
◇ 3                                   ◇ Q 8 7
♣ 7 6 3 2                             ♣ 10 8 4
                    ♠ K J 8
                    ♡ Q 10 5
                    ◇ K 10 6 5
                    ♣ A K 9
```

South opened with a strong no-trump which North confidently raised to Three No-Trumps. West leads ♠ 6 and South takes East's ♠ 10 with ♠ J. With seven top tricks it is necessary to establish the diamonds. Do you play for the drop with nine, missing the queen? Before deciding, you must consider what will happen if you lose a trick to the queen of diamonds. Presumably the opponents will continue with their spades, the suit they lead. How are you placed?

You still have ♠ K 8, but West is marked with ♠ A Q. For one thing, East put up ♠ 10 which was apparently his highest. Furthermore, applying the rule of eleven, ♠ 6 was led and assuming this to be fourth highest there are five spades higher than the six missing from West. Dummy has one (♠ 7), you have three (♠ K J 8) and East has played ♠ 10. West's suit is headed by ♠ A Q 9 6. So if opponents continue with spades you are only safe if you play last. In other words East is the danger hand and must be kept out.

Accordingly lead ◇ 5 to ◇ A and return ◇ 2, covering

East's ◊ 8 with ◊ 10, thus ensuring that the only person who can take the trick apart from yourself is West, the safe hand. Suppose West does hold the queen of diamonds and wins and switches to a heart. You must play the ace. You dare not risk the finesse because if East has the king and returns a spade you are down.

It would be equally correct to lead ◊ J from the table which might tempt East to cover with ◊ Q. But East should not do this as he can hardly gain by so doing.

Third example:

Dealer South. Love all.

```
                    ♠ A Q 8
                    ♡ 8 6
                    ◊ K 9 7 4 2
                    ♣ Q 9 6
    ♠ 9 6 5                        ♠ 10 7 3 2
    ♡ A J 10 9 5                   ♡ 7 3 2
    ◊ J 6                          ◊ Q 8 5
    ♣ 8 5 3                        ♣ K J 2
                    ♠ K J 4
                    ♡ K Q 4
                    ◊ A 10 3
                    ♣ A 10 7 4
```

South	West	North	East
1 ♣	Pass	1 ◊	Pass
2 NT	Pass	3 NT	Pass
Pass	Pass		

West leads ♡ J, taken in hand with ♡ Q. East's failure to play ♡ A suggests that West had led top of an inside sequence, his suit being headed by A J 10 9. Therefore South, with ♡ K 4 left must be careful to keep East out of the lead. Needing additional tricks the most promising suit is diamonds, in which one trick must be lost unless the queen and jack fall to the ace and king. There is no definite finesse position as the queen and jack are missing.

It is necessary to give up a trick, steering the lead into West's safe hand. Start by crossing to dummy with a spade and lead ◇ 2. When East follows with ◇ 5 put on ◇ 10. In other words duck into West's hand. If he carries on with hearts you will make a trick with your king but if he switches to clubs you will win with the ♣ A, and play ace and another diamond. Providing every one follows to the ace (i.e. second round) you will win four tricks in diamonds.

The play of the diamonds depended on being able to lose to West. Had East started with Q J x it would not have been possible to prevent him winning a trick.

In the next example South needs to be careful about entries, apart from the necessity of keeping out the danger hand.

Dealer North. Game all.

```
              ♠ A K 5 3
              ♡ K Q 10 3
              ◇ 8 3
              ♣ J 10 3
♠ Q 9                        ♠ J 10 7 2
♡ 7 2                        ♡ J 9 8 5 4
◇ Q J 7 2                    ◇ 6 5
♣ A Q 9 7 5                  ♣ 8 2
              ♠ 8 6 4
              ♡ A 6
              ◇ A K 10 9 4
              ♣ K 6 4
```

South	West	North	East
		1 ♠	Pass
2 ◇	Pass	2 ♡	Pass
3 NT	Pass	Pass	Pass

(repeated for convenience)

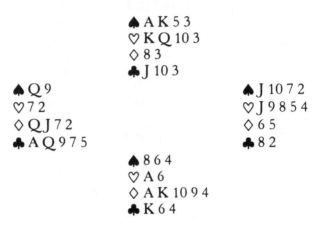

```
                    ♠ A K 5 3
                    ♡ K Q 10 3
                    ◇ 8 3
                    ♣ J 10 3
♠ Q 9                                    ♠ J 10 7 2
♡ 7 2                                    ♡ J 9 8 5 4
◇ Q J 7 2                                ◇ 6 5
♣ A Q 9 7 5                              ♣ 8 2
                    ♠ 8 6 4
                    ♡ A 6
                    ◇ A K 10 9 4
                    ♣ K 6 4
```

West leads ♣ 7 and the rule of eleven shows that East holds only one card in clubs above the seven. You cannot afford to play low from dummy as East might hold ♣ 8 or ♣ 9. As it is ♣ 10 wins the first trick, marking West with ♣ A Q and others. With eight top tricks the best suit to set up is diamonds since only queen and jack are missing. To trick two lead ◇ 8, playing low from hand and losing to West's ◇ J. If West continues clubs he gives you your ninth trick with your king. Instead he switches to ♡ 7 and you should stop and think before playing from the table. You may be tempted to try the ten, hoping it might win, or you might play low, hoping East plays the jack. But neither of these things happen and if you play low East plays the eight and you have to win with the ace. When the queen of diamonds does not fall you are in difficulties as you have no entry back to your hand. When West switches to ♡ 7 at trick 3 you must win in dummy and lead ◇ 3, again finessing to West. Now you are safe as the ace of hearts will be an entry for the fifth diamond.

In the next example your line of play cannot be determined until after the first trick.

Dealer South. East-West vul.

```
                    ♠ Q J 8
                    ♡ Q 7
                    ◇ J 10 4
                    ♣ A K 10 8 6
    ♠ 9 7 4                          ♠ 10 5 3 2
    ♡ A J 9 6 3                      ♡ 10 8 2
    ◇ K 7 3                          ◇ 8 6 5
    ♣ 7 2                            ♣ Q 4 3
                    ♠ A K 6
                    ♡ K 5 4
                    ◇ A Q 9 2
                    ♣ J 9 5
```

South	West	North	East
1 ◇	Pass	2 ♣	Pass
3 NT	Pass	Pass	Pass

West leads ♡ 6 and you have to decide which card to play from the table. As explained earlier, with a doubleton honour in dummy and no good supporting card for your king, it is best to play high. When the queen wins the first trick, West is marked with the ace and so East is the danger hand to be kept out. With seven top winners the extra tricks can be obtained either from clubs or diamonds. By leading ◇ J from dummy you can make absolutely certain that East will not get in, for if he has the king of diamonds you will capture it with your ace.

As it is, West wins with ◇ K and switches to a club. You must not be tempted to finesse, for that would risk defeat if East wins with ♣ Q and returns a heart. You can count nine tricks with three spades, one heart, three diamonds and two clubs. Suppose that East had held the ace of hearts

(repeated for convenience)

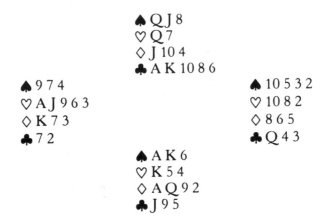

```
                    ♠ Q J 8
                    ♡ Q 7
                    ◇ J 10 4
                    ♣ A K 10 8 6
    ♠ 9 7 4                          ♠ 10 5 3 2
    ♡ A J 9 6 3                      ♡ 10 8 2
    ◇ K 7 3                          ◇ 8 6 5
    ♣ 7 2                            ♣ Q 4 3
                    ♠ A K 6
                    ♡ K 5 4
                    ◇ A Q 9 2
                    ♣ J 9 5
```

and won the first trick. He would return ♡ 10 which you would allow to win and continue with his third heart, forcing out your king.

Now the situation has changed. Whereas before you still held king and another heart which served to protect the suit if led from the left, you now have no stopper left and West probably has the remaining two, both winners. West has now become the danger hand and must be kept out. So the correct play is to lead ♣ J and finesse. East wins with ♣ Q but has no heart to return. Looking at dummy he may well lead a diamond. You must play your ace as you cannot afford to risk a finesse. Moreover you have nine tricks with four clubs, three spades, one heart and one diamond. It might be thought that South might still have succeeded had he played low from dummy at trick one and played low also from his hand. Then, if West won the next heart lead and cleared the suit, South winning with the king, it would be safe to finesse clubs towards East. But a good defender would duck the heart return, allowing dummy's ♡ Q to win, leaving his partner a third heart to return if he got in.

The next example occurred in a competition where all the competitors at some time play the same hands. This is one of the fascinating aspects of duplicate bridge, as it is called, for it is possible to compare what you have done with what has occured at other tables.

Dealer North. Love all.

```
                    ♠ Q 4 3
                    ♡ K Q J 6
                    ◊ A J 10 8
                    ♣ Q 8
    ♠ 8 2                               ♠ A J 10 9 6
    ♡ 10 9 4 3 2                        ♡ 8 7
    ◊ 6 4 2                             ◊ K 7 3
    ♣ K 7 4                             ♣ 5 3 2
                    ♠ K 7 5
                    ♡ A 5
                    ◊ Q 9 5
                    ♣ A J 10 9 6
```

South	West	North	East
		1 ♡	1 ♠
2 ♣	Pass	2 ◊	Pass
3 NT	Pass	Pass	Pass

West led ♠ 8, top of partner's bid suit, and the play varied according to what happened on the first trick. At some tables South played ♠ Q, taken by ♠ A, and held up ♠ K until the third round. Others played low from dummy, allowed ♠ 8 to win and came in later with ♠ K. It amounted to the same thing in that East held the remainder of the spades. West had no more and this meant that East was the danger hand. Accordingly they led ace and another heart to get to dummy and played ♣ Q. The finesse lost to West who returned a diamond. Not risking the finesse, South played ◊ A, cashed two hearts, and led a club making ten tricks.

(repeated for convenience)

```
                    ♠ Q 4 3
                    ♡ K Q J 6
                    ◇ A J 10 8
                    ♣ Q 8
    ♠ 8 2                           ♠ A J 10 9 6
    ♡ 10 9 4 3 2                    ♡ 8 7
    ◇ 6 4 2                         ◇ K 7 3
    ♣ K 7 4                         ♣ 5 3 2
                    ♠ K 7 5
                    ♡ A 5
                    ◇ Q 9 5
                    ♣ A J 10 9 6
```

This was quite good play in so far as it recognized the need to keep East out of the lead. But good defence would have defeated it. Going back to the point when South played ace and another heart and led ♣ Q, suppose West does not play the king. South probably finesses again and loses. West returns a diamond and South cannot get back to his hand to enjoy the clubs. Even if he takes the second club with the ace he will be a trick short. Alternatively, suppose he leads a low heart to dummy after winning with ♠ K and establishes clubs. Admittedly he now has entry to his hand with ♡ A to make the clubs but he is cut off from the table and cannot make the hearts. Others found a better line of play. They played low from dummy, East played low and South won with ♠ K. This left dummy with ♠ Q 4 which would provide protection if East led and dummy played last. This meant keeping out West. Therefore ◇ Q was next led, the finesse losing to East. Since a spade return would give away a trick East returned a club but South can now count nine tricks with three diamonds, four hearts, one spade and one club.

Problems sometimes arise when you hold one certain trick in the opponent's suit and may have two if you win the first round. It all depends on which defender is likely to get in when you establish your long suit. Consider this example:

Dealer South. Love all.

```
              ♠ K J
              ♡ A 8 7
              ◇ A Q 10 8 5
              ♣ 6 3 2
♠ Q 9 8                      ♠ 10 5 4 3 2
♡ Q 10 3                     ♡ 6 5 4
◇ 3 2                        ◇ K 7 4
♣ A 10 8 7 4                 ♣ Q 5
              ♠ A 7 6
              ♡ K J 9 2
              ◇ J 9 6
              ♣ K J 9
```

South opens with a weak no-trump (12-14 points) and is raised to Three No-Trumps.

West leads ♣ 7 and East plays ♣ Q. South has five top winners in the other suits and must make a trick in clubs. If he takes ♣ Q with ♣ K he may make a second trick with the jack. Suppose he wins the first round with ♣ K, leaving himself with ♣ J 9, can he be sure of a second club trick?

Applying the rule of eleven, the four cards outstanding above the seven of clubs are all accounted for. You hold K J 9, East has played ♣ Q, and therefore West started with ♣ A 10 8 7 and possibly another. East is the danger hand because if he returns a club through you, West will cover whatever you play.

To make the contract you must establish diamonds. Even if the hearts were well placed and you made all four you would still be short of a trick. There is only one feasible way to play the diamonds and that is to lead the jack and finesse against the king. If this fails East is in and that is what has to be avoided. The correct play therefore is to play low to ♣ Q. East will return ♣ 5 and your ♣ J draws ♣ A, a third

round being taken by your king. Now you can finesse
diamonds safely as East has no more clubs to lead.

Suppose your diamond holding had been different:

A 10 8 5 4   (dummy)

K J 9 3   (you)

It would now be safe to win the opening lead with ♣ K as
it would be possible to keep East out by leading ◊ A and
following with a low diamond and finessing ◊ J, not
minding if West gained the lead. In this case you are
missing the queen and, as we have seen earlier, it is
possible to finesse against a queen either way. But you can
only finesse one way against a king.

Here is a similar example:

Dealer South. Game all.

```
                    ♠ 9 3 2
                    ♡ K 6
                    ◊ A 9 6 3
                    ♣ A 9 6 3
    ♠ A 10 6 5 4                      ♠ J 7
    ♡ 10 5 3                          ♡ J 9 8 7 2
    ◊ 7 5                             ◊ K 8 4
    ♣ J 8 7                           ♣ Q 5 4
                    ♠ K Q 8
                    ♡ A Q 4
                    ◊ Q J 10 2
                    ♣ K 10 2
```

South	West	North	East
1 NT	Pass	3 NT	Pass
Pass	Pass		

West leads ♠ 5 and East plays ♠ J. Do you take it and hope for a second spade trick? Your extra tricks are to come from diamonds and you will have to lead ◇ Q and finesse into East's hand. If that fails a spade return through your remaining honour will be fatal. Therefore, hold up, rather as if you held A x x. By the time your stopper is knocked out East will have no further spades and he will be no danger to you.

Here is a further example:

Dealer North. Love all.

```
                    ♠ K 7 4
                    ♡ K 6 4
                    ◇ A J 10 9 6 5
                    ♣ 2
  ♠ Q 10 9                        ♠ J 8 6 3
  ♡ J 9 5                         ♡ Q 10 8 3
  ◇ 8 4                           ◇ K 2
  ♣ A 10 7 6 3                    ♣ K 8 5
                    ♠ A 5 2
                    ♡ A 7 2
                    ◇ Q 7 3
                    ♣ Q J 9 4
```

South	West	North	East
		1 ◇	Pass
3 NT	Pass	Pass	Pass

West leads ♣ 6 taken with ♣ K and ♣ 8 returned. The rule of eleven shows West to have led from A 10 7 6 with probably a fifth card as East, with four, would have returned fourth best. It is tempting for South to cover with ♣ Q or ♣ J, hoping that West will win and return the suit. But West will realize that he would be leading into a tenace, either Q 9 or J 9, and he would play low. Now when the diamond finesse fails East returns his ♣ 5 and West has three winners.

Again, South must retain his stopper as long as possible. He covers ♣ 8 with ♣ 9. West can win with ♣ 10 and cash ♣ A, clearing his suit. But East is also cleared of clubs and can do no harm when he gets in with the king of diamonds.

12. Timing

So far we have only dealt with situations where it has been necessary to establish one suit to provide the extra tricks necessary for the contract. The usual advice given to beginners is to go for the long suit first. That advice is excellent providing that the suit is long enough, but it may become necessary to set up more than one suit and then it does not follow that the longer suit should be attacked first.

Consider this hand:

Dealer South. North-South vul.

```
                    ♠ Q 10 6 2
                    ♡ 10 2
                    ◇ A J 10 7 6
                    ♣ K 7
   ♠ A 8 3                          ♠ 9 7 5 4
   ♡ K 9 8 7 6                      ♡ J 5 4
   ◇ 4 2                            ◇ K 5
   ♣ 9 5 4                          ♣ Q J 6 3
                    ♠ K J
                    ♡ A Q 3
                    ◇ Q 9 8 3
                    ♣ A 10 8 2
```

South	West	North	East
1 NT	Pass	2 ♣	Pass
2 ◇	Pass	3 NT	Pass
Pass	Pass		

In reply to South's strong no-trump call North bids Two Clubs (Stayman) asking for a four-card major. When South denies possession of either four cards in hearts or spades, North converts to Three No-Trumps.

West leads ♡ 7 covered by ♡ 10, ♡ J and ♡ Q. South has five top winners and the natural inclination is to play the queen of diamonds to set up the longest suit. If West holds the king there are plenty of tricks, but if East wins and returns a heart South will be in difficulty. He will hold up his ace until the third round and play off the rest of the diamonds, but he will then have only eight tricks. Needing one more he will play a spade hoping East has the ace, but unfortunately West has it and also two winning hearts to defeat the contract.

South should have played ♠ K at trick two. If it wins he can, if he wishes, switch to diamonds, but as his spades are quite strong he can afford to play another. Assume West wins the first or second round and plays ♡ K, South ducks and takes the third round. He next leads ◊ Q and finesses. East wins but has no heart to return. If he had the suit would have divided 4–4 and it would not matter. East's ace of spades having been forced out early, there is no way in which he can regain the lead to play his winning hearts. If East had held the ace of spades it would have made no difference.

The principle can be stated as follows:

When it is necessary to establish more than one suit in a no-trump contract first attack the suit in which the danger hand has a possible entry card. In the absence of any bidding the danger hand is probably that which leads, in this case, West. Of the two important cards, king of diamonds and ace of spades, the only entry card West could have is the ace of spades. If he had the king of diamonds it would be of no value as dummy held the ace.

Some further examples may help to clarify the position.

Dealer South. East-West vul.

```
                  ♠ 6 4
                  ♡ Q 10 4
                  ◇ K 9 6 5
                  ♣ A 10 8 5
♠ K 10 8 7 5                      ♠ J 9 2
♡ A 8 7                          ♡ 9 6 5 2
◇ 8 4 3                          ◇ Q J 7 2
♣ 3 2                            ♣ K 6
                  ♠ A Q 3
                  ♡ K J 3
                  ◇ A 10
                  ♣ Q J 9 7 4
```

South	West	North	East
1 ♣	Pass	1 ◇	Pass
2 NT	Pass	3 NT	Pass
Pass	Pass		

West leads ♠ 7 to ♠ J and ♠ Q. There are five top tricks (two spades, two diamonds, one club) and four more are needed. Clubs is the longest suit and if the finesse succeeds you will make overtricks. But if the finesse loses you will have four clubs, two spades and two diamonds, total eight. You need a heart trick. You are therefore in the position of needing to establish more than one suit.

Which is the danger hand? West. He probably led his best suit.

What card of entry can he hold? Ace of hearts. King of clubs will be valueless.

So at trick two lead ♡ K. If West wins, hold up spades until the third round and then finesse clubs towards East. If ♡ K wins, switch at once to clubs. You only need one heart trick and if you continue you could run into trouble if East holds five with the ace, plus king of clubs.

Another example:

Dealer North. North-South vul.

```
                ♠ K 8
                ♡ K Q 7
                ◇ A 8 7 2
                ♣ Q 9 8 7
♠ 9 5 4                        ♠ Q J 10 7 2
♡ 10 9 6 5 4                   ♡ A 3
◇ J 9 6                        ◇ Q 10 5
♣ K 2                          ♣ 5 4 3
                ♠ A 6 3
                ♡ J 8 2
                ◇ K 4 3
                ♣ A J 10 6
```

South	West	North	East
		1 ◇	1 ♠
3 NT	Pass	Pass	Pass

West leads ♠ 9, top of partner's suit, and dummy wins with ♠ K. There are five top tricks and it is necessary to make up the deficit from hearts and clubs.

East is the danger hand as he called spades and presumably has five or six headed by Q J 10. His only entry can be the ace of hearts. To trick two lead ♡ 7. If East plays low, win with ♡ J and return ♡ 2 to ♡ Q and ♡ A. East returns ♠ Q which you allow to win and take the continuation with ♠ A. Next cross to dummy with ◇ A. It would be dangerous to use your last heart. Finesse clubs and West wins but has no spade left, and East is without an entry.

A final example:

Dealer South. Love all.

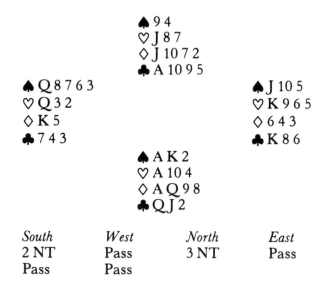

	♠ 9 4	
	♡ J 8 7	
	◊ J 10 7 2	
	♣ A 10 9 5	

♠ Q 8 7 6 3		♠ J 10 5
♡ Q 3 2		♡ K 9 6 5
◊ K 5		◊ 6 4 3
♣ 7 4 3		♣ K 8 6

	♠ A K 2	
	♡ A 10 4	
	◊ A Q 9 8	
	♣ Q J 2	

South	*West*	*North*	*East*
2 NT	Pass	3 NT	Pass
Pass	Pass		

West leads ♠ 6 to ♠ 10 and ♠ K. With the familiar five top tricks South needs to establish both clubs and diamonds. It is tempting to finesse in both suits but that would result in defeat. You might wish to finesse diamonds early having correctly decided that West is the danger hand. But to get to dummy it is necessary to use the ace of clubs which you cannot afford. West's only entry is the king of diamonds if he has it, so play ◊A followed by ◊ Q. West wins and returns a spade which you duck and take the third round with your ace.

Next finesse clubs into the safe East hand. Having no more spades East may lead a heart, but you must play ♡ A as you can see your nine tricks with three diamonds, three clubs, two spades and one heart. The hand was a little more difficult because you had tempting finesses in two suits. Had your diamonds been K Q 9 8 it would have been easier to see that you needed to attack West's possible entry.

When needing to establish more than one suit it is often

helpful to decide which opponent you would prefer to have the lead the first time you lose a trick. This often amounts to attacking the entry of the danger hand, as we have described above, but sometimes it may be difficult for the danger hand to continue with his suit.

Dealer South. Game all.

```
                     ♠ A
                     ♡ Q J 8 2
                     ◇ J 10 9
                     ♣ K Q 10 6 3
♠ Q 9 7 4 2                              ♠ 10 8 5 3
♡ K 6 4 3                                ♡ 10 9 5
◇ 7 2                                    ◇ K Q 8 5
♣ 8 4                                    ♣ A 7
                     ♠ K J 6
                     ♡ A 7
                     ◇ A 6 4 3
                     ♣ J 9 5 2
```

South	West	North	East
1 ♣	Pass	1 ♡	Pass
1 NT	Pass	3 NT	Pass
Pass	Pass		

West leads ♠ 4 taken with ♠ A. With only four top tricks South looks to his long suit, clubs. But this will only bring the total to eight and the safest way to make one more is in hearts, for even if the finesse loses there will be one more trick.

Holding ♠ K J it is clearly desirable to lose early to West because he cannot continue his suit without giving you an extra trick. If you play clubs you do not know who has the ace. As it is East will win and return a spade through your K J and West's suit will become established. Better to lead ♡ Q. If the finesse wins all is well. If West wins he cannot profitably continue spades. Now you make two spades, two hearts, one diamond and four clubs.

Here is another example:

Dealer South. North-South vul.

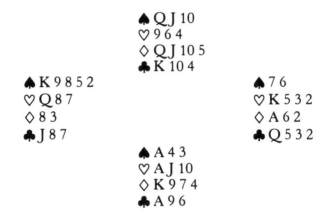

♠ Q J 10
♥ 9 6 4
♦ Q J 10 5
♣ K 10 4

♠ K 9 8 5 2
♥ Q 8 7
♦ 8 3
♣ J 8 7

♠ 7 6
♥ K 5 3 2
♦ A 6 2
♣ Q 5 3 2

♠ A 4 3
♥ A J 10
♦ K 9 7 4
♣ A 9 6

South opened a strong no-trump (16-18) and North raised to Three No-Trumps with nine points and three tens. West leads ♠ 5 and ♠ 10 wins the first trick. South has five top tricks and by establishing diamonds he can bring the total to eight, needing one more.

The best chance lies in hearts. If the missing honours are divided, as is most likely, two finesses should provide an extra trick. That is to say, if a low heart is led from the table and ♥ 10 played, losing to either ♥ Q or ♥ K, South will be left with a simple finesse against the remaining honour. The problem is which suit to play first. Applying the principle given above, where do you want the lead to be when you lose your first trick. Clearly West, because he cannot play spades again without giving you an extra trick.

A heart return will save you the trouble and worry of a second finesse and a club will do you no harm and would, in effect, give you a third club trick. At trick two, therefore, you lead ♥ 4, covered by ♥ 3, ♥ 10 and ♥ Q. West's only safe lead is a diamond which does no good but equally no harm. East wins with ♦ A and returns ♠ 6. When in with ♠ A, South plays off his diamonds, ending in dummy, and takes a second heart finesse. When this succeeds he has nine tricks. Had West held both king and queen of hearts the contract fails, but this would have been against the normal probabilities. Suppose that South had played diamonds first. East wins and returns a spade, establishing his partner's suit. Eventually West gets in with a heart to defeat the contract.

A final example:

Dealer South. Game all.

```
              ♠ 5 4 2
              ♡ K J 8
              ◇ Q J 10
              ♣ K 10 9 2
♠ K 10 9 6 3               ♠ 8 7
♡ 9 4 2                    ♡ Q 7 6 3
◇ K 7 4                    ◇ 9 6 3 2
♣ 4 3                     ♣ A 7 5
              ♠ A Q J
              ♡ A 10 5
              ◇ A 8 5
              ♣ Q J 8 6
```

West leads ♠ 6 against Three No-Trumps and South wins with ♠ J. There are five top tricks and the clubs can provide three more. An extra trick could be made in hearts if declarer guessed rightly which way to finesse. But an extra trick is certain by finessing diamonds even if the finesse fails. Again, it is important to let West in early as he cannot safely return spades. You do not know where the ace of clubs is. If it is with East a spade return will clear West's suit and a subsequent losing diamond finesse will be fatal. But you do know who will win a diamond trick if the finesse fails. Therefore cross to dummy with ♡ K and lead ◇ Q. West wins and his best return is a diamond. Now you knock out the ace of clubs and make nine tricks with two spades, two hearts, two diamonds and three clubs.

13. Blocking Opponent's Suit

Earlier we referred to blocking a suit. This usually resulted in failing to play the high card from the shorter suit with a solid holding, the consequence being that there were a number of winning cards that were wasted because there was no means of reaching them.

In this section we are going to consider the position where, as declarer, you can block the opponent's suit. In a sense a simple hold up (v. page 20) is a form of blocking play inasmuch that it may cut one hand off from another and deprive a defender of an opportunity to cash winners.

But the term blocking play usually refers to a slightly different situation.

Dealer South. Love all.

```
                    ♠ Q 4 3
                    ♡ J 10 8 7
                    ◇ A 5
                    ♣ Q 10 9 8
     ♠ 8 7 2                          ♠ 10 9 6 5
     ♡ A 9                            ♡ 6 5 4 3
     ◇ K J 7 6 3                      ◇ Q 8
     ♣ 7 6 5                          ♣ 4 3 2
                    ♠ A K J
                    ♡ K Q 2
                    ◇ 10 9 4 2
                    ♣ A K J
```

South	West	North	East
2 NT	Pass	3 NT	Pass
Pass	Pass		

West led ◇ 6 on which ◇ 5 was played from the table. East won with ◇ Q and returned ◇ 8 to ◇ A. South had eight sure winners but had to play hearts and West unfortunately held the ace, and three winning diamonds to defeat the contract. With thirty high card points between the two hands this was a big disappointment.

More thought should have been given to the play to the first trick. The contract is only in danger if West started with a five card suit, in which case East has two. It is a fair assumption that West does not hold K Q J for his natural lead would be the king, top of the sequence. Therefore, if East has two cards they must be K X, Q X or J X. If ◊ A is played from the table on the opening lead what can East do? Suppose he plays ◊ 8. South next leads hearts and West is in with ♡ A. He can play ◊ 3 to ◊ Q but East cannot return the suit. Alternatively he can lay down ◊ K, felling ◊ Q but then South's ◊ 10 will become a trick. Which will also be the case if East tried to unblock by playing his ◊ Q on ◊ A.

Most text books on play will cite this situation with the brief advice that with A x in dummy and 10 x x x in your hand and a low card led, you play the ace to block the suit. But this is more easily remembered and recognized if you understand why it happens. That is why I have spent a certain amount of time and space explaining it.

You will now be in a position to cope with the next example which is of a similar nature.

Dealer South. East-West vul.

```
              ♠ K Q 6 2
              ♡ A Q J 3
              ◊ A J
              ♣ 9 6 4
♠ A 9                          ♠ 10 8 7 4 3
♡ 8 7                          ♡ 9 6 5 4 2
◊ Q 10 7 4 3                   ◊ K 6
♣ Q 10 8 2                     ♣ 5
              ♠ J 5
              ♡ K 10
              ◊ 9 8 5 2
              ♣ A K J 7 3
```

(repeated for convenience)

```
                    ♠ K Q 6 2
                    ♡ A Q J 3
                    ◇ A J
                    ♣ 9 6 4
  ♠ A 9                              ♠ 10 8 7 4 3
  ♡ 8 7                              ♡ 9 6 5 4 2
  ◇ Q 10 7 4 3                       ◇ K 6
  ♣ Q 10 8 2                         ♣ 5
                    ♠ J 5
                    ♡ K 10
                    ◇ 9 8 5 2
                    ♣ A K J 7 3
```

South	West	North	East
1 NT	Pass	2 ♣	Pass
2 ◇	Pass	3 NT	Pass
Pass	Pass		

South should have opened One Club but being not vulnerable and an addict of the weak no-trump, the sight of twelve high card points was all he needed to bid One No-Trump. North investigated a major suit fit by calling a conventional Two Club and the final contract was Three No-Trumps, against which West led ◇ 4. South played ◇ J from dummy, East won and returned the suit.

South saw seven tricks with the possibility of making more from clubs or spades. He cashed ♣ A K in case the queen might fall. When this did not happen he tried spades but West had the ace and the contract finally went two down. The diamond position is virtually the same as in the previous hand. South's holding is headed only by the nine but dummy has ace and jack. So by playing ◇ A at trick one the opponent's suit would be blocked.

The next example probably comes within the classification of blocking plays, but its effect is to immobilise the suit insofar as it is not possible for the defender to continue playing his suit without giving away a trick.

Dealer South. North-South vul.

```
                    ♠ 9 8 4 2
                    ♡ Q 10 6
                    ◇ A J 6 5
                    ♣ 9 6
   ♠ 7 6 5 3                         ♠ Q J 10
   ♡ 8 2                             ♡ A J 9 7 4
   ◇ Q 10 8 4                        ◇ 7 2
   ♣ A 3 2                           ♣ 7 5 4
                    ♠ A K
                    ♡ K 5 3
                    ◇ K 9 3
                    ♣ K Q J 10 8
```

South	West	North	East
1 ♣	Pass	1 ◇	1 ♡
3 NT	Pass	Pass	Pass

West led ♡ 8 to which dummy played ♡ 6, East ♡ 7 and South ♡ K. South started on his clubs and West won with the ace and returned ♡ 2. East collected four tricks to defeat the contract. It would have made no difference had ♡ 10 been played to the first trick as East would have covered with ♡ J, leaving himself a strong holding over dummy.

North pointed out that had South ducked the opening lead he could have made his game because West would be unable to return a heart when in with the ace of clubs. But South contended that had East held the ace of clubs, as was likely on his overcall, he would be safe to win the opening lead with ♡ K. But had South played ♡ Q on the opening lead it would not have mattered where the ace of clubs was. East wins with ♡ A as he cannot gain by not doing so. If he returns a low heart South can safely play low as dummy will win with ♡ 10. West's lead is clearly his highest and East holds A J 9 x x. East probably switches to ♠ Q but South has now gained time and will be able to establish clubs whilst still holding a heart stopper.

Another example:

Dealer North. North-South vul.

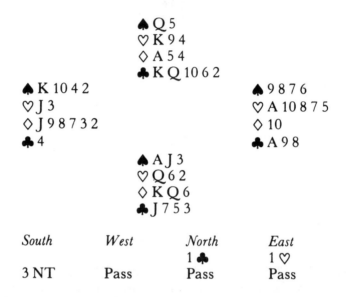

	♠ Q 5	
	♡ K 9 4	
	◇ A 5 4	
	♣ K Q 10 6 2	

South	West	North	East
		1 ♣	1 ♡
3 NT	Pass	Pass	Pass

West leads ♡ J and the correct play is to put up ♡ K from the table. It will not now matter who has the ace of clubs. As it happens East holds it, and South would have been all right to play low from the table and win in hand with ♡ Q. But exchange ♣ A for ♠ K, giving East a fair non-vulnerable overcall, and the contract would be defeated as West would get in with ♣ A and return a low heart.

It is likely that East has ♡ 10 for his call but it does not matter. Suppose East takes ♡ K with ♡ A and switches to a spade. South should win and clear clubs. If West should hold the ten of hearts the suit will be blocked.

On this hand South's correct play to trick one can be found by applying the rule of eleven.

Dealer South. Game all.

```
                    ♠ A 5 2
                    ♡ Q J 7
                    ◇ K J 10 9 8
                    ♣ 9 2
     ♠ 10 8 4                         ♠ J 9 6 3
     ♡ K 5 4                          ♡ 9 8 6 2
     ◇ 2                              ◇ 7 6 3
     ♣ K 10 7 6 5 4                   ♣ A J
                    ♠ K Q 7
                    ♡ A 10 3
                    ◇ A Q 5 4
                    ♣ Q 8 3
```

South	West	North	East
1 NT	Pass	3 NT	Pass
Pass	Pass		

West leads ♣ 6, East wins with ♣ A and returns ♣ J. It is easy to know what to do seeing all four hands, but assume only your hand and that of dummy is visible. South has his contract all right providing he can avoid the loss of too many tricks in clubs. West's lead is presumably fourth best so that there are five higher clubs than the six, divided between South, North and East. South can see three (♣ 9, ♣ Q and ♣ 8), East has played ♣ A and returned ♣ J, so West has all the remaining clubs higher than the six. So it will be fatal to cover the knave as West will take with ♣ K and play off the rest. South's only chance is to play low and hope East has no more clubs.

This hope is realised when East switches to a heart which South gratefully wins with his ace and makes his contract with five diamonds, three spades and one heart. Suppose West had led ♣5 and not ♣6. What difference would it make? In this case there would be six outstanding clubs above the five and East, after returning ♣J, holds one more. It is now correct for South to cover with ♣Q as his only real hope is that East's remaining club is the ten, in which case the suit will be blocked after West has won the queen with the king and returned a third round.

This next example is less easy:

Dealer South. Love all.

```
                  ♠ 4
                  ♡ K 6 4
                  ◇ K Q 10 6 2
                  ♣ A 8 6 3
  ♠ K 8 7 5 3                      ♠ Q J 10
  ♡ Q 8 3                          ♡ J 10 9 7
  ◇ A 4 3                          ◇ 8 7
  ♣ Q 4                            ♣ J 10 9 7
                  ♠ A 9 6 2
                  ♡ A 5 2
                  ◇ J 9 5
                  ♣ K 5 2
```

South	West	North	East
1 NT (12-14)	Pass	3 NT	Pass
Pass	Pass		

West leads ♠5, East plays ♠10 and South ducks. East returns ♠Q. What should South do?

On the lead there are six cards above the five missing from West's hand. South has three and East three. The play to the first trick and the second indicates that East has Q J 10, so South should win with ♠A and attack diamonds. West wins and can lead a low spade to East's ♠J but the suit is now blocked and East cannot continue, so is forced to switch. Had South played low again, East would have continued with ♠ J and, if South still held off, West would overtake with ♠ K and clear the suit, still having the ace of diamonds as entry.

This final example of a blocking play might well be missed.

Dealer North. North-South vul.

```
                    ♠ 4 3
                    ♡ A Q 7
                    ◊ K Q 10 9 7
                    ♣ A J 4
♠ Q 7 2                             ♠ A 9 8 6 5
♡ J 9 8 3                           ♡ 10 5 2
◊ 5 4                               ◊ A 6 3
♣ 10 9 5 2                          ♣ K 8
                    ♠ K J 10
                    ♡ K 6 4
                    ◊ J 8 2
                    ♣ Q 7 6 3
```

South	West	North	East
		1 ◊	1 ♠
1 NT	Pass	2 NT	Pass
3 NT	Pass	Pass	Pass

South's One No-Trump after an intervening bid is apt to be a little better than just five or six or seven points. Once North raises to Two No-Trumps, South with a maximum bids game. West leads ♠ 2 and South can see his contract if he can set up the diamonds. His main worry is losing too many spade tricks in the meantime.

East wins the opening lead with ♠ A and returns ♠ 6. Deciding to hold up as long as possible South plays ♠ J which West wins and clears his partner's suit. As East holds the ace of diamonds it can be seen that the contract is doomed. South should have given more thought to the lead. If it were top of partner's suit East would have held a seven card suit headed by ace queen and might have pre-empted.

It was more likely to be a low card from three headed by an honour, which could only be the queen. So South's correct play is to put up the king. If West plays low the suit will be blocked when East gets in with ◊ A and returns a spade. West can try a club but South will play for safety and put up ♣ A and run off nine tricks. If West tries to unblock by playing ♠ Q under ♠ K, South's jack will be a winner.

14. Avoiding Unnecessary Finesse

I believe it was the late S.J. Simon who stated the simple fact that the easiest way to make Three No-Trumps is to count nine tricks. This may appear to be a somewhat obvious fact but disregard of this advice results in many contracts being needlessly defeated, often due to unnecessary finesses being taken.

Dealer South. Love all.

```
              ♠ J 8 5
              ♡ K 3
              ◊ A Q 10 5
              ♣ K Q J 4
♠ A Q 9                      ♠ 7 6 4 2
♡ 9 8 6 5 4                  ♡ Q 10 7
◊ 2                          ◊ K J 9 6
♣ 10 7 6 3                   ♣ 8 2
              ♠ K 10 3
              ♡ A J 2
              ◊ 8 7 4 3
              ♣ A 9 5
```

South opened a weak no-trump and was raised to Three No-Trumps. West led ♡ 5 which gave South a good start and there were eight top tricks. To trick two South led ◊ 3 and finessed ◊ 10, losing to ◊ J. East returned ♡ 10 to ♡ K and the closed hand was entered with ♣ A to take a further diamond finesse. But when West discarded ♠ 9 prospects looked bleak. Having to abandon diamonds, South tried ♠ 5 to ♠ 10 but this lost to ♠ Q and a third heart finally cleared West's suit, the ace of spades provided the entry. South reckoned he was very unlucky. He explained to his partner all about the percentages in favour of the diamond honours being divided, coupled with the 68% chance of the five cards being split 3–2.

What he overlooked was that by playing spades at trick two, regardless of the position of ace and queen, he was bound to make one trick and that was all he needed.

Frequently the mistake is to take an unnecessary finesse on the opening lead.

Dealer South. Game all.

```
                    ♠ A J 10 9
                    ♡ 9 7 4
                    ◊ J 8 3
                    ♣ Q 9 3
    ♠ 8 7 6 5 4                     ♠ K 2
    ♡ K 6 2                         ♡ Q 10 8 3
    ◊ 6 2                           ◊ A 7 4
    ♣ 7 5 4                         ♣ 10 8 6 2
                    ♠ Q 3
                    ♡ A J 5
                    ◊ K Q 10 9 5
                    ♣ A K J
```

South	West	North	East
2 NT	Pass	3 NT	Pass
Pass	Pass		

West led ♠ 5, preferring fourth best to ♠ 8, top of a sequence. This turned out to be a good choice as it coaxed South into a rash play of ♠ 9 from dummy. East won with ♠ K and made the good return of ♡ 10, carefully selecting the card to beat dummy. South covered with ♡ J, losing to

♡ K and ♡ 6 was returned. It did not matter what was played from the table as East was well placed to cope.

So this promising looking contract went down when East regained the lead with ◊ A. South should have reckoned that he had five top tricks and that he could make four more from diamonds. He might not have envisaged the danger from the heart, it was not all that obvious. Had he done so he should have played dummy's ♠ A immediately and set up the diamonds while he had control of each suit.

This is easier to recognise:

```
                   ♠ A J 5
                   ♡ A 5
                   ◊ Q 10 9 6 3
                   ♣ 6 3 2
♠ 10 8 6 4 2                        ♠ K 3
♡ 10 9 3                           ♡ J 8 6 4
◊ 7 4                              ◊ A 2
♣ K 5 4                           ♣ J 10 9 8 7
                   ♠ Q 9 7
                   ♡ K Q 7 2
                   ◊ K J 8 5
                   ♣ A Q
```

South	West	North	East
1 ♡	Pass	2 ◊	Pass
3 NT	Pass	Pass	Pass

West leads ♠ 4. You have five top tricks and diamonds must provide four. At the time you establish your long suit it is essential that every suit should be under control. Therefore play ♠ A at trick one and attack diamonds. The opponents can take their king of spades but you still hold a stopper. But consider what happens if you take the spade finesse. East wins and switches to ♣ J and you will be two down.

If offered the chance of a finesse at trick one, ask yourself
   (a) Is the finesse necessary?
   (b) If it fails what can happen?

Applying that to the present deal the answer to (a) is No, and to (b) they may attack clubs through my A Q.

On this hand South thought he was playing safely. He wasn't.

Dealer South. Love all.

```
                    ♠ A 4
                    ♡ 6 4 3 2
                    ◇ A Q 4 2
                    ♣ K J 9
   ♠ J 9 8 6 2                        ♠ K 10 7
   ♡ 8 7 5                            ♡ K Q J 10
   ◇ 5 3                              ◇ J 10 9 7
   ♣ Q 7 3                            ♣ 8 2
                    ♠ Q 5 3
                    ♡ A 9
                    ◇ K 8 6
                    ♣ A 10 6 5 4
```

South opened a weak no-trump and North decided to bid Three No-Trumps and not use Stayman to look for a heart fit. West led ♠ 6 and South lost no time in playing ♠ 4 from dummy. After all, there was a good chance of making the queen on the opening lead. Even if East held the king of spades, playing low from dummy ensured that the queen became a trick. East won with ♠ K and switched to ♡ K. This was an annoying development. South played low and won the second round perforce with ♡ A. Having learned all about safe hands and danger hands he led ♣ 4 to ♣ K and returned ♣ J, finessing when not covered. East had to be kept out and there was every chance that West had no more hearts. But he had and South went down.

Had South stopped to ask himself the two questions put above he would have done better.

(a) Was the finesse necessary? No, because providing he finessed clubs towards West, as he did, the spades were protected with Q x in his hand and the lead coming from his left.

(b) If it fails, what can happen? A heart switch.

The danger was more heavily concealed on this hand, but the rule of eleven might have averted the disaster.

Dealer South. Game all.

```
                     ♠ Q 3
                     ♡ A 9 7 2
                     ◇ A 8 7 5 4
                     ♣ 9 2
  ♠ 9 8 7 6 5                            ♠ J 10
  ♡ 6 4                                  ♡ K Q 5 3
  ◇ 10 3                                 ◇ Q J 9
  ♣ K 7 6 4                              ♣ J 10 8 5
                     ♠ A K 4 2
                     ♡ J 10 8
                     ◇ K 6 2
                     ♣ A Q 3
```

South	West	North	East
1 ♠	Pass	2 ◇	Pass
3 NT	Pass	Pass	Pass

There did not seem to be much point in leading a spade and South's strong bidding made a club unattractive. So West selected ♡ 6 which seemed quite innocuous to South as he played low from dummy. He reckoned to make three tricks in this suit. But East won with ♡ Q and switched to ♣ J. South put up his ace and hoped to lose a diamond trick to West. This did not happen and East got in and continued with ♣ 10 to put the contract one down.

Applying the rule of eleven there should be only five hearts above the six divided between the hands of North, East and South. But South could see six and therefore West's lead was not fourth best. More likely top of nothing. Therefore South should have put up ♡ A at trick one and ducked a round of diamonds. The hearts were still protected as were the spades and clubs and nine tricks would have been made with three spades, one heart at least, four diamonds and a club.

In this final example an unnecessary finesse resulted in disaster in an unexpected way.

Dealer South. East West vul.

```
                  ♠ K Q 2
                  ♡ A Q J 2
                  ◊ 2
                  ♣ Q J 10 9 2
  ♠ J 7 5                          ♠ A 10 9 3
  ♡ 9 7 5 4 3                      ♡ K 10 8
  ◊ 5 3                            ◊ 9 8 7
  ♣ K 8 3                          ♣ A 7 5
                  ♠ 8 6 4
                  ♡ 6
                  ◊ A K Q J 10 6 4
                  ♣ 6 4
```

South opened Three No-Trumps and all passed. This is what is commonly known as the "gambling Three No-Trump opening bid". Originally an integral part of the British Acol System it has been adopted widely. The bid promises a long (seven cards at least) completely solid minor suit with virtually nothing outside. If the partner's hand is quite unsuited, being too weak in controls, the reply is Four Clubs which the opener will either pass, if it is his suit, or convert to Four Diamonds.

The standard opening lead against this bid is an ace in order to remain on lead when dummy is exposed. To give away the lead early will probably be fatal as declarer will have run off his long suit.

West did not have an ace and so took a chance with ♡ 4. South saw no risk in finessing as every suit was protected. East won and returned a diamond. South was able to make all his diamonds but in the process it was impossible to find discards from dummy without giving up protection. Sad to relate the contract was one down. South should have put up ♡ A at trick one and led ♠ K at trick two. This would have ensured his ninth trick.

15. Attacking Suit with Inevitable Losers

As I stated at the beginning of this book it is not easy for a beginner to play a card that he knows will be taken, but to attack a suit with inevitable losers is often correct play. You are only giving to the opponents the tricks they are certain to win. The examples that follow are all low contracts, often the most difficult to make owing to the combined strength being evenly divided between the two sides.

Dealer South. Game all.

```
                    ♠ Q 10 9 7
                    ♡ K 9 4
                    ◇ 6 4 3 2
                    ♣ K 6
  ♠ K J 6                              ♠ A 8 2
  ♡ J 10                               ♡ Q 8 5 2
  ◇ K 10 8                             ◇ Q J
  ♣ 10 8 5 4 2                         ♣ Q 9 7 3
                    ♠ 5 4 3
                    ♡ A 7 6 3
                    ◇ A 9 7 5
                    ♣ A J
```

South	West	North	East
1 ♡	Pass	1 ♠	Pass
1 NT	Pass	Pass	Pass

West leads ♣ 4 to ♣ 6, ♣ Q and ♣ A. South can see five tricks and needs two more. Numerically his best suit is diamonds but at best he can expect one extra trick from the suit and that will involve losing two. Meanwhile he will lose at least three clubs and two spades and will be down. An even break in hearts will provide one more trick but that will not solve the problem. The only suit that can yield two tricks is spades. It requires that West holds the jack. So at trick two South leads ♠ 3, West plays ♠ 6 and ♠ 9 is played from the table, losing to ♠ A. This confirms that West holds the jack. East returns ♣ 3 and ♣ K and the closed hand is entered with ♡ A for another spade lead. West can win with the king and cash his three clubs but South will regain the lead with ◇ A and the two spade winners in dummy make up the two tricks needed.

You may say it was lucky West held the jack of spades, but if that card had been with East the contract would have failed. But the defenders would always have been able to take three spades when they liked.

Dealer North. East-West vul.

```
                    ♠ 6 5 4
                    ♡ A Q 10
                    ◇ A K 7 6 4
                    ♣ 4 3
  ♠ 10 2                              ♠ A Q J 9 8
  ♡ 5 4 3 2                           ♡ 8 7 6
  ◇ Q J 10                            ◇ 9 2
  ♣ K 10 9 6                          ♣ A 5 2
                    ♠ K 7 3
                    ♡ K J 9
                    ◇ 8 5 3
                    ♣ Q J 8 7
```

South	West	North	East
		1 ◇	1 ♠
1 NT	Pass	Pass	Pass

West leads ♠ 10 which East correctly overtakes with ♠ J in case his partner has no more. It does not matter whether South wins or not. Assume he plays low and East continues with ♠ 8, taken with ♠ K. There are six top tricks and the natural inclination may be to go for the diamonds. With a normal 3–2 split it should be possible to make four diamonds, one spade and three hearts – contract with an overtrick. But stop to consider what will be lost. East must surely have a five card suit for his overcall, so you will lose four tricks in spades. You must lose two clubs so that the moment you give up a diamond to establish your suit you have virtually conceded the seventh trick.

You must forget the diamonds apart from the ace and king and look for your extra trick in clubs. Provided that you lead from the table towards your queen knave you will make a trick unless both ace and king are on your left. This is improbable and East must have one top club on his overcall. Therefore, after winning with ♠ K, cross to the table with ♡ Q and lead a club. If East plays low put up ♣ J, losing to West who has no spade. If he returns a heart, win with ♡ A and lead a club. East wins and cashes his spades, but you make the rest. It was important to use hearts as entries to dummy as you hold three stoppers. It was also necessary to ensure that you had a high heart as entry to your hand.

The important principle is that in playing clubs you were only giving to the opponents the tricks they were bound to win, but in so doing you established a valuable trick for yourself.

Careful attention to entries is needed in this hand.

Dealer North. Game all.

```
              ♠ A K 10 5
              ♡ J 5 4 3
              ◇ Q 3
              ♣ A 10 6
♠ 3 2                       ♠ J 9 8 4
♡ K 10 9 7                  ♡ A 6
◇ A K 6                     ◇ J 7 5 4
♣ Q 8 7 3                   ♣ 9 5 4
              ♠ Q 7 6
              ♡ Q 8 2
              ◇ 10 9 8 2
              ♣ K J 2
```

South	West	North	East
		1 ♠	Pass
1 NT	Pass	Pass	Pass

West leads ♡ 7 to ♡ A and ♡ 6 is returned, covered by ♡ 8, ♡ 9 and ♡ J. South has six top tricks and there are various chances of making the seventh. An even division of

(*repeated for convenience*)

```
                    ♠ A K 10 5
                    ♡ J 5 4 3
                    ◇ Q 3
                    ♣ A 10 6
    ♠ 3 2                            ♠ J 9 8 4
    ♡ K 10 9 7                       ♡ A 6
    ◇ A K 6                          ◇ J 7 5 4
    ♣ Q 8 7 3                        ♣ 9 5 4
                    ♠ Q 7 6
                    ♡ Q 8 2
                    ◇ 10 9 8 2
                    ♣ K J 2
```

spades, or the jack falling, would do, or a successful finesse in clubs. The best plan is to attack diamonds, the suit in which the opponents are sure to have three winners but which will ultimately provide you with one.

At trick three lead ◇ Q, losing to ◇ K. West cashes his two hearts, East discarding a diamond, and a club, and you ♠ 6. West switches to ♠ 3 and this is where you need to be careful. If you play low from table and win in hand with ♠ Q, and follow with ◇ 10, West will win and play ♠ 2. You take in dummy but need to cross to your hand with ♣ K to play a third diamond. You also have to discard from dummy whose remaining cards are

♠ A 10   ♡ –   ◇ –   ♣ A 10

Whichever ten you discard, East will win with ◇ J and return a card to your singleton ace, and you will lose the last trick to either the queen of spades or clubs.

But suppose you win West's spade switch at trick six with ♠ K and lead ◇ 3. West wins and returns a spade, taken in hand with ♠ Q, and ◇ 10 is led, losing to East. You still have the king of clubs as an entry for your now established ◇ 8.

PART THREE

The Play of the Hand in Suit Contracts

There are two main differences between the play of the
hand in a suit contract and the play in no-trumps.

In a suit contract you have more control over the hand.
There is not the same fear that an opponent will be able to
lead out a long established suit against you, for in a suit
contract you can stop him with a trump. This presupposes
that you have an adequate supply of trumps. If you keep
having to use a trump in this way you may run short and
the hand may go out of control. Also, there are more ways by
which you can win tricks in a suit contract. A common
example is by ruffing losing cards with small trumps in the
shorter hand.

16. When to Draw Trumps

In the majority of hands it is correct to draw trumps early.
That is to say, to remove the trumps from your opponents.
If you have tricks to make in other suits or you have a strong
suit other than trumps, it is common sense that you should
protect yourself from losing to an adverse ruff.

Dealer South. Love all.

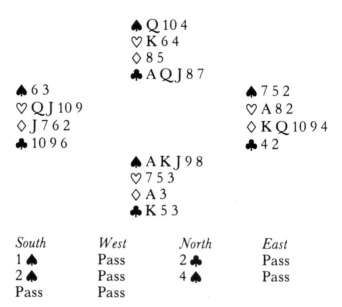

	♠ Q 10 4	
	♡ K 6 4	
	◇ 8 5	
	♣ A Q J 8 7	
♠ 6 3		♠ 7 5 2
♡ Q J 10 9		♡ A 8 2
◇ J 7 6 2		◇ K Q 10 9 4
♣ 10 9 6		♣ 4 2
	♠ A K J 9 8	
	♡ 7 5 3	
	◇ A 3	
	♣ K 5 3	

South	West	North	East
1 ♠	Pass	2 ♣	Pass
2 ♠	Pass	4 ♠	Pass
Pass	Pass		

West leads ♡ Q and South has to decide whether or not to cover with the king. East must surely hold ♡ A as West would be unlikely to make an opening lead from ace – queen. The principle of 'covering an honour with an honour' does not really apply as South has no card in either his hand or that of dummy which is likely to become a winner as a result of covering West's queen with the king. South's best chance is to keep playing low from the table in the hope that East started with ace and one other heart, and might be compelled to play his ace on the second round. As it happens the defenders take the first three tricks, East winning the third, and ◇ K is returned to dummy's weak suit.

South must take this with his ace as he cannot afford to lose any more tricks. He has two strong suits to play – spades and clubs. It would be a mistake to play clubs next as it would not be long before one defender had no more and would trump. This is a clear case for taking out the trumps first.

It is important to count the trumps that are played, for it is dangerous to leave a small trump around that you could afford to draw. Equally you may leave yourself short if you take an unnecessary round.

Here, when both opponents follow suit to the first two rounds you know there is only one left and this you can afford to draw. Having removed the trumps from your opponents you turn your attention to the clubs. As these are solid you again follow the principle stated earlier that you start with the high card from the short hand. Assuming that the third round of trumps was taken in your own hand, you now play ♣ K and follow with ♣ 5 to ♣ J and cash ♣ A. You next play ♣ Q and, having no more clubs, you discard your worthless ◇ 3. Had you started by playing ♣ A and ♣ Q and taking the third round in your hand with ♣ K, the suit would be blocked. There would be no way to get back to dummy to play ♣ J and discard your diamond.

Dealer South. North-South vul.

```
                    ♠ 7 3
                    ♡ K 10 6
                    ◇ A K J 8 7
                    ♣ Q 6 5
  ♠ K 10 8 6 2                      ♠ Q J 9 5
  ♡ 4 3                             ♡ 7 5 2
  ◇ 10 9 6                          ◇ 4 2
  ♣ J 10 9                          ♣ A K 7 3
                    ♠ A 4
                    ♡ A Q J 9 8
                    ◇ Q 5 3
                    ♣ 8 4 2
```

South	West	North	East
1 ♡	Pass	2 ◇	Pass
2 ♡	Pass	4 ♡	Pass
Pass	Pass		

West leads ♣J, top of his sequence, and South is powerless to avoid losing the first three tricks. A spade is led at trick four which South wins, needing to make the rest. The position is similar to the previous hand. South has strong hearts and diamonds. He draws trumps in three rounds and then plays diamonds, being careful to lead ◊Q early to avoid blocking the suit. The losing ♠4 is discarded on the fourth round of diamonds led from the table.

In the next round South's trumps are not solid and he had to rely on a finesse.

Dealer South. Game all.

```
                    ♠ A 8 5 2
                    ♡ Q 10 5
                    ◊ Q 8 6
                    ♣ K 7 6
  ♠ K 7 3                              ♠ 6
  ♡ 8 7 3                              ♡ 9 6 4 2
  ◊ A 9 7                              ◊ 5 4 3 2
  ♣ J 10 9 2                           ♣ A Q 8 5
                    ♠ Q J 10 9 4
                    ♡ A K J
                    ◊ K J 10
                    ♣ 4 3
```

South	West	North	East
1 ♠	Pass	3 ♠	Pass
4 ♠	Pass	Pass	Pass

North's jump response was a limit bid showing about ten or eleven high card points and promising at least four cards in support of partner's suit. If South had a very moderate opening bid he could pass, but he has quite a good hand and is fully justified in bidding game.

West leads ♣J and the defence take the first two tricks but South ruffs the third club. He has lost two tricks and must lose another in diamonds, so cannot afford to lose a trick in trumps. He is missing the king and he must hope that this card is on his left so that it can be captured by dummy's ace.

South leads ♠Q and when West plays low, dummy follows with ♠ 2. When ♠Q wins the trick, in other words, the finesse succeeds. South continues with ♠J and eventually West's ♠K is captured by ♠A and no trick in trumps is lost.

South's play was correct for he had an even chance of winning the trick by finessing. Had he put up ♠A he would certainly have won the trick but it would have been most unlikely that the king would have fallen. It may be said he was lucky, but remember he was unlucky with dummy's king of clubs which fell to East's ace.

Here is another example of finessing in trumps.

Dealer South. Love all.

```
                    ♠ K 7 4
                    ♡ 9 3
                    ◇ Q 10 7 6
                    ♣ A Q 10 9
   ♠ J 10 9 6                        ♠ A Q 8 3
   ♡ A 5                             ♡ Q 6 4
   ◇ 9 8 3                           ◇ J 5 4 2
   ♣ 7 6 5 3                         ♣ 8 4
                    ♠ 5 2
                    ♡ K J 10 8 7 2
                    ◇ A K
                    ♣ K J 2
```

South	West	North	East
1 ♡	Pass	2 NT	Pass
4 ♡	Pass	Pass	Pass

North's response was a limit bid showing about 11-12 high card points and was not forcing. South correctly decided that a game was possible and that it would be safer to play in a suit than in no-trumps and bid four hearts. Had he bid Three Hearts it would have been a sign off and North would have passed.

(repeated for convenience)

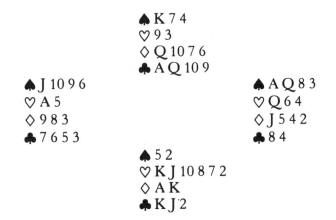

West led ♠ J and dummy's king fell to the ace. South ruffed the third round of spades and was now confronted with the problem of avoiding the loss of more than one trump. He is missing the ace and the queen. The position of the ace is unimportant as it is always going to win a trick, but the position of the queen matters a great deal. To prevent the queen winning a trick it is essential to be in a position to cover it with the king and this means that the queen must be assumed to be in East's hand, i.e. on South's right. Furthermore, it is all important that the trump should be led from dummy so that East plays before South. To lead away from the closed hand would almost certainly result in the loss of two tricks.

At trick four, having ruffed the spade, South crosses to the table by playing ♣ 2 to ♣ 9. He next leads ♡ 9. When East follows with ♡ 4, South plays ♡ 2 and West wins with ♡ A. What conclusions can South draw from this? East must surely hold ♡ Q, for why should West use the ace to take the nine?

West returns a club and South has to decide whether to win the trick in his hand or dummy's. After winning this trick he intends to lead a trump from the table. Therefore he should play ♣ Q and continue with ♡ 3 to which East follows with ♡ 6, South with ♡ 8 and West with ♡ 5. Counting trumps, there have been two complete rounds (eight) and one was used to ruff a spade. Therefore there is one left, the queen, and this will fall when the king is led.

Care may be needed if the trump suit is not solid. If one of your high cards is captured by a higher honour, one of the lower cards will become promoted to trick taking rank. Consequently it is important to play towards honours where possible.

Dealer South. Love all.

```
                    ♠ 4 3
                    ♡ K 7 2
                    ◊ K J 6 3
                    ♣ A 8 7 4
  ♠ 10 7                            ♠ A J 2
  ♡ Q 10 8 6                        ♡ J 9 5
  ◊ 8 7                             ◊ Q 10 9 4 2
  ♣ K Q J 10 6                      ♣ 9 3
                    ♠ K Q 9 8 6 5
                    ♡ A 4 3
                    ◊ A 5
                    ♣ 5 2
```

South is declarer in a slightly ambitious contract of four spades, against which West leads ♣ K. If South can make five out of his six trumps he is home. As he is missing the ace, jack and ten he cannot afford to lose one of his top honours to the ace, so he must hope that the ace of spades is on his right. After winning with ♣ A he leads ♠ 3 from the table, East plays low and ♠ Q wins. This is a promising start and dummy is re-entered with ♡ K to lead ♠ 4. It does not matter whether or not East goes up with the ace as only one trump trick will be lost.

Had West held the ace and captured South's queen, a second trump would have been lost and declarer might then have tried the finesse of ◊ J in the hope of discarding a losing heart. As the cards lie this would have failed.

17. When Not to Draw Trumps

In the previous section it was correct in each case to draw
trumps early. The actual handling of the trump suit may
have varied, depending on whether it was solid or a finesse
was necessary. But in such instances declarer had tricks to
make outside the trump suit and there was no valid reason
for not playing trumps at once.

One of the earliest lessons given to beginners is that they
must draw trumps. Indeed, the most dreadful prospects are
spelled out if they disregard this so-called rule! They are
told that many players are homeless and sleeping on
London's Embankment because they neglected to draw
trumps. In fact, as I have written elsewhere, the population
on the Embankment is cosmopolitan, there being as many
in that unhappy state because they drew trumps as those
who omitted to do so.

There are two main situations where trumps are now
drawn at once.

(A) NEED TO RUFF IN DUMMY

Whilst it seldom gains a trick to ruff in the stronger hand, it
is an advantage to ruff in dummy which usually contains
fewer trumps.

Dealer South. East-West vul.

```
                ♠ Q J 2
                ♡ J 9
                ◊ J 8 5 4
                ♣ A K 6 4
   ♠ 8 7                        ♠ 6 5 3
   ♡ Q 8 6 5                    ♡ 10 7 4 2
   ◊ A K 6                      ◊ Q 10 7 2
   ♣ Q 10 7 5                   ♣ J 8
                ♠ A K 10 9 4
                ♡ A K 3
                ◊ 9 3
                ♣ 9 3 2
```

The bidding went:

South	West	North	East
1 ♠	Pass	2 ♣	Pass
2 ♠	Pass	4 ♠	Pass
Pass	Pass		

West leads ◇ A and East encourages with ◇ 7. West continues with ◇ K and ◇ 6, South ruffing the third round with ♠ 4. Counting his winners, South can see five in trumps and two each in clubs and hearts, a total of nine. An extra trick might be obtained from clubs if the suit is evenly divided, but a much better chance is provided by the hearts. After cashing ♡ A and ♡ K South will have one and dummy none. By leading ♡ 3 and ruffing on the table an extra trick will be made. It can easily be seen that if South draws trumps as soon as he is in, dummy's spades will fall on to South's and a total of five spades will result.

It may be necessary to lose a trick before you can ruff.

Dealer South

```
                  ♠ 8 3
                  ♡ 9 3 2
                  ◇ A K 9 7 4
                  ♣ K 5 3
♠ K J 10 6                      ♠ Q 7 4 2
♡ 10 8 7                        ♡ 5
◇ 6 2                           ◇ Q J 10 8
♣ Q J 10 7                      ♣ A 9 8 2
                  ♠ A 9 5
                  ♡ A K Q J 6 4
                  ◇ 5 3
                  ♣ 6 4
```

South	West	North	East
1 ♡	Pass	2 ◇	Pass
3 ♡	Pass	4 ♡	Pass

(repeated for convenience)

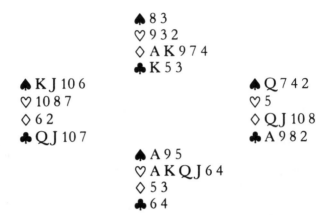

West led ♣ Q and the defence won the first two tricks, South ruffing the third round. South played off ♡ A and K and was disappointed that two rounds had not cleared trumps. Finding himself a trick short he played ace and another spade with a view to ruffing his third on the table. This was a good plan, but he put it into effect too late because West won the second spade lead with ♠ 10 and promptly returned ♡ 10, removing the last trump from the table. South should have played spades before touching trumps.

It may be possible to make more than one extra trick by ruffing in dummy.

Dealer South. Game all.

```
                ♠ A K 3 2
                ♡ J 10 3
                ◇ 6 3
                ♣ 6 4 3 2
♠ J 8 7                          ♠ Q 10 6 5
♡ 8 7 5                          ♡ 4
◇ Q 10 4                         ◇ K J 9 8
♣ K Q 10 9                       ♣ A J 8 5
                ♠ 9 4
                ♡ A K Q 9 6 2
                ◇ A 7 5 2
                ♣ 7
```

South	West	North	East
1 ♡	Pass	1 ♠	Pass
3 ♡	Pass	4 ♡	Pass
Pass	Pass		

West led ♣ K, East encouraged with ♣ 8 and West continued with ♣ 9 to ♣ A, ruffed by South with ♡ 2. South counted nine top tricks and rejected the idea of cashing ♠ A K and ruffing a spade or ruffing a club for he realized that he would only be making tricks with the trumps he had already reckoned he could make.

He needed to make tricks with dummy's trumps and led ◇ A, followed by ◇ 2. East won and did his best by returning a trump. South won in hand with ♡ 9, ruffed ◇ 6 with ♡ 10, returned to hand with a club ruff and trumped his last diamond with ♡ J. Thus he made eight tricks with trumps plus three top winners for eleven tricks in all. The defence could have saved one trick by leading a trump earlier.

The next example is an unspectacular part score but it involves a ruff in dummy, combined with the importance of leading towards honours.

Dealer South. Love all.

```
                    ♠ K 5 4
                    ♡ 6 5 2
                    ◇ 6 2
                    ♣ A Q 9 7 2
♠ Q J 10 9                              ♠ A 7 2
♡ J 8                                   ♡ A 10 7
◇ J 10 8 5                              ◇ Q 9 7 4
♣ K 6 4                                 ♣ J 10 8
                    ♠ 8 6 3
                    ♡ K Q 9 4 3
                    ◇ A K 3
                    ♣ 5 3
```

South	West	North	East
1 ♡	Pass	2 ♣	Pass
2 ♡	Pass	Pass	Pass

South has a borderline opening, but if the hand is passed originally it is far more dangerous to come in later. West leads ♠ Q and the defence take the first three tricks, switching to diamonds to South's king.

This is basically a hand where it is correct to draw trumps, but owing to the nature of the trump suit it is important to lead from dummy towards the honours. At trick five ◇ A is cashed followed by ◇ 3, ruffed in dummy with ♡ 2. A low trump is played from the table, East plays low and ♡ Q wins. Dummy is re-entered with a successful club finesse and ♡ 6 led. East can only make his ace and South makes an overtrick. Had trumps been led from the closed hand at least two trump tricks would have been lost.

Sometimes it is possible for declarer to trump losing cards alternately in his own hand and dummy. This method of play is called cross-ruffing. By never drawing trumps it may be possible to make all or many of the trumps separately.

Dealer East. East-West vul.

```
              ♠ A J 9 3
              ♡ 8
              ◊ 8 7 5 3
              ♣ A 6 5 2
♠ 7 4                          ♠ 6 5
♡ Q 10 5 2                     ♡ K J 7 6
◊ K Q J 10                     ◊ A 9
♣ J 9 8                        ♣ K Q 10 4 3
              ♠ K Q 10 8 2
              ♡ A 9 4 3
              ◊ 6 4 2
              ♣ 7
```

East opened 1 ♣ and South overcalled with 1 ♠ and eventually became declarer in 4 ♠.

West led ◊ K which East overtook with ◊ A to unblock and the defence won the first three tricks. West switched to a club, taken with the ace. South next played ♡ 8 to ♡ A and ruffed ♡ 3 in dummy with ♠ 3 and proceeded to ruff clubs in his hand, and hearts on the table. In effect he made two tricks with his red aces, made three tricks by ruffing hearts in dummy and all his own five spades.

It may be necessary to time the entries carefully to avoid finding yourself in the wrong hand at the wrong moment.

Dealer South. East-West vul.

```
                    ♠ Q 6 4 2
                    ♡ Q J 10 9 6
                    ◇ 8 4
                    ♣ 8 6
    ♠ A K 9 5                        ♠ J 10 8 3
    ♡ 5 4                            ♡ 8 3
    ◇ A J 9 2                        ◇ K 10 5
    ♣ Q 9 7                          ♣ J 10 4 3
                    ♠ 7
                    ♡ A K 7 2
                    ◇ Q 7 6 3
                    ♣ A K 5 2
```

South	West	North	East
1 ♡	Dbl:	3 ♡	Pass
4 ♡	Pass	Pass	Pass

South overlooked the fact that his partner's bid of 3 ♡ after West's take-out double was purely defensive and did not promise much apart from trumps. He was tempted to go one more for game, having good controls, and was lucky in that West did not lead off with a trump.

Instead West led ♠ A and switched to ♡ 5 which South won in his hand with ♡ K. He played ♣ A K and ruffed ♣ 2 with ♡ 9, ruffed ♠ 4 with ♡ 2 and ruffed ♣ 5 with ♡ 10 and ♠ 6 with ♡ 7. Now he wanted to be in dummy to ruff another spade. But he wasn't and led a diamond. West won and returned a trump and the contract ended down one.

South mistimed it. He should have won the second trick in dummy and ruffed a spade. Then cross-ruffed clubs and spades. The point to remember in cross-ruffing is to count up the number of ruffs you need and ensure that you have the necessary entries. In the present hand South needs to ruff three spades in his hand which means he must lead spades three times from dummy, which in turn means he requires three entries. There are two entries by ruffing two clubs and the third entry is provided by taking the trump lead on the table at trick two.

A cardinal principle in cross-ruff play is to cash the side winners first, that is to say top cards in suits which are not involved in the cross-ruff.

The reason is that while you are merrily trumping backwards and forwards an opponent who is unable to follow suit and cannot over-trump will take the opportunity to discard losers and when you later try to make your top cards they get trumped.

Dealer North. Love all.

```
                    ♠ A J 9 3
                    ♡ 8
                    ◇ A 8 7
                    ♣ A 7 6 5 3
  ♠ 4                                  ♠ 7 6 5
  ♡ Q J                                ♡ K 10 7 6 5 2
  ◇ Q 10 5 3 2                         ◇ J 4
  ♣ Q 10 9 8 2                         ♣ K J
                    ♠ K Q 10 8 2
                    ♡ A 9 4 3
                    ◇ K 9 6
                    ♣ 4
```

South	West	North	East
		1 ♣	Pass
1 ♠	Pass	3 ♠	Pass
4 NT	Pass	5 ♠	Pass
6 ♠	Pass	Pass	Pass

West leads ♡ Q taken with ♡ A. South has four top tricks apart from spades and therefore needs to make eight tricks with trumps. This he can do by ruffing three hearts in dummy and using club ruffs to return to his hand.

In other words, cross-ruffing hearts and clubs. If, however, he sets out on this campaign at once East will shortly run out of clubs and discard diamonds. It is important to cash the ace and king of diamonds before starting the cross-ruff.

Dealer East. Love all.

	♠ 3	
	♡ K Q 6	
	◇ K J 9 2	
	♣ 10 8 4 3 2	
♠ Q 9 6 4 2		♠ 10 8
♡ J 9 7 4 2		♡ A 10
◇ –		◇ 7 6 5 3
♣ Q 9 7		♣ A K J 6 5
	♠ A K J 7 5	
	♡ 8 5 3	
	◇ A Q 10 8 4	
	♣ –	

South	West	North	East
			1 ♣
2 ♠	Pass	2 NT	Pass
3 ◇	Pass	5 ◇	Pass

South preferred a jump overcall to double as his hearts support was weak. West leads ♣ 7 and South ruffs. If he can ruff three spades in dummy he has ten tricks and needs a heart. He must establish the heart quickly and make his side winner before the opponents have a chance to discard their losers.

At trick two South leads ♡ 3 to ♡ Q and ♡ A. East does his best by returning a trump, won with ◇ 8. South leads ♡ 5 to ♡ K and then proceeds to cross-ruff spades and clubs.

The most spectacular example of cashing in side winners early is this hand of many years ago, which became known as the Four Trump Slam.

Dealer South. Game all.

```
                    ♠ A
                    ♡ Q J 8 4 2
                    ◊ A Q J 6 3
                    ♣ A 10
  ♠ J 10 8                            ♠ 6 4 2
  ♡ 9 7 6                             ♡ 10 5 3
  ◊ 10 9 7                            ◊ 5 4
  ♣ J 4 3 2                           ♣ 9 8 7 6 5
                    ♠ K Q 9 7 5 3
                    ♡ A K
                    ◊ K 8 2
                    ♣ K Q
```

With a grand slam to be made in spades, hearts, diamonds or no-trumps, South actually found himself declarer in 6♣! This came about through a bidding misunderstanding when South, endeavouring to show some control in clubs, created the impression with his partner that he had a suit, and was left in. Of course, had West led a trump the hand would have collapsed, but West led ♠ J.

South won with dummy's ace, crossed to ♡ A K and cashed ♠ K Q, followed by ◊ K, and ◊ 2 to ◊ A. South discarded his last diamond on ♡ Q which brought his total of tricks to eight. He made four more by cross-trumping spades and diamonds, neither opponent having been able to over-ruff.

(B) NEED TO DISCARD LOSER EARLY
The other occasion when it is wrong to play trumps at once is where you need to discard a loser quickly and you do not hold the top trump.

Before proceeding to give examples this is a convenient moment to mention the importance of counting losers. In no-trumps it is usually best to count winners, but in suit contracts you should count both winners and losers. First see whether the number of tricks needed are available and next look to see what tricks may be lost, for the number of potential winners does not always balance with the number of possible losers.

Dealer North. North-South vul.

```
                    ♠ K Q J 8 6
                    ♡ Q 8 4
                    ◇ J 3
                    ♣ A Q 2
     ♠ 10 7 4                        ♠ 9 5
     ♡ A                             ♡ 5 3 2
     ◇ K Q 10 9 4                    ◇ 8 7 6 5
     ♣ 10 7 5 4                      ♣ J 9 8 3
                    ♠ A 3 2
                    ♡ K J 10 9 7 6
                    ◇ A 2
                    ♣ K 6
```

South	West	North	East
		1 ♠	Pass
2 ♡	Pass	4 ♡	Pass
4 NT	Pass	5 ◇	Pass
6 ♡	Pass	Pass	Pass

West leads ◇ K taken with ◇ A. If you count your potential winners you expect to make five out of six hearts, probably all five spades, three clubs, one diamond – a total of fourteen tricks. You may wonder why you did not bid a grand slam. But consider the losers. There is an inescapable loser in trumps and, on the lead, a loser in diamonds. Suppose that you decide to draw trumps at once. West will win and lead ◇ Q. You would not be worried had the lead been a club or spade, but the diamond has left you with two losers. You cannot afford to give up the lead while you have a losing diamond in each hand.

In order to discard your diamond you must look for a suit in which one hand has more cards than the other. There are two such suits, spades and clubs. As you hold between you only five clubs there is every chance that the suit will go round three times. Therefore lead ♣ K, follow with ♣ 6 to ♣ Q and cash ♣ A, throwing ◇ 2.

The next example is less easy because you have to establish a suit before you can get a discard.

Dealer South. Love all.

```
                  ♠ J 10 6 3
                  ♡ K Q 3
                  ◇ 8 5 4
                  ♣ A J 3
  ♠ A K                            ♠ 4 2
  ♡ 10 9 4 2                       ♡ A 8 7 6
  ◇ Q J 10 6                       ◇ 9 7 3
  ♣ 6 4 2                          ♣ 9 8 7 5
                  ♠ Q 9 8 7 5
                  ♡ J 5
                  ◇ A K 2
                  ♣ K Q 10
```

South	West	North	East
1 ♠	Pass	3 ♠	Pass
4 ♠	Pass	Pass	Pass

West leads ◇ Q Counting winners you have three clubs and two diamonds on top, and you expect to make three spades and two hearts. Looking at the losers you have two top trumps and a top heart which are inevitable and also the third diamond. You must discard your small diamond and this can be done on a heart. But you have to force out the ace of hearts first.

At trick two lead ♡ J. Assume East wins and returns a diamond, win with ◊ A and play ♡ K Q discarding ◊ 2. Had you led trumps at trick two you would have been too late. A diamond would force out your ace and the defence would make a diamond trick as soon as they regained the lead with a heart.

Dealer South. East-West vul.

```
              ♠ K Q 9 8
              ♡ J 7 4 2
              ◊ A 7
              ♣ A 7 2
  ♠ A 5 3 2                    ♠ 10 7 6 4
  ♡ 3                          ♡ A
  ◊ Q J 10 5                   ◊ K 9 8 4
  ♣ K 10 8 4                   ♣ J 9 5 3
              ♠ J
              ♡ K Q 10 9 8 6 5
              ◊ 6 3 2
              ♣ Q 6
```

South	West	North	East
3 ♡	Pass	4 ♡	Pass
Pass	Pass		

West leads ◊ Q which must be taken with ◊ A. There is a potential loser in each suit and as nothing can be done about the hearts, spades and diamonds, it is essential to avoid the club loser. If you lead a trump East will win, cash ◊ K and switch to a club, hoping to set up a trick while his partner has the ace of spades, likely on the opening weak bid. At trick two lead a low spade and force out the ace. Opponents can cash ◊ K and play a club, but you can discard your losing club on ♠ K before they get in again.

18. Avoiding Unnecessary Finesse

Just as in no-trumps, many suit contracts fail due to taking an unnecessary finesse. On this hand a combined count of thirty high card points proved insufficient to make a game. It was declarer's carelessness that was his downfall.

Dealer South. Game all.

```
                    ♠ K 8 2
                    ♡ A 6 5
                    ◇ 8 4 2
                    ♣ A Q J 6
   ♠ 10 7 6 3                        ♠ 9
   ♡ 10 7 4 3                        ♡ K 9 8
   ◇ A 5 3                           ◇ Q J 10 7
   ♣ 10 9                            ♣ 8 5 4 3 2
                    ♠ A Q J 5 4
                    ♡ Q J 2
                    ◇ K 9 6
                    ♣ K 7
```

South	West	North	East
1 ♠	Pass	2 ♣	Pass
2 NT	Pass	3 ♠	Pass
4 ♠	Pass	Pass	Pass

South's rebid of Two No-Trump showed 15-16 points and North's Three Spades was forcing offering the choice between Four Spades, if South held five, or Three No-Trump. West led ♡ 3 and South decided to try and win with his jack. East won with ♡ K and switched to ◇ Q and South lost the first four tricks.

Had he counted his winners he could see five spades, four clubs and one heart. If you are in a position to win the first ten tricks it is an awful pity to lose the first four. Had South put up ♡ A, drawn trumps, cashed four clubs, discarding two diamonds, he would have made eleven tricks.

If you are offered the chance of a finesse on the opening lead you should ask yourself:

(a) Is the finesse necessary?

(b) If not, is there any danger in taking it?

Lack of care would result in disaster on this hand.

Dealer North. Love all.

```
                    ♠ A 4 3 2
                    ♡ 8 7 6
                    ◇ A 6
                    ♣ K Q 10 9
    ♠ 7 5                              ♠ 10 9
    ♡ 9 4 2                            ♡ K Q J 5
    ◇ J 9 7 4 2                        ◇ K 10 8 3
    ♣ A 6 5                            ♣ 4 3 2
                    ♠ K Q J 8 6
                    ♡ A 10 3
                    ◇ Q 5
                    ♣ J 8 7
```

South	West	North	East
		1 ♣	Pass
1 ♠	Pass	2 ♠	Pass
4 ♠	Pass	Pass	Pass

West leads ◇ 4 and you have to decide whether you play ◇ A or ◇ 6. Counting winners, you have five spades, two aces and you should make three tricks in clubs. In other words you should have ten tricks.

Counting losers you could lose one diamond, one club and two hearts, a total of four. Again the number of winners does not balance with the number of losers, but one of your small hearts can be discarded on the fourth club, providing that you can force out the ace of clubs before you have had to play your ace of hearts.

Play ◇ A at trick one and draw trumps, using high trumps from your hand, leaving the ace in dummy as an entry in case the ace of clubs is held up. After drawing trumps, establish clubs. The defence can take their ◇ K and switch to hearts but you are in control as you still have the ace.

Applying the two questions given above, the answers would have been –

    (a) No. There are ten tricks.

    (b) Yes. A heart switch will be fatal as the clubs are not established.

An unnecessary finesse on the next hand resulted in declarer losing the first five tricks.

Dealer South. North-South vul.

```
                    ♠ K 4
                    ♡ Q 10 8 7
                    ◇ J 3 2
                    ♣ A J 9 5
      ♠ J 9 7 6 3                    ♠ Q 10 8 2
      ♡ 6 5 3                        ♡ 2
      ◇ K 10 6 4                     ◇ A 9 8
      ♣ 2                            ♣ K 8 7 4 3
                    ♠ A 5
                    ♡ A K J 9 4
                    ◇ Q 7 5
                    ♣ Q 10 6
```

South	West	North	East
1 ♡	Pass	3 ♡	Pass
4 ♡	Pass	Pass	Pass

West led ♣ 2 and South played low from dummy. East won and returned ♣ 3 which West ruffed. A diamond return enabled West to get a second club ruff and the king of diamonds put the contract two down.

Counting winners there are two in spades and five in hearts and it should be possible to make three in clubs. Provided that South does not try to make a trick in

(repeated for convenience)

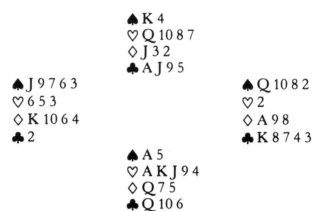

♠ K 4
♡ Q 10 8 7
◇ J 3 2
♣ A J 9 5

♠ J 9 7 6 3
♡ 6 5 3
◇ K 10 6 4
♣ 2

♠ Q 10 8 2
♡ 2
◇ A 9 8
♣ K 8 7 4 3

♠ A 5
♡ A K J 9 4
◇ Q 7 5
♣ Q 10 6

diamonds he is all right. Counting losers, no spades or hearts, one club and two diamonds.

Coming back to the two questions:

    (a) No need to finesse. There are ten tricks and only three apparent losers.

    (b) Yes, dangerous to finesse. Risk of club ruff. There might also be a diamond ruff.

Suppose, however, that South's diamonds were 10 7 5 instead of Q 7 5. It would be now correct to finesse the club at trick one because with three losing diamonds you cannot afford to give away the king of clubs. The only chance is that West has it. But, of course, with the actual deal, the finesse was completely unnecessary.

In the last hand the risk of a ruff may not have been entirely obvious, although the lead may have looked suspicious. But there are occasions when a ruff is extremely likely and the best way to avoid it is to get trumps out quickly, declining any finesse.

Dealer South. Game all.

```
              ♠ 10 8 7 3
              ♡ A K 2
              ◇ K 10 8
              ♣ Q 5 4
♠ K 5                           ♠ 4 2
♡ Q J 10 8 7 3                  ♡ 9
◇ 4 3 2                         ◇ Q J 7 6 5
♣ K 7                           ♣ 10 9 8 6 3
              ♠ A Q J 9 6
              ♡ 6 5 4
              ◇ A 9
              ♣ A J 2
```

South	West	North	South
1 ♠	2 ♡	4 ♠	Pass
Pass	Pass		

West leads ♡ Q, taken with ♡ K. South expects to lose one club, no diamond, one heart and can afford one spade. There is, however, the risk of losing a fourth trick to a heart ruff. West has overcalled at the two level and probably holds a six card suit, leaving East with a singleton.

West is likely to hold the king of spades so if you finesse in trumps, West will win and lead ♡ J, East ruffing your ♡ A. You will later lose a club and a heart. As you can afford to give a trick to the king of trumps, but cannot afford a heart ruff, play ace and another trump. If trumps are 2–2 there is no problem. If East should have started with K x x he cannot get a ruff in hearts as he cannot put his partner in. If he leads a club you put up the ace and draw his trump.

The situation is similar with this next hand –

Dealer West. Game all.

```
                    ♠ A 10 2
                    ♡ Q J 5 4
                    ◇ K Q
                    ♣ K Q 6 2
♠ K Q 9 5 4                              ♠ 8 3
♡ K 6                                    ♡ 3 2
◇ A 10 9 3                               ◇ 8 7 6 4 2
♣ 9 5                                    ♣ J 10 8 3
                    ♠ J 7 6
                    ♡ A 10 9 8 7
                    ◇ J 5
                    ♣ A 7 4
```

South	West	North	East
	1 ♠	Dbl:	Pass
3 ♡	Pass	4 ♡	Pass
Pass	Pass		

West leads ♠ K which should be taken in dummy as East might have a singleton. The only obvious losers are one spade, one diamond and a trump. But there is the danger of a spade ruff. You are not dependent on capturing the king of hearts and in any case it is almost certainly with West. Therefore play ace and another trump to prevent the threatened spade ruff.

19. Entries

The importance of entries applies equally to suit contracts as to no-trumps.

Dealer North. North-South vul.

```
                    ♠ A K Q
                    ♡ A Q 3
                    ◊ A K Q J 10 4
                    ♣ 7
    ♠ J 10 9                          ♠ 7 3 2
    ♡ J 9 6 5                         ♡ K 7 2
    ◊ 8 7                             ◊ 9 6
    ♣ K Q J 6                         ♣ A 10 9 8 2
                    ♠ 8 6 5 4
                    ♡ 10 8 4
                    ◊ 5 3 2
                    ♣ 5 4 3
```

South	West	North	East
		2 ♣	Pass
2 ◊	Pass	3 ◊	Pass
3 NT	Pass	5 ◊	Pass
Pass	Pass		

South was surprised to find himself declarer in Five Diamonds with his miserable hand. When he picked it up he expected to be defending against a slam. However, after his partner's game forcing bid of Two Clubs he stoically kept the bidding open and, having given an initial negative reply of Two Diamonds, became the declarer.

West led ♣ K and continued the suit and dummy ruffed the second round with ◊ 4. There being no entry to the closed hand two heart tricks were lost for down one. The contract should have been made. The second club must be ruffed with an honour. Trumps are cleared in two rounds and the three top spades are played. When all follow,

South's ♠ 8 becomes a winner. Moreover, there is an entry to hand with the five of diamonds. South not only makes his contract but can take the heart finesse for an overtrick. This fails but at least game has been made.

An important point to remember is this. If you have a solid trump suit, always make a practice of ruffing with a medium trump, not your lowest. Once trumps have been drawn the ace of trumps and the two have the same value.

Here is a further example:

Dealer South. Love all.

```
                    ♠ 9 5
                    ♡ Q 6 4
                    ◇ K Q J 10 6
                    ♣ 7 4 2
  ♠ 6 4                          ♠ 7 3 2
  ♡ J 10 9 8                     ♡ A K 7 2
  ◇ 9 7 4                        ◇ 8 5 3 2
  ♣ K J 9 5                      ♣ Q 10
                    ♠ A K Q J 10 8
                    ♡ 5 3
                    ◇ A
                    ♣ A 8 6 3
```

South	West	North	East
2 ♠	Pass	3 ◇	Pass
4 ♣	Pass	4 ♠	Pass
Pass	Pass		

South opened with an Acol Two Bid, indicating at least eight playing tricks. Following North's positive reply he made a slam try with Four Clubs but North signed off. West leads ♡ J, the defence take the first two tricks and continue with a third heart.

As soon as dummy went down South should have noted the annoying diamond situation and realized that he needed an entry to the table. Luckily the nine of trumps is there, so the third heart is ruffed high. After cashing ◇ A,

South leads one high trump followed by ♠ 8 to ♠ 9 and plays off his diamonds, discarding clubs. It is correct to play a high spade from hand first, for by taking two rounds of trumps you minimize the risk of a diamond ruff. In fact you gain an overtrick as the defender with the third trump has to follow to four rounds of diamonds.

In the next hand South needed to overtake a winning card in order to be in the right hand.

Dealer South. Love all.

```
                    ♠ 8 3 2
                    ♡ A J 10 9
                    ◊ 5 4 3
                    ♣ 4 3 2
    ♠ -                             ♠ J 9 5 4
    ♡ 8 7 5 2                       ♡ 6 4 3
    ◊ K Q J 8                       ◊ A 9 2
    ♣ Q 9 7 6 5                     ♣ K J 10
                    ♠ A K Q 10 7 6
                    ♡ K Q
                    ◊ 10 7 6
                    ♣ A 8
```

South	West	North	East
2 ♠	Pass	2 NT	Pass
3 ♠	Pass	4 ♠	Pass
Pass	Pass		

South's opening bid was Acol and was forcing for one round, the response of Two No-Trump being negative. However, North's heart values justified raising to game.

West led ◊ K and the defence took the first three tricks, switching to ♣ J taken in hand with ♣ A. South laid down ♠ A and found out the distribution when West discarded a club.

South now had two things to do. He had to discard his losing club and also catch East's jack of trumps by leading from dummy, and finessing. To trick six he led ♡ K and continued with ♡ Q, overtaking with ♡ A. He next played ♡ J and discarded ♣ 8, and followed with a trump, taking the marked finesse against East's jack. If one hand is short of entries, the best possible use must be made of them.

Dealer South. Love all.

```
                    ♠ A 9 3
                    ♡ 5 3
                    ◊ J 8 4 3 2
                    ♣ Q 7 2
   ♠ Q J 10 7                        ♠ 5 4 2
   ♡ K 9 8                           ♡ 6 2
   ◊ Q 10 7                          ◊ K 9 5
   ♣ K 8 6                           ♣ 10 9 5 4 3
                    ♠ K 8 6
                    ♡ A Q J 10 7 4
                    ◊ A 6
                    ♣ A J
```

South	West	North	East
1 ♡	Pass	1 NT	Pass
4 ♡	Pass	Pass	Pass

South's hand is on the border of an Acol Two Bid but the same contract should be reached.

West leads ♠ Q. South can reckon on making five tricks in hearts, two spades, one diamond and one club, total nine. Dummy has one entry, the ace of spades. If the first trick is taken on the table, what is led next? It may seem to be a good moment to finesse trumps but even if your ♡ 10 wins you are no better off unless East started with king and one other so that the king will fall. You cannot get back to dummy to repeat your finesse.

A better alternative is to lead ♣ 2 and finesse ♣ J. If this succeeds at least you have achieved something. But if the finesse loses, as it does, there is no way in which you can reach ♣ Q. It should certainly be possible to make two tricks from clubs but you must be careful to make sure you can get to them.

Take the opening lead in hand with ♠ K and play ♣ A, followed by ♣ J. West wins and whatever he returns you must get to dummy with ♠ A to cash ♣ Q. You are also in dummy to take the trump finesse as well.

The next example is less straightforward.

Dealer South. East-West vul.

```
              ♠ K 5
              ♡ A 9 4
              ◊ J 9 7 6
              ♣ Q J 10 9
♠ Q 10 7                    ♠ 3 2
♡ K 8 6                     ♡ Q J 10 5
◊ K 8 5 2                   ◊ Q 10 3
♣ K 7 6                     ♣ 8 5 4 3
              ♠ A J 9 8 6 4
              ♡ 7 3 2
              ◊ A 4
              ♣ A 2
```

South	West	North	East
1 ♠	Pass	2 NT	Pass
4 ♠	Pass	Pass	Pass

Had West been one of those players brought up on the dictum "never lead from a king" and not wishing to lead from the spade holding, it is doubtful whether the hand would ever have got started. But West, in fact, led ◊ 2, although a heart would have worked out best. South played ◊ 9 from dummy, East played ◊ 10 and South ◊ A. South's first thoughts were to get the trumps out and he began with ♠ 4 to ♠ K, and ♠ 5 to ♠ J, losing to ♠ Q. West returned ◊ 5 to ◊ Q and East switched to ♡ Q, forcing out ♡ A. The hand was not going well for South and the situation did not improve when he led ♣ Q and unsuccessfully finessed,

(repeated for convenience)

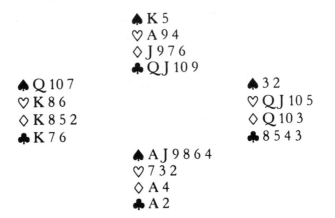

losing to ♣K. With the clubs blocked the contract finally ended two down.

There are, as is shewn, potentially five losers and some use must be made of the clubs. With limited entries to dummy there is little point in crossing to the table and leading ♣Q as the suit will be blocked. Much better to lead ace and another club at tricks two and three. West wins and leads ♦5 to East's ♦Q and ♡Q is returned, taken with dummy's ace.

Something needs to be done about trumps at this stage and the best plan is to lead ♠5 to ♠A and return ♠4 to ♠K. If both opponents follow there is one trump outstanding, probably the queen. South next leads ♣Q, discarding ♡3.

Provided no one is short in clubs and also has the remaining trump, the contract is safe. South plays ♣J, throwing his remaining heart, and the defender holding the outstanding trump can ruff.

Although it is usually an advantage to ruff with small trumps in dummy, you may endanger the entry position by doing so.

Dealer East. East-West vul.

```
              ♠ Q
              ♡ Q 5 3
              ♢ 6 4 3 2
              ♣ Q J 10 8 7
♠ 9 5 4 3 2                    ♠ A K J 8 7
♡ 9 8 2                        ♡ K J 10
♢ 7                           ♢ J 10 9
♣ 5 4 3 2                      ♣ 9 6
              ♠ 10 6
              ♡ A 7 6 4
              ♢ A K Q 8 5
              ♣ A K
```

South	West	North	East
			1 ♠
Dbl:	2 ♠	3 ♣	Pass
4 ◇	Pass	5 ◇	Pass
Pass	Pass		

Vulnerability prevented West from bidding higher over the double, defensively.

West led ♠ 3, East won with ♠ K and made the good return of ♠ A. South ruffed in dummy with ◇ 2 and drew trumps which unfortunately did not fall in two rounds. He cashed ♣ A K and tried to get to dummy with ♡ Q, but this failed as it was bound to do as North-South had twenty seven high card points between them and East had opened the bidding.

South should have discarded a heart from dummy at trick two and not ruffed. South wins whatever is returned and clears the trumps in three rounds. He cashes ♣ A K and gets to dummy by leading ◇ 5 to ◇ 6 to play off the good clubs.

On the next hand West's opening lead created an awkward problem for declarer.

Dealer South. Game all.

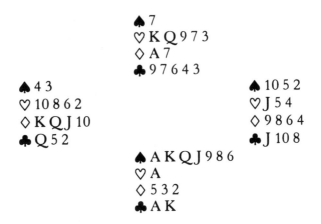

```
            ♠ 7
            ♡ K Q 9 7 3
            ◇ A 7
            ♣ 9 7 6 4 3
♠ 4 3                          ♠ 10 5 2
♡ 10 8 6 2                     ♡ J 5 4
◇ K Q J 10                     ◇ 9 8 6 4
♣ Q 5 2                        ♣ J 10 8
            ♠ A K Q J 9 8 6
            ♡ A
            ◇ 5 3 2
            ♣ A K
```

After starting with a game forcing Two Clubs and getting a positive response of Two Hearts, South was hopeful of a grand slam. But when his Blackwood enquiry located only one ace and one king in partner's hand he decided to settle for Six Spades.

West led ◇ K and this posed a problem. Having the bare ace of hearts there would be no means of getting back to dummy if the ace of diamonds were played.

He considered playing ◇ A and returning ◇ 7 with a view to ruffing but realized that this would never work as the opponents would lead a trump. South found the right answer. He ducked in dummy. If the laws permitted a player to lead two cards at once West would play a diamond and a trump, one card removing the entry and the other preventing a ruff. But such action not being allowed West decided to play a second diamond, knocking out the ace. South entered his hand with ♡ A, ruffed his last diamond on the table, came back with ♣ A and drew trumps, claiming twelve tricks.

On the next hand declarer had to resort to desperate measures to find an extra entry.

Dealer South. Love all.

```
              ♠ A 6 5
              ♡ 7 6 5 4
              ◊ A J 5
              ♣ J 10 9
  ♠ 10 9 8                    ♠ J 7 3 2
  ♡ –                         ♡ K 9 3 2
  ◊ Q 10 7 6 2                ◊ 9 8 3
  ♣ A K Q 4 2                 ♣ 8 3
              ♠ K Q 4
              ♡ A Q J 10 8
              ◊ K 4
              ♣ 7 6 5
```

South	West	North	East
1 ♡	2 NT	Dbl:	3 ◊
Pass	Pass	3 ♡	Pass
4 ♡	Pass	Pass	Pass

West's Two No-Trump was the Unusual No-Trump convention, indicating two minor suits probably 5–5 or 6–5 in shape. This convention, if not abused, can often pave the way for an economical sacrifice bid, despite the fact that the opponents have by far the stronger hands in points. If a minor suit fit can be discovered it is surprising how much you can do.

Reverting to the play of the hand, West led out ♣ A K Q and switched to ♠ 10 taken in dummy with ♠ A. Having lost three tricks, South cannot afford to lose another so it must be assumed that the king of hearts is with East.

At trick five ♡ 4 was led and ♡ 10 won, but West's discard of a club showed that East still had three hearts and two more finesses would be needed so consequently two

(repeated for convenience)

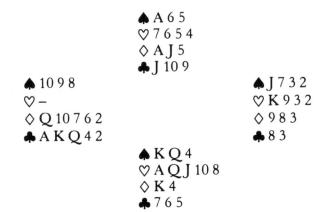

more entries to the table. The ace of diamonds was one, but where was the other? South led ◊ 4 and when West played low finessed ◊ J, which held. The chances of this succeeding were much improved by West's Two No-Trump overcall, implying strength in minor suits, but even without this the finesse would offer the only real chance. It was now possible to finesse twice against East's king of trumps and make the contract.

South was lucky on two counts. Firstly that the finesse of ◊ J won, but this, as we have said, was quite likely. Secondly, that West was not an expert, for a good defender sitting West could foil South's plan by putting ◊ Q on ◊ 4 and blocking the second entry. This is quite logical because if South has the king of diamonds he can always make three tricks by finessing. Nevertheless this type of play is very often missed at the table, even by international players.

20. Ruffing Out Suits

It was explained earlier that there is seldom any advantage in ruffing in the closed hand, as in doing so you merely make a trick with a trump that was always good and in addition you run the risk of weakening your trumps. There are occasions, however, that you trump low cards in your hand in order to establish a long suit. To do this you must, of course, have plenty of trumps.

Consider this example:

Dealer North. Game all.

```
              ♠ A K 9 8 6 5
              ♡ A K 10 8 6
              ◊ 2
              ♣ 3
♠ Q J 7 3                      ♠ 10
♡ –                            ♡ 4 3 2
◊ K 10 8 7 6 3                 ◊ Q J 5
♣ Q J 10                       ♣ K 9 8 7 6 4
              ♠ 4 2
              ♡ Q J 9 7 5
              ◊ A 9 4
              ♣ A 5 2
```

South	West	North	East
		2 ♠	Pass
3 ♡	Pass	4 NT	Pass
5 ♡	Pass	7 ♡	Pass
Pass	Pass		

West led ♣ Q. South won and decided that the hand was a simple cross-ruff. He trumped a club in dummy, returned with ◊ A and trumped a diamond in dummy. He could not afford to return to hand with a trump so played off ♠ A K with a view to cross-ruffing. But East ruffed the second round and that was the end of South's grand slam.

(*repeated for convenience*)

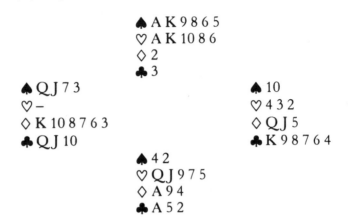

♠ A K 9 8 6 5
♡ A K 10 8 6
◊ 2
♣ 3

♠ Q J 7 3
♡ –
◊ K 10 8 7 6 3
♣ Q J 10

♠ 10
♡ 4 3 2
◊ Q J 5
♣ K 9 8 7 6 4

♠ 4 2
♡ Q J 9 7 5
◊ A 9 4
♣ A 5 2

South's basic plan was wrong. The hearts are solid and dummy's two singletons are covered by the two aces. That leaves the spades, with a combined holding of eight. There are five outstanding which are likely to be divided either 3–2 or 4–1. In view of the unbalanced nature of North's hand the spades may well be 4–1. Therefore, the suit should be cleared in four rounds. Trumps must be drawn first and despite the fact that all three are in the same hand, there will still be two in each of the North-South hands. South next plays ♠ A and ♠ K and ruffs ♠ 5 in hand. Dummy is re-entered by trumping a club and fourth spade is ruffed with declarer's last trump.

West's four spades have now all been played, leaving dummy with two winners. South next plays ◊ A, ruffs a diamond in dummy, and the two good spades complete thirteen tricks. Had all five spades been in the same hand it is doubtful whether the contract would be made with the trumps splitting 3–0.

In order to establish extra tricks by ruffing out a suit it is necessary to reach the relevant hand and this, again, involves entries. The importance of entries was discussed earlier but they play an important part in the present topic.

Dealer South. Love all.

```
                    ♠ K 5 4
                    ♡ J 8 3
                    ◊ 6 3
                    ♣ A K 8 5 4
  ♠ J 10 9 6                        ♠ A Q 7
  ♡ 7 4 2                           ♡ 5
  ◊ K 10 9 8                        ◊ Q J 7 5 4
  ♣ 3 2                             ♣ Q J 10 9
                    ♠ 8 3 2
                    ♡ A K Q 10 9 6
                    ◊ A 2
                    ♣ 7 6
```

South	West	North	East
1 ♡	Pass	2 ♣	Pass
3 ♡	Pass	4 ♡	Pass
Pass	Pass		

West leads ♠ J. As the lead is unlikely to be from the ace, and the queen is also marked on the right, so it is correct to play low from dummy in the hope that East has ace–queen only. When East follows to the first round with ♠ 7 there is no way of avoiding the loss of the first three tricks.

East switches to ◊ Q which is won with ◊ A and a count of tricks reveals a total of nine, leaving one to be found. This will have to come from the clubs and will be possible if the adverse six cards are divided no worse than 4–2.

To trick five South plays ♡ A and follows with ♣ 7, cashing ♣ A K. He next leads ♣ 4 which he is careful to ruff high with ♡ 10. He can now enter dummy by leading ♡ 6 to ♡ 8 and continue with ♣ 5, ruffed with ♡ Q, this establishing ♣ 8 on the table. Ruffing with ♡ Q (or ♡ K) was necessary as ♡ 9 is needed to enter dummy with ♡ J to cash ♣ 8 for the tenth trick.

A further example:

Dealer East. North-South vul.

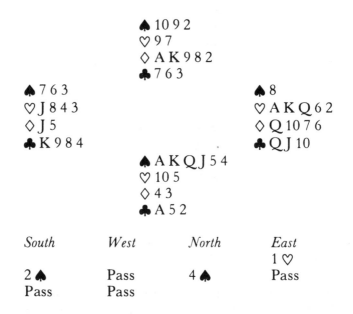

	♠ 10 9 2	
	♡ 9 7	
	◊ A K 9 8 2	
	♣ 7 6 3	
♠ 7 6 3		♠ 8
♡ J 8 4 3		♡ A K Q 6 2
◊ J 5		◊ Q 10 7 6
♣ K 9 8 4		♣ Q J 10
	♠ A K Q J 5 4	
	♡ 10 5	
	◊ 4 3	
	♣ A 5 2	

South	*West*	*North*	*East*
			1 ♡
2 ♠	Pass	4 ♠	Pass
Pass	Pass		

South's jump overcall is strong but not forcing. It promises a good suit that requires little support and around seven playing tricks. North has two sure tricks and a five card suit so decides to bid game.

West leads ♡ 3, East wins with ♡ Q, cashes ♡ A and switches to ♣ Q. South wins and faces the same problem as in the previous example. He must set up diamonds and he needs outside entries to the table.

After playing off ♠ A, he plays ◊ A K and ruffs the third round with an honour. He crosses to dummy with ♠ 9 and ruffs a diamond high. He re-enters dummy with ♠ 10 at the same time drawing the last trump from the opponents and cashes ◊ 9 for the contract.

In the majority of cases establishing tricks by ruffing requires a long suit, at least five. But there are occasions where an additional trick can be obtained from a suit of four cards.

Dealer North. North-South vul.

```
                    ♠ A 10 6
                    ♡ A Q 7
                    ♦ A 9 4 3
                    ♣ A 5 4
    ♠ 8 5                           ♠ 7 3 2
    ♡ J 10 9 6 4                    ♡ 8 5 3 2
    ♦ Q 7                           ♦ J 8 2
    ♣ Q 10 9 3                      ♣ 8 6 2
                    ♠ K Q J 9 4
                    ♡ K
                    ♦ K 10 6 5
                    ♣ K J 7
```

South	West	North	East
		1 NT (16-18)	Pass
3 ♠	Pass	4 ♠	Pass
4 NT	Pass	5 ♣	Pass
7 ♠	Pass	Pass	Pass

North's response to the Blackwood 4 NT showed either no aces or four. South could have no doubts and with all aces and kings bid the grand slam.

West leads ♡ J taken with ♡ K and the contract might appear to depend on a successful finesse in clubs unless the queen and jack of diamonds were to fall on the ace and king. But a far better chance exists. Draw three rounds of trumps ending in dummy and cash ♡ A Q, discarding ♦ 6 5. Next play ♦ 3 to K, ♦ 10 to ♦ A, and ruff ♦ 4 in hand. If the adverse cards are divided 3–2, the most likely split as explained earlier, dummy's ♦ 9 is now a winner on which can be thrown ♣ 7.

The position is not really different from having ◊ A 9 6 5 4 3 in dummy and ◊ K 10 in your hand where it is easier to see that the suit can be ruffed out. Here there are still eight cards between the two hands and by shedding two of them so that the third round can be trumped an extra winner is produced.

In the next example a suit divided 4–3 was ruffed out.

Dealer South. Love all.

```
                    ♠ A 9 8 4
                    ♡ K J 3
                    ◊ 8 2
                    ♣ A K 6 4
    ♠ K                              ♠ Q 2
    ♡ 10 8 6 4                       ♡ 9 7 5 2
    ◊ Q J 10 7 5                     ◊ K 9 6 4
    ♣ 10 8 7                         ♣ Q J 5
                    ♠ J 10 7 6 5 3
                    ♡ A Q
                    ◊ A 3
                    ♣ 9 3 2
```

After South opened One Spade North pushed the bidding to an ambitious contract of Six Spades. West led ◊ Q taken with ◊ A. With a certain loser in trumps South had to avoid a loser in diamonds and this was only possible if an extra trick could be developed in clubs.

Before touching trumps, South played three rounds of hearts, discarding ♣ 2 on the jack. He next played ♣ A and ♣ K and ruffed ♣ 4 in hand. Luckily the outstanding cards were evenly divided so that ♣ 6 in dummy became a winner. A trump was led to the ace and ♣ 6 led and ◊ 3 discarded. East could ruff if he wished with the master trump, but South made his little slam.

Some further examples of ruffing out suits will be given later when we discuss timing.

South had a choice between two possible lines of play on this hand.

Dealer South. Love all.

```
              ♠ 8
              ♡ K 3
              ◊ A 8 6 4 3
              ♣ A K 6 4 2
♠ Q J 10 9 5 4                    ♠ 7 6 3 2
♡ 6 5                             ♡ 9 7 2
◊ 10                              ◊ K Q J
♣ J 9 5 3                        ♣ Q 10 8
              ♠ A K
              ♡ A Q J 10 8 4
              ◊ 9 7 5 2
              ♣ 7
```

South was declarer in Six Hearts and West led ♠ Q. A diamond would have turned out better, but the top of the sequence was a reasonable choice. South won and could see eleven top tricks. There were two chances of making a twelfth, one being to hope that the adverse diamonds were divided 2–2 and the other to establish an extra club. To succeed with the latter alternative required the clubs to be divided 4–3 which is more likely to happen than that the diamonds should divide 2–2. Without introducing unnecessary complications about odds and percentages it is quite helpful to remember this fairly simple fact.

An even number of cards usually divide in the second best way, e.g. four cards outstanding are more likely to be 3–1 than 2–2 and six cards more likely to be 4–2 than 3–3. An odd number of cards usually divides well, e.g. five cards are more often split 3–2 than 4–1 and seven cards more often 4–3 than 5–2.

Having decided to establish an extra trick in clubs, South led ♣ 7 to ♣ A and ruffed ♣ 2 in hand with ♡ 8. He entered dummy by leading ♡ 4 to ♡ K and ruffed ♣ 4 in hand with ♡ 10. This meant that three rounds of clubs had been played so that if one defender started with four his last would fall on the king of clubs. South drew the outstanding trumps, crossed to dummy with ◇ A and played ♣ K followed by the established ♣ 6.

The next example is again a slam.

Dealer South. Love all.

```
              ♠ J 8 3
              ♡ A Q 3
              ◇ J 6
              ♣ K 9 8 6 3
 ♠ 5                          ♠ Q 7 4
 ♡ J 6 3                      ♡ 10 9 8 7
 ◇ K Q 9 3 2                  ◇ 10 7 5 4
 ♣ Q J 4 2                    ♣ 10 5
              ♠ A K 10 9 6 2
              ♡ K 5 4
              ◇ A 8
              ♣ A 7
```

South is declarer in Six Spades, and West leads ◇ K, taken with ◇ A. South plays off ♠ A K but is disappointed when West discards. With a loser in trumps some way must be found of discarding ◇ 8. South plays ♣ A and ♣ 7 to ♣ K, returning ♣ 6. It does not help East to ruff with his master trump as the losing diamond will be discarded. So East discards a heart and South ruffs. South leads ♡ 4 to ♡ Q and plays a fourth club, East again discarding a heart. Re-entering dummy with ♡ A the fifth (good) club is led and ◇ 8 discarded. It was lucky that East held four hearts but as against that the queen of spades might have fallen in two rounds or the clubs might have been 3–3.

21. Simple Avoidance Plays. Danger Hand. Safe Hand

Just as when playing in no-trumps, it may be important which opponent gains the lead. The principle consideration is the protection of honour cards, particularly a king which has no queen or ace to bolster it up.

Dealer South. Love all.

```
              ♠ K 9 2
              ♡ 8 4 3
              ◇ A Q J 5 3
              ♣ 8 7
♠ 5                              ♠ Q 7 4
♡ A 9 5                          ♡ Q J 10 2
◇ 9 6 4 2                        ◇ 7
♣ J 10 9 6 5                     ♣ K Q 4 3 2
              ♠ A J 10 8 6 3
              ♡ K 7 6
              ◇ K 10 8
              ♣ A
```

South	West	North	East
1 ♠	Pass	2 ◇	Pass
2 ♠	Pass	3 ♠	Pass
4 ♠	Pass	Pass	Pass

West leads ♣J to ♣A. There are certainly ten tricks available but care is needed not to lose four tricks in the process. The weakness is in hearts where three tricks could be lost if East were to get in and lead through your king. If, in addition, you lost a trick in trumps you would be down.

Remembering the importance of being the last to play holding an unsupported king, you lead ♠3 to ♠K and return ♠2 and finesse ♠10 when East follows with ♠7. It will not matter if West wins with the queen because no lead that he can make will cause you any worry.

Dealer South. Game all.

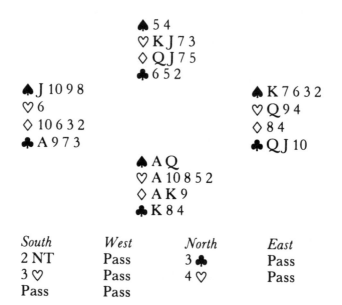

South	West	North	East
2 NT	Pass	3 ♣	Pass
3 ♡	Pass	4 ♡	Pass
Pass	Pass		

The opening bid indicated 20–22 high card points and the response of Three Clubs was Stayman asking for a four card major suit. This succeeded in locating the good heart fit. West led ♠ J, taken with ♠ Q. South was one of those players who had learned "never finesse with nine" and played off ace and king of trumps, West signalling with ♣ 7. South did his best to recover by switching to diamonds. Had East held three it would have been possible to discard a losing club on the fourth round. But East ruffed the third round and returned ♣ Q to defeat the contract.

Had South appreciated the danger of losing three clubs he might have followed the plan explained in the previous hand and finessed the trumps into West's 'safe' hand.

The danger is less apparent in this hand.

Dealer North. East-West vul.

```
                    ♠ A Q 5
                    ♡ A J 8
                    ◊ J 10 9 4 2
                    ♣ J 6
    ♠ 9 6 4                          ♠ K 8 7 2
    ♡ Q 5 3                          ♡ 6
    ◊ A 5 3                          ◊ 8 7
    ♣ 8 4 3 2                        ♣ A K Q 10 9 5
                    ♠ J 10 3
                    ♡ K 10 9 7 4 2
                    ◊ K Q 6
                    ♣ 7
```

South	West	North	East
		1 ◊	2 ♣
2 ♡	Pass	3 ♡	Pass
4 ♡	Pass	Pass	Pass

West leads 2 ♣. East wins, and South ruffs the club continuation. The tricks are there in the shape of five hearts at least, four diamonds and one spade, possibly more. South has lost one club and must lose a diamond. He may also lose a trump as he is missing the queen, and possibly also a spade. Too many losers. He can, however, avoid the spade loser by discarding his losers on the diamonds. But this can be done only after drawing trumps. Provided that the opponents can be prevented from setting up a spade trick before trumps are drawn all should be well.

The only opponent who can attack spades profitably is West and therefore West is the danger hand to be kept out. Once this point has been established the play becomes reasonably easy. Lead ♡ 10 and play low from dummy unless West plays the queen. When ♡ 10 wins, draw trumps and set up the diamonds, playing king and queen first. West wins and leads a spade but you play ♠ A and carry on with the diamonds, getting rid of your spades, to make an overtrick.

It would not have mattered had East held ♡ Q, as he could not attack spades without giving you a free finesse. It was also technically correct to lead ♡ 10 initially not ♡ K, just in case West held all four trumps.

The examples given so far have all involved careful handling of the trump suit. But it may equally be essential to prevent the danger hand getting in with a side suit.

Dealer West. East-West vul.

```
              ♠ K Q J 6 4
              ♡ K 7 3
              ◊ 7 2
              ♣ 7 3 2
♠ A 2                        ♠ 10 9 5 3
♡ 10 8                       ♡ 6
◊ Q J 10 6 4                 ◊ K 8 5 3
♣ A Q 6 5                    ♣ 10 9 8 4
              ♠ 8 7
              ♡ A Q J 9 5 4 2
              ◊ A 9
              ♣ K J
```

South	West	North	East
	1 ◊	1 ♠	Pass
4 ♡	Pass	Pass	Pass

West leads ◊ Q and South can see seven tricks in hearts, one in diamonds and at least two in spades. Looking at the losers, there is one in spades, one in diamonds and probably two in clubs if East gets in. So long as West has the lead there is no danger. So ◊ Q must be allowed to win, you playing ◊ 9. West cannot do better than continue his suit. You win, draw trumps and lead a spade. West will win with ♠ A and can do no better than cash ♣ A, for otherwise he may not make it. But this establishes your king. Had you won the opening lead East would have later got in with ◊ K and led a club.

Suppose East had held ♠ A? In the first place there is nothing you could do as a player with an ace is more often than not going to win with it. In the second place, it was almost impossible for East to have it. North and South have between them 24 high card points and on the lead of ◊ Q East has ◊ K, accounting for three more = 27 points. Take away West's ace of spades and he is left with 9 points. Moreover East, with the ace of spades and some diamonds headed by the king might have supported his partner to 2 ◊.

Dealder South. Game all.

```
                    ♠ Q 9 8 4
                    ♡ A 4
                    ◊ 6 3 2
                    ♣ A J 10 9
   ♠ 5 2                              ♠ 7 3
   ♡ K Q 10 7                         ♡ J 9 8 5
   ◊ A 9 8 7                          ◊ Q J 10 4
   ♣ 8 7 4                            ♣ Q 6 3
                    ♠ A K J 10 6
                    ♡ 6 3 2
                    ◊ K 5
                    ♣ K 5 3
```

South	West	North	East
1 ♠	Pass	3 ♠	Pass
4 ♠	Pass	Pass	Pass

West leads ♡ K and South can count eight top tricks with five trumps, two clubs and one heart. One extra trick can be made by ruffing a heart in dummy and at least one extra trick can be made from clubs. In other words there are ten tricks available, but checking up on losers will reveal that you might lose two diamonds, one club and one heart.

Again, the danger lies in diamonds where you only hold the king so the hand to be kept out is East. Therefore the first move must be to play low from dummy at trick one as you have nothing to fear if West is on play. West probably continues hearts. You draw trumps in two rounds ending in your hand and lead your third heart which you ruff on the table. You next lead ♣J and if East plays low, you do likewise, not minding if West wins with the queen. Whatever happens you have ten tricks. Had you taken the first trick in hearts you could not be sure of keeping East out on the second round.

South's trump finesse on this hand might appear unusual, but he had a valid reason for taking it.

Dealer South. Love all.

```
                    ♠ —
                    ♡ 7 4 3
                    ◇ A K 8 7 4 3
                    ♣ J 10 6 4
♠ K Q 10 9 2                          ♠ A J 6 5 4
♡ 2                                   ♡ J 9 8 6
◇ 10 9 5                              ◇ 6
♣ A Q 8 5                             ♣ 9 7 3
                    ♠ 8 7 3
                    ♡ A K Q 10 5
                    ◇ Q J 2
                    ♣ K 2
```

After a competitive auction in which East-West had bid spades, South became declarer in Five Hearts. West led ♠ K which was ruffed in dummy. South could see eleven tricks providing he could draw trumps and later make his diamonds. But it sounded from the bidding as though the hearts might be badly divided, and if the knave did not fall it would be impossible to enjoy the diamonds, without the opponents getting in with a trump, and taking tricks in clubs and spades.

If a trick in trumps were lost early, dummy would offer protection against a spade lead by a trump being there for ruffing. And if East could be kept out the club position would be protected. So at trick two South led ♡ 4 and finessed ♡ 10. If West had won, a club lead would establish declarer's king and a spade could be ruffed on the table. As it was, ♡ 10 held, trumps were drawn and twelve tricks were made.

22. Timing

This involves various factors in the play of the hand where it is important in which order suits are played and how suits are played. In the following hand success depends on one out of two important cards being favourably placed.

Dealer South. North-South vul.

```
                    ♠ 3 2
                    ♡ A Q 7 5
                    ◇ 7 5 3
                    ♣ K Q 9 3
      ♠ 8 7 6                      ♠ 9 5
      ♡ 10 8 6 4                   ♡ K J 9
      ◇ K Q J                      ◇ 9 8 6 2
      ♣ A 8 2                      ♣ J 10 7 5
                    ♠ A K Q J 10 4
                    ♡ 3 2
                    ◇ A 10 4
                    ♣ 6 4
```

South	West	North	East
1 ♠	Pass	2 ♣	Pass
3 ♠	Pass	4 ♠	Pass
Pass	Pass		

West leads ◇ K and South can see eight top tricks. He must also make at least one club so he can be sure of nine.

(repeated for convenience)

```
              ♠ 3 2
              ♡ A Q 7 5
              ◇ 7 5 3
              ♣ K Q 9 3
♠ 8 7 6                        ♠ 9 5
♡ 10 8 6 4                     ♡ K J 9
◇ K Q J                        ◇ 9 8 6 2
♣ A 8 2                        ♣ J 10 7 5
              ♠ A K Q J 10 4
              ♡ 3 2
              ◇ A 10 4
              ♣ 6 4
```

There are two possible ways to make a tenth. One is to find West with the ace of clubs and the other to find West with the king of hearts. The problem is which suit to try first. The answer is clubs, because if the ace is with East, which means you can only make one trick in clubs, you are still alive to try the heart finesse. If on the other hand you finesse hearts first and lose, you are down for certain.

Having decided to play clubs before hearts, do you first draw trumps?

Suppose you do and then lead a low club to dummy and ♣ Q wins, you cannot get back to your hand. You can afford to play one top trump and then lead a club. When ♣ Q wins you return to hand with a trump and draw the opposing trumps. Now lead your second club. Assume West puts up his ace and cashes two diamonds, you take the rest as your losing heart is discarded on ♣ K.

If East holds ♣ A you will have to rely on the heart finesse and if that, too, fails you can tell your friends what an unlucky player you are. It was important to win the opening lead, otherwise West might switch to a heart.

We have discussed the technique of ruffing out suits to provide additional winners. The examples that follow are a little more complicated than those given earlier as matters of timing are involved.

Dealer South. Love all.

```
                    ♠ A 5 4
                    ♡ J 5 4
                    ◊ A Q 10 8 7
                    ♣ 4 2
♠ 10 3 2                              ♠ 8 6
♡ A Q 2                              ♡ K 10 8 7
◊ 4 2                                ◊ J 9 6 5
♣ K Q J 10 9                         ♣ 8 6 5
                    ♠ K Q J 9 7
                    ♡ 9 6 3
                    ◊ K 3
                    ♣ A 7 3
```

South	West	North	East
1 ♠	2 ♣	2 ◊	Pass
2 ♠	Pass	4 ♠	Pass
Pass	Pass		

West leads ♣ K and there are nine sure tricks. You might have thought of allowing ♣ K to win, intending to take the continuation and ruff your third club in dummy. But you cannot afford to do that because West might switch to hearts and you would lose the first four tricks. The best chance is in diamonds. With a combined total of seven including the three top honours there is a fair chance that the jack will fall, but it is by no means a certainty and a better way should be found if possible.

Take the first trick with ♣ A and play ♠ K and ♠ Q. This will establish whether the outstanding trumps are split 3–2. When each opponent follows suit you know you can draw the last trump with dummy's ace. Leaving that as an entry you play ◊ K followed by ◊ 3 to ◊ Q. When all follow there are two outstanding diamonds which may be both with East, both with West, or divided. Next lead ◊ 8 and ruff in hand with ♠ J, return to dummy with ♠ A, drawing West's ♠ 10, play ◊ A on which ◊ J must fall and ◊ 10 is your extra trick.

Had the trumps been found to be 4–1 this plan would not be possible and it is doubtful if you could do better than simply draw trumps and play diamonds, hoping the jack fell. But when you found the trumps were 3–2 it was a near certainty that the contract would be made by ruffing a low diamond in hand. Success on the next hand depended on declarer knowing how many entries he needed to establish and enjoy his suit.

Dealer South. Love all.

```
              ♠ A 10 2
              ♡ 7 5 2
              ◊ A J 8 7 3
              ♣ A 3
  ♠ 9 7 5                      ♠ 4
  ♡ K 10 3                     ♡ Q J 9 4
  ◊ 4 2                        ◊ K Q 10 9
  ♣ Q J 10 7 6                 ♣ K 9 5 2
              ♠ K Q J 8 6 3
              ♡ A 8 6
              ◊ 6 5
              ♣ 8 4
```

South	West	North	East
1 ♠	Pass	2 ◊	Pass
2 ♠	Pass	4 ♠	Pass
Pass	Pass		

West led ♣ Q which South correctly won, not wanting a heart switch. With nine top tricks he sought his tenth in diamonds and played ace and another. East won, cashed ♣ K and returned ♡ Q. South won and played ♠ K followed by ♠ 3 to ♠ 10 and led ◊ 7 from the table and ruffed. Had the adverse diamonds been evenly divided all would have been well. As it was, he could cross to dummy with ♠ A and ruff a fourth diamond, but there was no further entry to score the winner.

His partner suggested leading ♠ 2 to ♠ K at the second trick and playing a diamond to ◊ J and ◊ Q. But this would not work either, as East would return a low club to West's ♣ J and West could lead a trump, leaving South an entry short.

In order to make an extra diamond and allowing for a likely 4–2 split South must be prepared to lose one round, ruff twice and finally get back to dummy to play the winner. He needs three entries and as the ace of clubs has gone he has exactly three left (♠ A 10 and ◊ A). Playing ace and another diamond is a waste of an entry. The correct sequence of play is a low diamond at trick two, taken by East who cashes ♣ K and returns ♡ Q to ♡ A. South next lays down ♠ K and follows with ◊ 6 to ◊ A (entry no.1) and ruffs ◊ 7 with ♠ J. He re-enters dummy with ♠ 10 (entry no.2) and ruffs ◊ 8 with ♠ Q. He finally crosses to dummy with ♠ A (entry no.3) to make ◊ J and his tenth trick.

The next is a cross-ruffing hand and as we stated in an earlier hand (p. 118) the number of entries will correspond to the number of times you may need to ruff.

Dealer South. Love all.

```
                    ♠ 10 8 6 4 2
                    ♡ 9 5 4 2
                    ◊ Q
                    ♣ A J 3
        ♠ 5                             ♠ K Q
        ♡ Q 10 3                        ♡ A K 8 7
        ◊ K J 9 7 4                     ◊ 8 5
        ♣ 10 8 6 2                      ♣ K 9 7 5 4
                    ♠ A J 9 7 3
                    ♡ J 6
                    ◊ A 10 6 3 2
                    ♣ Q
```

(repeated for convenience)

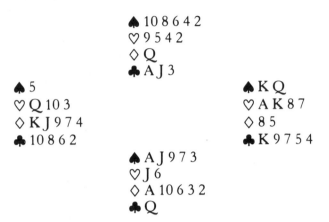

♠ 10 8 6 4 2
♡ 9 5 4 2
◊ Q
♣ A J 3

♠ 5
♡ Q 10 3
◊ K J 9 7 4
♣ 10 8 6 2

♠ K Q
♡ A K 8 7
◊ 8 5
♣ K 9 7 5 4

♠ A J 9 7 3
♡ J 6
◊ A 10 6 3 2
♣ Q

South opened One Spade and North, regarding his distribution in a favourable light, bid Four Spades. West leads ♣ 2 and the first point is that ♣ A must be played at once. To finesse would risk inevitable defeat if East held the king. With singletons in each hand the plan must be to cross-ruff. Suppose South leads ♠ 2 to ♠ A, followed by ◊ A and ◊ 2, ruffed in dummy, followed by a club ruff and diamond ruff. East has no diamonds but is wise to discard. South ruffs a club in hand and leads a fourth diamond which dummy ruffs and, again, East discards.

The situation at this stage is that South still holds a losing diamond but cannot get back to his hand. He plays a heart from the table, East wins and now leads ♠ K, removing dummy's last trump. Needing to ruff four diamonds in dummy South needs four entries to his hand and he has them with ◊ A, ♠ A and two club ruffs. When he played ♠ A followed by ◊ A he telescoped two entries and was one short.

The entries must be used in the correct order. If, for example, South leads ◊ Q to ◊ A and ruffs a diamond and next ruffs a club and leads another diamond, East can over-ruff, put his partner in with a heart and over-ruff again in diamonds. The sequence of play must be to win the first trick with ♣ A and lead ◊ Q to ◊ A and ruff ◊ 2 with ♠ 2.

Next lead ♠ 3 to ♠ A and ruff another diamond. It does not matter whether or not East over-ruffs as South has another two entries to his hand by trumping clubs.

The stratagem of ducking which was described in Part 2 relating to no-trumps also plays its part in suit contracts.

Dealer South. Game all.

```
                    ♠ 3 2
                    ♡ A K 9 8 6
                    ◊ 9 8 7 3
                    ♣ 7 2
      ♠ 5 4                           ♠ 10 6
      ♡ J 5                           ♡ Q 10 7
      ◊ K J 10 2                      ◊ 6 5 4
      ♣ Q J 10 8 5                    ♣ K 9 6 4 3
                    ♠ A K Q J 9 8 7
                    ♡ 4 3 2
                    ◊ A Q
                    ♣ A
```

South	West	North	East
2 ♣	Pass	2 ♡	Pass
4 NT	Pass	5 ◊	Pass
5 NT	Pass	6 ◊	Pass
6 ♠	Pass	Pass	Pass

Having received a positive reply to his game forcing opening of Two Clubs, South decided to launch into Blackwood as he was clear in his mind that the final contract would be spades.

West leads ♣ Q and South can see eleven tricks. After drawing trumps one possibility would be to finesse diamonds but that would be staking all on an even money chance, rather like spinning a coin. With eight hearts between the two hands there is a good chance of a 3–2 division of the others, in which case the suit would be cleared in three rounds. But if the ace and king are played first there is no hope of getting back to dummy.

(repeated for convenience)

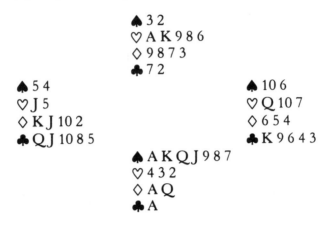

```
              ♠ 3 2
              ♡ A K 9 8 6
              ◇ 9 8 7 3
              ♣ 7 2
♠ 5 4                        ♠ 10 6
♡ J 5                        ♡ Q 10 7
◇ K J 10 2                   ◇ 6 5 4
♣ Q J 10 8 5                 ♣ K 9 6 4 3
              ♠ A K Q J 9 8 7
              ♡ 4 3 2
              ◇ A Q
              ♣ A
```

Supposing you decide to duck an early round, playing low from hand and putting on dummy's eight. East wins, say, with ten and returns a diamond. Now you have an awkward decision, whether to finesse or put on the ace, trusting that the hearts are evenly divided. As this represents a better mathematical chance, you win and play a second heart, but unfortunately West discards. You can no longer establish the hearts and you have already played your ace of diamonds so you cannot finesse. To make things worse it transpires that East had the king of diamonds.

Ducking a heart was right in principle but the correct play is to win the first round with ace or king. If no high cards fall return a low heart and if each opponent follows suit you have no further worries as the only remaining heart must fall on the next lead to dummy. If, on the other hand, one opponent discards, marking the other with four you are still in a position to rely on the diamond finesse.

There is also a further possibility. Suppose on the first round East follows with an honour, say, the jack. He might have jack bare, jack–ten or jack–queen. Now play ♡ 8 or ♡ 9 from dummy. If East discards, West will win and you can now take a marked finesse against the remaining honour.

Alternatively you can get back to hand by ruffing a club and lead a heart towards dummy and if West started with something like ♡ Q 10 x you may make an overtrick. The important point to grasp is that establishing the hearts is much better than relying on the diamond finesse, and it is better to play off one top honour in dummy than to give away the first round.

It may be necessary to duck a round in a side suit before drawing trumps as dummy may need to have a trump to protect against the loss of too many tricks elsewhere.

Dealer South. North-South vul.

```
                ♠ A K 7 3
                ♡ 6 5
                ◊ Q 9 7 4 3
                ♣ 6 5
  ♠ J 9 5                          ♠ Q 10 2
  ♡ 7 4 2                          ♡ 10 3
  ◊ K 8 5                          ◊ J 10 6 2
  ♣ K J 9 4                        ♣ A 10 3 2
                ♠ 8 6 4
                ♡ A K Q J 9 8
                ◊ A
                ♣ Q 8 7
```

South	West	North	East
1 ♡	Pass	1 ♠	Pass
3 ♡	Pass	4 ♡	Pass
Pass	Pass		

West leads ♡ 2 to ♡ 10 and ♡ J. There are nine top tricks and no possibility of ruffing a club in dummy as the defence will lead another trump. Nor is there any real chance of establishing an extra diamond. That leaves spades and if the suit breaks evenly the fourth spade in dummy will be good.

You cannot afford to draw trumps at once because when you give up an early spade trick you will be likely to lose three tricks in clubs. At trick two you lead a spade and play low from dummy. East wins and returns a club and the defence win two tricks and switch to trumps. You draw the rest of the trumps, cash ◇ A and lead a spade to ♠ A. You can now ruff a low diamond in hand on the offchance that the king falls. When it doesn't, lead your last spade and when each opponent follows the fourth spade is your tenth trick. The term 'duck' has two meanings. One is to play a small card and surrender a trick that might have been won, in order to preserve an entry. The other is to refuse to win a trick in order to keep control. We have just given examples of the former type. The second, which is analogous to the hold-up in no-trumps, is employed to retain control in trumps.

Dealer South. Love all.

```
                    ♠ 4 3
                    ♡ J 4
                    ◇ A Q J 4 2
                    ♣ A J 3 2
  ♠ Q J 10                            ♠ 7 2
  ♡ A K Q 10                          ♡ 7 4 2
  ◇ 8 7                               ◇ 10 9 6 5
  ♣ Q 8 7 6                           ♣ K 10 5 4
                    ♠ A K 9 8 6 5
                    ♡ 9 8 6 3
                    ◇ K 3
                    ♣ 9
```

South	West	North	East
1 ♠	Pass	2 ◇	Pass
2 ♠	Pass	3 ♣	Pass
3 ♠	Pass	4 ♠	Pass
Pass	Pass		

West leads ♡ A and switches to ♠ Q. There are plenty of tricks once the trumps are out but the difficulty is that a trick must be lost in trumps and South has four losing hearts. Suppose he takes ♠ A and ♠ K and plays diamonds intending to discard hearts, West will ruff the third and defeat the contract. South must duck ♠ Q, playing low from his hand. If West continues spades South can draw trumps and make all his diamonds and the ace of clubs. West can only cash one more heart as dummy will ruff a third. By ducking the trump switch South has retained control.

To ruff in the closed hand may be an embarrassment if you do not have an adequate supply of trumps and in order to retain trump control it may be wise on occasions not to ruff.

Dealer South. Love all.

```
                    ♠ J 7 3
                    ♡ K 6
                    ◇ K J 6 4
                    ♣ K 6 4 3
  ♠ K Q 10 8                        ♠ A 9 5 4 2
  ♡ 9 8 7 2                         ♡ 5 3
  ◇ 10 5 3                          ◇ 9 8 7
  ♣ A 5                             ♣ 9 8 7
                    ♠ 6
                    ♡ A Q J 10 4
                    ◇ A Q 2
                    ♣ Q J 10 2
```

South	West	North	East
1 ♡	Pass	2 NT	Pass
3 ♣	Pass	4 ♣	Pass
4 ♡	Pass	Pass	Pass

As it happens Five Clubs might be easier, but South had good hearts and, maybe, wanted his bonus for honours. West led ♠ K and continued with ♠ Q which South ruffed. South started drawing trumps but when East discarded on the third he was in trouble. If he drew West's trump he would be left with none and still had to clear the ace of clubs. So he played ♣ Q, West won and played another spade which forced declarer's last trump. South's best plan is to ruff the second spade and lead ♣J, hoping that West, if he has the ace, may play low thinking that South is trying to finesse. If ♣J wins South can draw trumps as he has ten tricks.

If West wins the first club lead and returns a spade, South must not ruff as he cannot afford to shorten himself further. Suppose he throws a club. If another spade is played dummy will be able to ruff and take the strain off South.

In the foregoing hand South's trumps were good and it was not so obvious that he could not afford to keep ruffing. The position is more clear when declarer has only four trumps and dummy three.

Dealer South. Love all.

```
                  ♠ Q 9 6
                  ♡ 7 4 3
                  ◇ A Q J 8 6
                  ♣ 4 3
  ♠ 7 5 3 2                        ♠ 8 4
  ♡ A K J 6                        ♡ Q 10 8 2
  ◇ 9 5 4                          ◇ 7 3
  ♣ Q 8                            ♣ K 10 6 5 2
                  ♠ A K J 10
                  ♡ 9 5
                  ◇ K 10 2
                  ♣ A J 9 7
```

South	West	North	East
1 ♣	Pass	1 ◇	Pass
1 ♠	Pass	2 ♠	Pass
4 ♠	Pass	Pass	Pass

North was wrong to support South's second suit with less than four cards but the final contract turned out to be a good one.

West led ♡ A and ♡ K and continued with ♡ 6. South could not spare a trump and so discarded a club. Now there was nothing the defence could do. Dummy would ruff another heart. East in fact switched to clubs, South won, drew trumps and made five diamond tricks for the contract.

The necessity for keeping trump control usually arises where declarer is short in a suit and is continually being forced to ruff. On this hand even a combined total of eight trumps might prove insufficient without care.

Dealer South. Love all.

```
                  ♠ K 4 3
                  ♡ K 7 6 5
                  ◇ K 7
                  ♣ 7 6 3 2
  ♠ Q 10 5                        ♠ 7 2
  ♡ J 10 8                        ♡ Q 9 4 2
  ◇ A 4                           ◇ 8 5 3 2
  ♣ K Q J 9 4                     ♣ A 10 5
                  ♠ A J 9 8 6
                  ♡ A 3
                  ◇ Q J 10 9 6
                  ♣ 8
```

South	West	North	East
1 ♠	2 ♣	2 ♠	Pass
3 ◇	Pass	4 ♠	Pass
Pass	Pass		

South's Three Diamonds was in the nature of a trial bid and as North had a good raise and a high honour in diamonds he bid game.

West led ♣ K and continued with a low club to ♣ A, ruffed in hand with ♠ 6. South next led ♠ 8, covered by ♠ 10 and ♠ K and returned ♠ 3, finessing ♠ J which lost to ♠ Q, West returned a club which South ruffed with ♠ 9. He needed to establish diamonds and when West got in with

◊ A and played another club, declarer's last trump, the ace, was forced out leaving West with ♠ 5 and dummy with ♠ 4.

Better timing would have made all the difference. South has one club loser, no heart loser, one diamond loser and can afford to concede a trump. His weakness is the singleton club. At tricks three and four he cashes ♠ A and ♠ K, leaving the queen outstanding. He next drives out ◊ A and ruffs the club return, leaving himself with ♠ J only. But all he needs to do is to play off winners and allow West to take his good trump when he likes.

23. Loser on Loser

There are several situations where it may pay to throw a card that is bound to lose on a losing trick in some other suit. We have just cited examples of declaring declining to ruff because he could not afford to spare a trump. Here is another example.

Dealer West. East-West vul.

```
              ♠ K J 8
              ♡ J 5
              ◊ K 8 5 2
              ♣ K 10 6 4
♠ 4                        ♠ 6 5 3 2
♡ A K 10 9 7 4             ♡ Q 8 6 3
◊ 9 6 4                    ◊ Q J 10
♣ A 7 5                    ♣ 8 3
              ♠ A Q 10 9 7
              ♡ 2
              ◊ A 7 3
              ♣ Q J 9 2
```

South	West	North	East
	1 ♡	Pass	2 ♡
2 ♠	3 ♡	4 ♠	Pass
Pass	Pass		

South had a choice between a direct overcall in spades or a take-out double. Had he doubled North might have had a problem about the action to take over a rebid in hearts.

West led his top hearts and South ruffed the second. He started drawing trumps but had to stop when West discarded. He could not afford to leave himself without a trump with the ace of clubs still outstanding. He therefore switched to ♣ Q to which West followed with ♣ 5 and East with ♣ 8. South continued clubs, West won with ♣ A and returned ♣ 7 for East to ruff and the defence later made a diamond.

South should have discarded a losing diamond on the second heart. Dummy would then be able to ruff if a third round were played. It would simply mean that declarer lost two hearts and no diamond instead of one heart and one diamond. The 4–1 trump split was unlucky, but there was an indication that trumps might split badly. North-South held between them 24 high cards points and East-West had bid up to three hearts vulnerable on 16 points, and would have made the contract. They must have been bidding up on distribution.

It is worth remembering that if your opponents have bid up on a minority of the points and, so far as you can judge, they were not being unduly rash, they must have distributional values to compensate for their lack of high cards.

In the next hand it was safer to discard a likely loser rather than risk an over-ruff or trump promotion.

Dealer East. Game all.

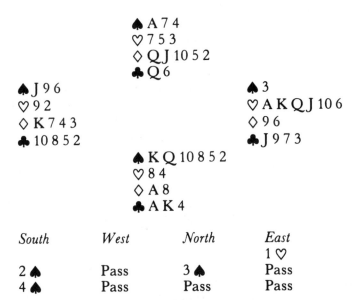

	♠ A 7 4	
	♡ 7 5 3	
	◇ Q J 10 5 2	
	♣ Q 6	

♠ J 9 6		♠ 3
♡ 9 2		♡ A K Q J 10 6
◇ K 7 4 3		◇ 9 6
♣ 10 8 5 2		♣ J 9 7 3

	♠ K Q 10 8 5 2	
	♡ 8 4	
	◇ A 8	
	♣ A K 4	

South	West	North	East
			1 ♡
2 ♠	Pass	3 ♠	Pass
4 ♠	Pass	Pass	Pass

West leads ♡ 9 to ♡ 10 and East continues with two more rounds. If South ruffs with ♠ 10 he will be over-ruffed with ♠ J and later he will have to rely on the diamond finesse which fails. If he ruffs with ♠ K or ♠ Q he is dependent on the jack falling or the diamond finesse. The safest plan is to discard ◇ 8 on the third heart, exchanging one loser for another. Now he can only be defeated by finding West with all four missing trumps.

To throw a loser on a loser may often be necessary to ruff out a suit and at the same time ensure that the lead does not get into the danger hand.

Dealer South. Love all.

```
                    ♠ 8 7 4
                    ♡ Q 10 9
                    ◇ A K J 5 4
                    ♣ A 8
♠ A Q J 6 2                         ♠ 10 5
♡ 8 4                               ♡ 6 3
◇ 7 2                               ◇ Q 10 9
♣ K Q J 6                           ♣ 10 9 7 5 3 2
                    ♠ K 9 3
                    ♡ A K J 7 5 2
                    ◇ 8 6 3
                    ♣ 4
```

South	West	North	East
1 ♡	1 ♠	2 ◇	Pass
2 ♡	Pass	4 ♡	Pass
Pass	Pass		

West leads ♣ K and South can see that he will need to establish dummy's diamonds. If East should get in, as will happen if the diamond finesse loses, a spade return will result in the loss of four tricks. This risk can be avoided by playing low from dummy at trick one. West probably continues his suit and South discards ◇ 3 on ♣ A. He has, in effect, lost one club and no diamond, instead of no club and possibly one diamond.

After winning with ♣ A he cashes ◇ A and leads ♡ 9 to ♡ A. He next leads ◇ 8 from his hand and when West follows, plays ◇ K and next ruffs a low diamond in hand, establishing ◇ J 5. These are cashed after dummy has been entered with ♡ 10, drawing the outstanding trumps.

Here is another example of ducking in order to avoid losing a trick to the danger hand.

Dealer West. Love all.

```
                    ♠ 6 3
                    ♡ A 2
                    ◇ Q 9 8
                    ♣ A J 9 7 4 3
♠ A J 9                                 ♠ Q 10 5 4
♡ K Q J 5 3                             ♡ 9 8 7 6 4
◇ 5 3                                   ◇ 4 2
♣ K 8 2                                 ♣ Q 10
                    ♠ K 8 7 2
                    ♡ 10
                    ◇ A K J 10 7 6
                    ♣ 6 5
```

South	West	North	East
	1 ♡	2 ♣	2 ♡
3 ◇	3 ♡	4 ◇	Pass
5 ◇	Pass	Pass	Pass

West leads ♡ K. The contract depends on being able to establish dummy's clubs, in which one trick must be lost. If East wins a trick in clubs he will lead a spade and as West is marked with the high cards on his opening bid South's king is likely to be captured.

If South allows ♡ K to win, West remains on lead. A heart continuation will enable South to discard a club on ♡ A. Now the clubs can be established by ruffing, South being careful to ruff with high trumps so that he can keep ◇ 7 and ◇ 6 to lead over to the higher trumps on the table.

On the next hand South was fully alive to the danger but could not find a solution.

Dealer South. North-South vul.

```
                    ♠ K Q 10
                    ♡ A 6 3
                    ◇ K 8 6 4
                    ♣ 7 4 2
  ♠ 8 2                              ♠ 5 4
  ♡ K Q J 9 4                        ♡ 8 7 2
  ◇ J 9 3                            ◇ Q 10 2
  ♣ A Q 5                            ♣ J 10 9 8 6
                    ♠ A J 9 7 6 3
                    ♡ 10 5
                    ◇ A 7 5
                    ♣ K 3
```

South	West	North	East
South	*West*	*North*	*East*
1 ♠	2 ♡	2 NT	Pass
4 ♠	Pass	Pass	Pass

West led ♡ K and South could see nine tricks. As the king of clubs appeared unlikely to make on the bidding, the best chance seemed to be to establish a diamond. After winning with ♡ A, trumps were drawn in two rounds and ◇ 4 was led from the table. East put up ◇ 10 which foiled declarer's plan to duck into West's hand. South won with ◇ A, led to ◇ K and returned ◇ 6 hoping that West held the queen and would have to take the third round. But East held the queen and the inevitable club return defeated the contract.

Again, if South is prepared to lose two hearts but no diamond instead of one heart and one diamond he will succeed. He plays low from dummy at trick one and notes what East plays. When East follows with ♡ 2 it appears that he has three and consequently when West continues with ♡ Q dummy plays low again. Now it is possible for South to discard a low diamond on ♡ A, leaving himself with ◇ A 7 opposite dummy's ◇ K 8 6 4. Three rounds of diamonds, including a third round ruff, establishes the fourth one on the table and a trump provides the entry.

Had East petered in hearts, playing ♡ 8 on the first round, South would have to win the second heart with the ace. He would then play ♠ K Q to draw trumps and lead ♡ 6 from the table and discard a diamond from hand, losing to West. The play to the first two tricks would have indicated East with ♡ 8 2 and West with ♡ K Q J 9 7 4.

Sometimes a loser on loser play can be employed to enable dummy to ruff in a safer suit. For example:

Dealer South. North-South vul.

```
                    ♠ 5 3
                    ♡ K 9 4
                    ◇ A 7 6
                    ♣ J 8 6 4 3
    ♠ K Q J 8 7 6                   ♠ 9 2
    ♡ 10 5                          ♡ J 8 3
    ◇ J 8 2                         ◇ Q 10 9 3
    ♣ Q 5                           ♣ K 10 9 2
                    ♠ A 10 4
                    ♡ A Q 7 6 2
                    ◇ K 5 4
                    ♣ A 7
```

South	West	North	East
1 ♡	1 ♠	2 ♡	Pass
4 ♡	Pass	Pass	Pass

West leads ♠ K and East encourages with ♠ 9, South playing ♠ 4. West continues with ♠ J, East plays ♠ 2 and South ♠ A. Assuming that the trumps are well divided there are nine top tricks. Nothing can be done with the clubs and there is no chance of ruffing a spade in dummy as East will over-ruff and to employ the king will set up a trump trick for the defence.

But by an exchange of losers a tenth trick can be found. South leads ♠ 10, West covers with ♠ Q and ◇ 6 is discarded from the table. It is now possible to ruff the third round of diamonds on the table. It needed East to hold four diamonds so that one discard on ♠ Q would not help.

On this hand a loser on loser play was needed to keep out the danger hand. Careful timing was necessary as there were also entry problems.

Dealer South. Game all.

```
                    ♠ J 10 6 2
                    ♡ Q J 8
                    ◇ 6 4 3
                    ♣ A Q J
       ♠ Q 5 4 3                    ♠ 9 8 7
       ♡ 6                          ♡ 7 3 2
       ◇ A 8 7 2                    ◇ Q J 10
       ♣ 10 9 8 7                   ♣ K 6 5 2
                    ♠ A K
                    ♡ A K 10 9 5 4
                    ◇ K 9 5
                    ♣ 4 3
```

South	West	North	East
1 ♡	Pass	1 ♠	Pass
3 ♡	Pass	4 ♡	Pass
Pass	Pass		

West led ♣ 10 and South can count nine top tricks. If the club finesse succeeds he is home or if the ace of diamonds is on his right he is safe. But a losing club finesse coupled with a bad lie of diamonds would result in defeat.

Not wishing to risk the finesse South puts up ♣ A. He next cashes ♠ A K and enters dummy with the lead of ♡ 4 to ♡ 8. He now plays ♠ J and if East covers he will ruff, return to dummy with a trump and make ♠ 10. As it is East plays low and South discards ♣ 4. West wins with ♠ Q and

(repeated for convenience)

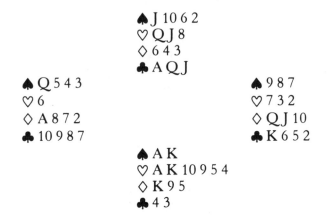

does best to return his last spade to prevent a discard being made on ♠ 10. East duly ruffs and South over-ruffs and enters dummy with ♡ J. He then leads ♣ Q, East covers with ♣ K and South ruffs, crosses to the table with ♡ Q and discards ◇ 5 on the winning ♣ J. Had East not covered ♣ Q, South would have discarded. The only tricks lost are one spade and two diamonds. Had declarer taken even one round of trumps before playing spades he would have been one entry short and would have been unable to make ♣ J for the tenth trick.

PART ONE

Introductory

1. Opening Leads

As the defence starts with the opening lead it is logical to discuss this first. In doing so it is convenient to divide the subject into:

    (a) Opening leads against no-trumps

    (b) Opening leads against suit contracts.

(a) *Against No-Trumps*

The main object must be to establish a long suit against the declarer. If you are able to lead a card to which the declarer is unable to follow suit either from his own hand or dummy, your card must win the trick for the very simple reason that there are no trumps.

If your partner has bid it is nearly always correct to lead his suit as a suit he considered strong enough to call is likely to be better than yours. If it turns out a complete failure you can ask him politely not to bid on rubbish. If, on the other hand, you lead your own suit, possibly because the opponents called strongly over your partner's bid, and it becomes apparent that had you trusted your partner the contract would have been defeated, you have between tricks one and thirteen to work out a good alibi for not leading his suit.

In leading partner's suit you lead the top card unless holding three or more cards with an honour, in which case you lead a low card. For example, assume the bidding was

South	West	North	East
No Bid	1 ◇	1 ♠	2 NT
No Bid	3 NT	All pass	

If your spade holding is any of the following, lead the top card

(1) ♠ 9 2   (2) ♠ Q 2   (3) ♠ 7 4 2   (4) ♠ Q J 2

In (4) you lead ♠ Q as you have a second honour in sequence.

If you hold three cards with an honour it is correct to play a low card. The reason for this can be seen in this example where South is declarer in No-Trumps after East has bid spades

                    ♠ 6 4
    ♠ Q 5 3   ♠ A 10 9 7 2
                    ♠ K J 8

It can be seen that if West leads ♠ Q, South will make two tricks in the suit whereas if ♠ 3 is led South will make only one. West has kept an honour behind or over the declarer. Thus in the sequence given above where partner has overcalled one diamond with one spade and East has called no-trump, lead the card underlined in each of the following

(5) ♠ J 7 2   (6) ♠ A 4 2   (7) ♠ 10 7 3

There is virtually no risk that partner will mis-read the position. In the example give above where ♠ 3 was led; if this were the highest card it would be a singleton as you (East) have ♠ 2. In that event South would hold ♠ K Q J 8 5 which would hardly make sense.

If your partner has not bid it is generally correct to lead your longest and best suit. If your suit is headed by a sequence including an honour, lead the top. Thus from

Q J 10 7 3	lead	Queen
J 10 9 6 4	lead	Knave
10 9 8 4 2	lead	Ten

If the top two cards are in sequence and the third one step below, treat as a sequence

K Q 10 7 5	lead	King
Q J 9 5 4	lead	Queen

The reason that you lead the top card of a sequence is this. Suppose you hold Q J 10 7 6 4 in any suit and lead the queen, you force out the ace. When you get in again, lead the knave and force out the king and your remaining cards are likely to be winners. If you were to lead a low card and dummy holds, say, K 3 and declarer A 9 2, he would win the first trick with the nine and make all three.

If you hold two or three cards in sequence headed by an honour together witn one higher honour, lead the top of the inside sequence. e.g. in each of the following lead the card underlined

(1) A 10 9 8 4   (2) K 10 9 8 3   (3) A J 10 7 4

In (3) although there are only two cards in sequence the knave is correct. Similarly in (1) and (2) if the suit was headed by A 10 9 or K 10 9 the ten would be correct as it might save partner playing a high honour in a case such as this

```
              J 4 3
K 10 9 7 6              Q 5 2
              A 8
```

If the seven is led and dummy plays low East's queen loses to the ace and the knave will later win a trick. If the ten is led, East has no need to play the queen unless the knave is played from the table.

If your long suit is not headed by a sequence it is usual to lead the fourth highest card, i.e. the fourth down from the top. Thus from

K 10 7 6 2 lead the six.

The reason for leading the fourth highest is that it enables partner to judge the length of the suit. In the above case, when you subsequently play the three it is clear that you have more than four. Similarly if the two is led the implications are that the suit contains four cards. It may also assist your partner to place the outstanding high cards by applying the Rule of Eleven (q.v.)

There are occasions where the lead of your longest suit is not practical. Suppose declarer had opened one heart and later bid three no-trumps as in the following sequence.

South	West	North	East
–	–	–	1 ♡
No bid	2 ◇	No bid	3 NT
All pass			

You hold   ♠ 8 7 6   ♡ Q 8 4 3 2   ◇ Q 7 3   ♣ 5 4

There can be little point in leading a heart as there cannot be much prospect of establishing winners in a suit bid by the opponent on your right. Your best choice is ♠ 8, an unbid major suit. Opponents are likely to bid major suits if they are good, to explore the possibility of an alternative contract but they may well conceal a minor. Other holdings which are liable to turn out badly are J x x x and K Q x x (the crosses denoting low cards of no value).

It is also unwise to lead from tenace holdings (i.e. two cards in the same suit where one ranks two degrees lower than the other) against a strong opening bid such as Two No-Trump, e.g.

West	East
	2 NT
3 NT	

Holding   ♠ J 10 9   ♡ K J 5 4   ◇ Q 10 2   ♣ Q 3 2 lead ♠ J, not ♡ 4.

Finally, beware of leading an unbid suit.

South	West	North	East
–	1 ♣	No bid	1 ♡
No bid	1 ♠	No bid	3 NT
All pass			

Do not lead a diamond as East is likely to be strong. Lead a spade through dummy's second suit, particularly if short.

(b) *Against Suit Contracts*

Here the alternatives are more varied. If partner has bid a suit it is wisest to lead it, again leading a low card if holding three headed by an honour. But if you hold the ace (e.g. A 6 3) lead the ace lest it later be trumped.

If your partner has not bid you have to make your own choice and the various possibilities are as follows

1. Top of a Sequence. K Q J   Q J 10   J 10 9
The card underlined is both safe and constructive; it is unlikely to give away an unnecessary trick.

2. A top card from a suit headed by A K. The advantage here is that you will probably win the first trick and will be in command when you see dummy. You will then be able to decide whether to continue with the suit or switch to another. In this you will be guided by your partner's play and that aspect will be explained under Signals.

From a suit headed by A K it is equally correct to lead either ace or king. But as the king is also led from a combination headed by K Q, difficulties may be encountered when a player leads the king which may be from either combination. For this reason the majority of modern players lead ace from ace–king.

This may also be a convenient moment to illustrate one of the fundamental differences between leading against No-Trumps and leading against a Suit contract. Holding, say, A K 8 5 4 against No-Trumps it would be correct to lead the five (fourth highest) and this is because you are planning on a long term policy. You do not mind giving an early trick to your opponents if you can make four later. By leading a low card it may well be possible if your partner gains the lead that he can return your suit, which may be divided in this way

J 7 6

A K 8 5 4   3 2

Q 10 9

South wins the first round. If East gets in and returns your suit you have four winners. In a suit contract you have to seek faster tricks. If you play a low card first your ace or king may later be trumped as suits rarely go round three times.

3. If you have no sequence and no suit headed by A K it is correct to lead fourth highest, but not if the suit is headed by the ace. You may lose to a singleton king or give declarer an unnecessary trick. It is rarely wise to lead an unsupported ace as the opponents will merely play their low cards. You should hope to capture a high honour with your ace.

Examples

(i)   ♡ K
    ♡ A 10 6 3 2   ♡ Q J 9 8
                       ♡ 7 5 4

(ii)   ♡ 6 4 2
    ♡ A 10 7 5   ♡ Q J 9
                       ♡ K 8 3

In (i) dummy's king wins and your ace is later trumped.

In (ii) South makes his king. Had you waited for the suit to be played to you South's king would be taken by your ace.

There is a common belief that it is a major crime to lead from a suit headed by the king. There is an element of risk attached but it may not necessarily be fatal.

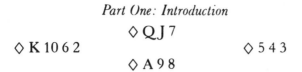

♢ QJ7

♢ K 10 6 2   ♢ 5 4 3

♢ A 9 8

If West leads ♢ 2 and dummy wins with ♢ J, West has certainly got off to a bad start. But providing he does not lead the suit again from his king he may still make it. All that has happened is that the king, normally a winner on the second round, has been relegated to the third.

A lead from a queen is more hazardous

♢ J 10 4

♢ Q 9 6 3   ♢ 7 5 2

♢ A K 8

West leads ♢ 3 and ♢ 10 wins. West will not make ♢ Q as a queen, normally a third round winner, has been relegated to the fourth. Or:

♢ K 10 3

♢ Q 6 5 2   ♢ J 8 4

♢ A 9 7

West leads ♢ 2. Dummy plays ♢ 3, East ♢ J and South ♢ A. Later South leads ♢ 7 and finesses ♢ 10 when West follows low. East–West have a natural winner providing their opponents open up the suit.

4. If none of the foregoing leads is available it may be best to play from a worthless suit. After all, it is up to you to get the game started and if you cannot find an attacking lead you will need to select a card that is unlikely to assist the declarer.

From three worthless cards some players lead the highest, i.e. top of nothing. Thus from 9 7 3 the nine would be played. This has the disadvantage of creating an ambiguity in partner's mind whether you hold two or three cards in the suit. For this reason modern players prefer to lead the middle card and follow with the highest. This method is usually referred to as MUD, standing for middle–up–down. Thus if from ♠972 the ♠7 is led, followed later by ♠9, the original holding was three, whereas ♠9 followed by ♠7 would show only two (doubleton).

5. Leads of doubletons and singletons are speculative. There are two main situations in which they are justified.

(a) Holding control in trumps but not many, e.g. A x x or K x x. In such a case you are likely to obtain the lead before trumps are completely drawn and if you can find partner with an entry you may get a ruff (trump). But if you hold length in trumps (e.g. A x x x) it is better to attack with your longest suit with the object of shortening declarer so that he runs out of trumps

(b) With a hopeless hand. For example the opponents have bid to four spades without any competitive action. You hold

♠ 7 3 2   ♡ 10 6 4 2   ◇ 2   ♣ J 7 4 3 2

It is logical to lead ◇ 2. The opponents have made no attempt to reach a slam and therefore your partner must have some high cards. If he has ◇ A and you can find him with another quick entry the contract will be defeated immediately. With a stronger hand the singleton would be a poor prospect as partner would be unlikely to have the necessary entries.

6. Finally there is the lead of a trump. There is a popular saying "When in doubt lead trumps". This is not entirely correct and there should be a rather more sound reason. Frequently the clue lies in the bidding. Suppose the bidding between East–West has been

West	East
–	1 ♡
2 ♡	2 NT
3 ♡	No bid

East, following a single raise, has rebid Two No-Trumps. He probably has an even shaped hand with about 17–18 high card points. West has a choice of action. With a balanced hand he can pass or bid Three No-Trumps. When he reverts to Three Hearts he clearly has a minimum raise on the first round and considers that his hand will be more helpful if hearts are trumps than in No-Trumps. This suggests that he is short in some suit and might provide tricks by trumping. Having reached this conclusion you lead a trump to try and prevent dummy ruffing.

Another situation is where the responding hand has indicated a preference for one or other of the opener's suits

(i)	*West*	*East*
	–	1 ♠
	1 NT	2 ♡
	No bid	

or

(ii)	*West*	*East*
	–	1 ♠
	1 NT	2 ♡
	2 ♠	No bid

In each of these auctions West has shown a poor hand in reply to the opening bid. In (i) it appears that East's rebid of Two Hearts suits West much better for otherwise he would have reverted to Two Spades. In (ii) West corrected to Two Spades, either because he had more spades than hearts or because there was little to choose between the two suits and the first bid suit was likely to be the better.

In such a case the lead of a trump is all the more mandatory if you have potential winners in the other suit. Thus in example (i) if you hold

♠ K J 9 3   ♡ 5 4   ♢ K 10 6 3   ♣ J 6 2

you would hope to make tricks in spades sitting over the original spade called. The only thing that might prevent you would be dummy being short and trumping. Therefore you would lead a trump to stop this occurring.

A third occasion where a trump lead is correct is when you hold a good hand and cannot expect much help from your partner. For example the bidding has been

West	*East*
	1 ♠
3 ♠	4 ♠

You hold   ♠ J 10 2   ♡ K J 8 2   ◇ A J 4   ♣ Q 10 7
With twelve high card points it is unlikely that partner will turn up with much. Moreover, there is no evidence on the bidding that there is a long side suit, although there could be. But it may well be that there is very little to spare and the contract may depend for success on a little assistance from the defence.

In defending against a contract such as Four Spades there are two ways of going about it. You can set out to win four tricks, or you can sit back and wait for the declarer to lose four tricks. The latter tactics would be described as passive defence and these are the measures you should adopt when you hold good defensive values. The lead should be ♠ 2 and not ♠ J in case partner should hold a singleton ♠ Q or ♠ K.

If a long suit is in evidence if may be necessary to attack,

West	*East*
	1 ♠
2 ◇	2 ♠
4 ♠	

Here West appears to hold a diamond suit and a passive game might not succeed as declarer may discard his losers on the established side suit.

Leading Against a Slam
This is often difficult and a large number of factors may influence upon your choice. Against either a small or grand slam in No-Trumps it is best to play a passive game and

select a lead that is unlikely to give away an unnecessary trick. Suppose the bidding has been brief:

West	*East*
	2 NT
6 NT	

You hold ♠ Q 6 3   ♡ K 9 7 4 3   ◇ 10 9   ♣ Q 5 3
Against Three No-Trumps you would lead ♡ 4 as your target is to make five tricks and this is most likely to be achieved if you attack with your longest suit. But against Six No-Trumps your target is two tricks and you must hope to make tricks with your honours resulting from unsuccessful finesses by declarer. With seven high card points your partner can hardly have one since the opponents are likely to hold thirty three.

Against a little slam in a suit contract you need to attack. You may need to risk leading from a king or queen in the hope of setting up a trick quickly for your side. The trump factor is all important. If there is a trick declarer has to lose, either a high card to be knocked out or a finesse which loses it is essential to have your second trick established.

A singleton is a possibility if the opposing bidding has indicated that an ace is missing. To lead an ace may or may not be right. If the bidding has been somewhat hit or miss

West	*East*
	1 ♠
3 ♠	6 ♠

it may be that they are lacking an ace and king of a suit.

The lead of an ace is also reasonable if you suspect a possible trump winner. Such would be the case if you held Q x x in trumps or you were void and your partner might well turn up with a trump trick due to a bad break.

In Duplicate pairs where every trick is important, it may be right to lay down an ace if you are satisfied that the slam is undefeatable and the best you can do is to prevent an overtrick.

Against a grand slam clearly the accent must be on safety. You do not need to establish a trick for when you get in. The lead of a trump is generally considered a standard lead as it is presumed that the trump suit is solid. It should be but is not always and I am not entirely convinced that pulling out a trump is always the right thing to do.

What if you hold an ace? It might appear that you have nothing to worry about. Play it and claim one down. But if the opponents are good players they are unlikely to bid a grand slam with a top loser. More likely they are void and, after trumping your ace, the king and queen may be established in the opposite hand. However, mistakes in bidding do occur even in the highest circles. In the European Championships in Torquay in 1961 the Italians bid a grand slam missing an ace and if our player had led ♣ A it would have won a trick. But he could not reasonaly anticipate such a bidding misunderstanding by his Italian opponents and led something else. He never made his ace and the grand slam was made.

Lead Directing Doubles

In some cases a double by your partner may demand the lead of a suit, in which case you no longer follow the standard principles set out above. There are two common instances

    1 Double of a Slam

    2 Double of Three No-Trumps.

As it is mathematically impractical to double a slam contract as the potential loss is far greater than the potential gain, the double of a slam by the player not on lead has a conventional meaning. It is called a "Lightner Double" having been originated by the late Theodore A. Lightner, an American, and member of the Culbertson team in the 1930s. The double demands an unusual lead.

That is to say not a suit bid by the defending side nor a trump. It usually asks for the lead of a suit bid by the declarer's side, often by dummy

South	*West*	*North*	*East*
			1 ♠
2 ♡	3 ◇	No bid	3 ♠
No bid	4 NT	No bid	5 ♡
No bid	6 ♠	Dbl.	All pass

West's Four No-Trumps was Blackwood and Five Hearts showed two aces. North's double of Six Spades rules out a heart or spade lead, and the answer is almost certainly a diamond, dummy's suit, as North is probably void. As the opponents stopped in six, evidently expecting to lose one trick, the slam is likely to be defeated as a first round ruff is not the trick they expected to lose.

The double of a final contract of Three No-Trumps usually requires the lead of dummy's suit, unless the defenders have bid, in which case the lead called for is the defender's bid suit. Thus

South	*West*	*North*	*East*
			1 ♠
No bid	2 ◇	No bid	2 NT
No bid	3 NT	Dbl.	All pass

South should lead a diamond.

South	*West*	*North*	*East*
	1 ◇	1 ♡	1 NT
No bid	2 NT	No bid	3 NT
No bid	No bid	Dbl.	All pass

South should lead a heart. He probably would anyway if he trusted his partner.

South	West	North	East
			1 ◊
1 ♠	2 ♣	No bid	2 NT
No bid	3 NT	Dbl.	All pass

South should lead a spade. Again, he might well have done so, but North's double indicates a helpful card, such as Q x.

If both defenders have bid and the final contract of Three No-Trumps is doubled the leader may have to use his own judgment.

To complete the discussion of opening leads there are two standard situations.

1 Against an opening bid of Three No-Trumps, indicating a long solid minor suit with little or nothing outside, it is advisable to lead an ace if you have one, in order to retain control when dummy goes down. If you lead a low card and declarer wins, you will not regain the lead until he cashes his seven card, or longer, suit.

2 If partner elects to pass your take-out double for penalties, thereby showing a solid holding in the opponent's suit, lead a trump, e.g.

South	West	North	East
1 ♡	Dbl.	No bid	No bid
No bid	All pass		

Holding ♠ K Q 10 8   ♡ 3   ◊ K J 7 4   ♣ A K 6 5
lead ♡ 3. The object must be to prevent declarer making tricks with low trumps. Treat the position as if you are playing the hand in hearts and you aim to draw trumps.

2 SIGNALS

When dummy is exposed declarer is in a better position in that he can see his partner's cards and can manipulate them to the best advantage. Although the defenders also see dummy, they cannot see their partner's cards. In order that the defending side makes the best use of their combined holding it is necessary that they co-operate, using established methods of signalling to indicate whether to continue with a certain suit or switch to another and, if so, which.

Most common of the signals is the high–low play, sometimes referred to as a "peter', to indicate a desire for a suit to be continued. Two possible reasons for wishing partner to carry on with a suit he has led are

(1) that you hope to win the third round with a high card, or

(2) that you have only two cards and will be able to trump.

In the following examples it is assumed that hearts are trumps

(a)

◊ 8 5 3

◊ A K 6 4   ◊ Q 7 2

◊ J 10 9

West leads ◊ A which probably implies possession of ◊ K, and East plays ◊ 7. West continues with ◊ K and East plays ◊ 2 (high–low). West plays a third diamond and East wins with ◊ Q. Had East held ◊ 9 7 2 he would have played his lowest card (◊ 2) as he would have no reason to think that a continuation of the suit would be beneficial.

(b)

◊ Q 5 3

◊ A K 10 6 4   ◊ 8 2

◊ J 9 7

West leads ◊ A and East plays ◊ 8. West continues with ◊ K and East plays ◊ 2. West continues with a third round and East trumps.

If partner leads a high card that you cannot beat the natural inclination is to play your lowest card. If, therefore, you play a card that can be identified as not your lowest there must be some reason for your having played it.

Usually a card is considered encouraging if it is six or higher. But the important factor is whether you are likely to hold a lower card than the one you played. If you hold 9 2 it is very convenient because the nine is a high card and easy to recognise. But if you hold 3 2 you can only play what you have been given. If your partner is observant and notices that the two has not appeared he should realize that you must have it, unless declarer is playing a cunning game, and that your three was not the lowest card you hold.

Similarly, if you play the seven and your partner can see all the cards which rank below he should know that you have played your lowest card. As the play of a "high" card is encouraging so also is the play of your lowest card a warning not to carry on unless you are sure of your ground.

Signals are not unlike traffic lights and if your partner plays, say, the two, it is a red light.

$$♡\,Q\,J\,8\,7$$
$$♡\,A\,K\,9\,5 \qquad\qquad\qquad ♡\,10\,6\,4\,2$$
$$♡\,3$$

West leads ♡ A and East plays ♡ 2. If West ignores the signal and continues with ♡ K, South trumps and Q J are established as winners

$$♡\,9\,7\,2$$
$$♡\,A\,K\,J\,6 \qquad\qquad\qquad ♡\,10\,4\,3$$
$$♡\,Q\,8\,5$$

West leads ♡ A and East plays ♡ 3. As ♡ 2 is in dummy East has played his lowest card and West should switch to another suit. If he plays off ♡ K, South will make ♡ Q. But if West switches and East later gets the lead and returns ♡ 10, South's ♡ Q is caught.

In discussing earlier (p. 13) the lead of ace or king from a suit headed by A K it was pointed out that difficulty might be experienced if the king were led first. Consider the following examples

(i)   ♡ 6 4 3

   ♡ K Q 10 9   ♡ J 8 2

                 ♡ A 7 5

(ii)   ♡ 6 4 3

   ♡ A K 10 9   ♡ J 8 2

                 ♡ Q 7 5

In hand (i) if West leads ♡ K and East plays ♡ 2, West should switch. He cannot afford to continue with his suit as South may hold ♡ A J 7 and has declined to win the first trick in the hope of a further lead into A J. On the actual lay out on hand (i) East should play ♡ 8 to encourage a further heart lead. But on hand (ii) East would be wrong to play ♡ 8 as West will next play ♡ A and South will make ♡ Q. East's correct play on hand (ii) is ♡ 2. West will switch to another suit and if East gets in and returns ♡ J, South's ♡ Q is caught. It is a pure guess for East to decide whether or not to encourage with ♡ 8 if West's lead can be either from A K or K Q.

It is justifiable to start a high–low peter with the knave, particularly if the second card is very low. But it is not sound to peter with the queen. In fact, if partner leads the ace of a suit, playing ace from ace–king, the play of the queen indicates the possession of the knave, unless it is a singleton, and requests partner to lead a low card to the next trick.

If partner leads a low card and the trick is taken in dummy, it is correct to follow with a high card to indicate some strength. For example

             North

             ◇ A 7 2

  ◇ 4 led   *East*

                        ◇ K 8 3

and ◇ A is played from the table, East should follow with ◇ 8 as he holds ◇ K.

The employment of the high–low signal can also be used to show distribution. For example

$$\heartsuit Q 3$$
$$\heartsuit A J 9 6 4 \qquad\qquad \heartsuit 10 8 7 5$$
$$\heartsuit K 2$$

West leads ♡ 6 against South's No-Trump contract and dummy wins with ♡ Q. East should follow with ♡ 8. Now, if West regains the lead and reading his partner for four cards, he can lay down ♡ A, knowing ♡ K is bare and will fall from South.

The play of a high honour by leader's partner, dummy having won the first trick, indicates a solid sequence.

$$\diamondsuit A 4 3$$
$$\diamondsuit 2 \text{ led} \qquad\qquad \diamondsuit K Q J 10$$

After West's lead of ◊ 2 against South's no-trump contract, dummy plays ◊ A. East plays ◊ K to show a solid sequence from the king down.

Another common use of the high–low signal to show distribution occurs where you need to inform partner at what point he should play an ace if a long suit is in dummy where there is no side entry

$$\diamondsuit K Q J 9 6$$
$$\diamondsuit 7 5 2 \qquad\qquad \diamondsuit A 4 3$$
$$\diamondsuit 10 8$$

Playing No-Trumps South leads ◊ 10 and East needs to know when to play ◊ A. To hold up too long could prove as expensive as not holding up at all. He will be guided by the order in which his partner plays his cards. On the above diagram West will play ◊ 2 on ◊ 10 and next ◊ 5 on ◊ 8. Playing in ascending order indicates an odd number of cards, in this case three. This leaves declarer with two and East can safely play his ◊ A on the second round.

Alter the lay-out to this

$\diamond$ K Q J 9 6

$\diamond$ 7 2 $\diamond$ A 4 3

$\diamond$ 10 8 5

Now West plays $\diamond$ 7 on the first round and $\diamond$ 2 on the next. This shows an even number of cards which must be two rather than four. East therefore knows South holds three and consequently keeps $\diamond$ A until the third round.

The practice of laying high–low to show distribution must not be used indiscriminately but only when you judge that it will help partner rather than the declarer. Here is an example where it would be quite wrong to peter

♣ K Q 6

♣ 8 2   ♣ J 7 5 3

♣ A 10 9 4

Suppose ♣ K is played from the table and East plays ♣ 5 and West ♣ 8. On ♣ Q East plays ♣ 3 and West ♣ 2. Now, unless the defenders are playing a very cunning game South can safely finesse ♣ 10 when East follows with ♣ 7 as each defender has obligingly advertised his length.

One of the most common signals is the discard of a high card to indicate a suit you wish partner to lead if he gets in. For example, suppose hearts are trumps and the clubs are distributed as follows

♣ K 7 3

♣ A Q J 8 2

South leads out trumps and on the third round East is unable to follow suit. He discards ♣ 8 to indicate the suit he would like his partner to lead when he has the chance.

Suppose South is declarer in No-Trumps and West has succeeded in establishing his diamonds, having two winners to cash, South having won the third round with his ace. Apart from his diamonds West holds ♣ A 9 4. At his first opportunity he should discard ♣ 9 to show where his entry lies.

3 Third Hand Play

After the opening lead and dummy has played it is the turn of the third player. A popular precept is "third player plays high". This is basically correct for if only low cards have been played by the first two players it is logical for the third hand to put up his highest in the hope of either winning the trick or forcing out a high card from the declarer and thereby helping partner. For example

♣ 7 6

♣ Q J 8 5 3   ♣ K 9 4

♣ A 10 2

Against No-Trumps West leads ♣ 5. East must play ♣ K for although ♣ K may be taken by ♣ A it has served a useful purpose as partner's ♣ Q J are now winners. Had East played ♣ 9 South would have won with ♣ 10.

In playing high it is usual to play the lower of equal cards viz

♠ 7 4 3

♠ K 10 8 2   ♠ Q J 5

♠ A 9 6

West leads ♠ 2 either against a suit or No-Trump contract. East should follow with ♠ J. If South wins with ♠ A West will know that his partner holds ♠ Q, for if South held that card he would surely take ♠ J with ♠ Q rather than with ♠ A. But if East plays ♠ Q on the opening lead, South wins with ♠ A and the position of ♠ J might be uncertain. In fact, providing East has played correctly, ♠ J must be in South's hand and West will need to wait for East to get in and return a spade through ♠ J x into

♠ K 10. Of course, if dummy has already played a card that is higher than you possess there is no longer any need for you to play high, as in this situation

♥ A 6

♥ Q 10 7 4 2   ♥ K 8 5 3

♥ J 9

Against either a suit contract or No-Trumps West leads ♥ 4 and declarer decides to win with ♥ A, there is no point in playing ♥ K. In fact you should play ♥ 8 to encourage, as was explained in the previous chapter on Signals.

It is not necessary always to play your highest card, particularly when there is an honour in dummy

♠ K 7 6

♠ J 9 5 2   ♠ A Q 4

♠ 10 8 3

West leads ♠ 2 and dummy plays ♠ 6, you play ♠ Q which is the lowest card available to win the trick. This is a somewhat obvious case, but it is often necessary to retain an honour over dummy.

(i)

♥ Q 7 6

♥ J 9 3 2   ♥ K 10 5

♥ A 8 4

(ii)

♠ Q 9 7

♠ K 10 8 6 4   ♠ A J 2

♠ 5 3

In (i) West leads ♥ 2 and dummy plays ♥ 6. East should play ♥ 10. This is not his highest card but he wishes to retain ♥ K over ♥ Q. Suppose East plays ♥ K. South wins with ♥ A and later makes ♥ Q. As it is, if South takes ♥ 10 with ♥ A that is the only trick he wins in that suit. If South had held ♥ J 8 4 he would win with ♥ J but he would have

always had one trick. If he held ♡ A J 4, leaving West with
♡ 9 8 3 2, playing ♡ K would give South three tricks
whereas playing ♡ 10 should restrict him to two.

In (ii) if East plays ♠ J on dummy's ♠ 7, after the lead of
♠ 6, South makes no trick in the suit. If South took ♠ J with
♠ K, East would still hold ♠ A over ♠ Q. In fact, providing
♠ 6 is West's fourth highest card, it is possible for East to
know that ♠ J will win by applying what is known as the
Rule of Eleven.

Rule of Eleven
If a lead can be assumed to be the fourth highest card held
in that suit, by subtracting the value of the card led from
eleven the balance remaining represents the number of
cards higher than the one led which are distributed
between the other three hands. Suppose you set out all the
cards in one suit, viz: A K Q J 10 9 8 7 6 5 4 3 2 and assume
as in hand (ii) above that the ♠ 6 is led, there are altogether
eight cards above the six. Of these three must be in the
hand that led, ♠ 6 being fourth highest. Therefore there
must be five in the other three hands.

Looking back at hand (ii) where ♠ 6 is led. Ticking off
the cards you can see (♠ Q 9 7 in dummy and ♠ A J in your
hand) partner's spade suit must be headed by ♠ K 10 8 6
and declarer has no card higher than ♠ 6.

Playing a card that is not your highest, in order to retain
an honour over dummy is termed finessing against dummy.
It should not be confused with finessing against partner,
which means failing to play your highest card when dummy
contains low cards and thereby allowing declarer to win a
trick to which he was not entitled. For example

                          ♣ 7 5
    ♣ A J 8 6 4   ♣ K 10 3
                          ♣ Q 9 2

West led ♣ 6 against South's No-Trump contract. If East
plays ♣ 10 South wins with ♣ Q. But if East plays ♣ K and

returns ♣ 10 the defence wins the first five tricks.

One situation where a finesse against partner is correct is where you need to prevent declarer holding up a stopper. The play is correct if you anticipate getting the lead early. Consider this hand

Dealer South. Love All.

```
                    ♠ K 7 6
                    ♡ 7 5
                    ◇ A Q J 10 4
   ♠ 9 3 2          ♣ Q 8 3         ♠ Q J 8 5
   ♡ J 9 8 6 4                      ♡ A Q 2
   ◇ 5 2                            ◇ K 7 6
   ♣ 10 5 2                         ♣ 9 7 6
                    ♠ A 10 4
                    ♡ K 10 3
                    ◇ 9 8 3
                    ♣ A K J 4
```

South	West	North	East
1 ♣	No bid	1 ◇	No bid
1 NT	No bid	3 NT	All pass

North–South were playing the weak No-Trump (12–14 points) so that the rebid would show a balanced hand of 15–16 points.

West leads ♡ 6. If East plays ♡ A and returns ♡ Q South will hold up his ♡ K until the third round. When East gets in with ◇ K he will have no heart to return and West will never get the lead to make his heart winners. East can see 12 points in his hand and 12 on the table. On the bidding South has 15–16 so at best West can hold one. It has to be hoped that he has led from five hearts headed by the knave. But South must be prevented from holding up ♡ K. If East plays ♡ Q on the first trick South must surely win, for West might have ♡ A J x x x. Now, when East gets in when the diamond finesse fails, he plays ace and another heart and

(*repeated for convenience*)

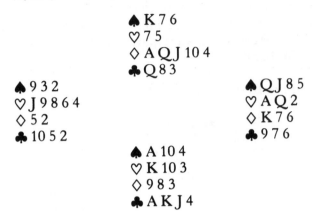

```
                    ♠ K 7 6
                    ♡ 7 5
                    ◇ A Q J 10 4
                    ♣ Q 8 3
♠ 9 3 2                              ♠ Q J 8 5
♡ J 9 8 6 4                          ♡ A Q 2
◇ 5 2                                ◇ K 7 6
♣ 10 5 2                             ♣ 9 7 6
                    ♠ A 10 4
                    ♡ K 10 3
                    ◇ 9 8 3
                    ♣ A K J 4
```

the contract is defeated. An important factor is that East is likely to get in early. Contrast the deal above with the following

Dealer South. Love All.

```
                    ♠ K 7 5
                    ♡ 6 4
                    ◇ Q 7 6 2
                    ♣ Q 10 8 3
♠ Q 10 4 3                           ♠ J 8 6 2
♡ J 9 8 7 5                          ♡ A Q 2
◇ K 3                                ◇ 5 4
♣ 9 5                                ♣ 7 6 4 2
                    ♠ A 9
                    ♡ K 10 3
                    ◇ A J 10 9 8
                    ♣ A K J
```

South	West	North	East
2 NT	No bid	3 NT	No bid

West leads ♡ 7. Here East should play ♡ A and follow with ♡ Q. South has shown 20 points and East and North share 14, leaving West with 6. East is unlikely to get in and therefore West will need an entry card of his own. He will in fact get in with ◊ K. If East were to play ♡ Q taken by ♡ K, West, when in with ◊ K, might not continue hearts as he might think ♡ Q was East's highest, leaving South with ♡ A 10.

The other situation in which it is correct to finesse against partner and not play your highest card is when holding K J x or more against a suit contract, as here

◊ 7 6

◊ 3 led   ◊ K J 8 4

East should play ◊ J. It is to be assumed that West has not led from an ace in a suit contract and therefore the ace is with South. If you play ◊ K, taken with ◊ A, and you later obtain the lead you may have to choose between trying to cash a diamond trick or switching to another suit. It depends on who holds ◊ Q. If ◊ J is played and is taken by ◊ A it is clear that West holds ◊ Q.

We have considered the position where partner has led a low card and you have played a card that was not your highest, but nevertheless was not low. The object was to retain an honour over dummy. There is no point in playing your highest card when it can hardly gain.

♡ Q J 10 3

♡ 2 led   ♡ K 7 6 4

Defending against a spade contract West leads ♡ 2 and ♡ 10 is played from dummy. It cannot gain to play ♡ K as South is marked with ♡ A. In fact if ♡ 2 is fourth highest South has a singleton ace.

The next example is less obvious

♠ J 10 3

♠ 2 led   ♠ Q 9 6 4

South opened Two No-Trumps and was raised to Three No-Trumps. West leads ♠ 2 and ♠ 10 is played from the table. Do not play ♠ Q but show some length with ♠ 6. South is marked with two spades and must have at least one honour by his opening bid of Two No-Trumps. If he has ♠ A x he will always make two tricks. If he has A K he will make three if you play ♠ Q. But if he has ♠ K x he will only make one trick if you withhold ♡ Q.

If partner, defending against No-Trumps, leads your suit which you bid, or leads a short suit in which you hold length, it may not necessarily be correct to play your highest card. This situation arises most often when partner's card is his highest. Consider this example

Dealer North. North–South Vul.

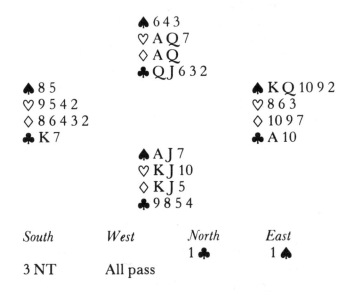

	♠ 6 4 3	
	♡ A Q 7	
	◊ A Q	
	♣ Q J 6 3 2	
♠ 8 5		♠ K Q 10 9 2
♡ 9 5 4 2		♡ 8 6 3
◊ 8 6 4 3 2		◊ 10 9 7
♣ K 7		♣ A 10
	♠ A J 7	
	♡ K J 10	
	◊ K J 5	
	♣ 9 8 5 4	

South	West	North	East
		1 ♣	1 ♠
3 NT	All pass		

Despite South's strong call of Three No-Trumps, West has no good reason not to lead his partner's suit. Suppose

East plays ♠Q on the first trick, South will play ♠7. If East continues with ♠10 South will win with ♠J. With eight top tricks he will need to make a trick in clubs. He leads ♣4 and West wins with ♣K but has no more spades. The contract is made with an overtrick. It would be no better if East won the club lead with ♣A. He could clear his suit but would have no entry. East should play ♠9 on the opening lead. South must win with ♠J, otherwise he makes only one trick. West wins the first round of clubs and returns his remaining spade enabling East to clear his suit while he still has an entry with ♣A.

Here is a second example

Dealer South. Love All.

```
                ♠ 4 2
                ♡ A J
                ◇ K Q 5 4
                ♣ J 10 8 7 2
  ♠ K 9 5 3                      ♠ J 8 6
  ♡ 7 6 2                        ♡ K 10 9 4 3
  ◇ 7 6 2                        ◇ J 9 8
  ♣ A Q 9                        ♣ 4 3
                ♠ A Q 10 7
                ♡ Q 8 5
                ◇ A 10 3
                ♣ K 6 5
```

South	West	North	East
1 ♠	No bid	2 ♣	No bid
2 NT	No bid	3 NT	All pass

There is nothing to be gained for West to lead his fourth highest spade into South's bid suit, so he leads ♡7, an unbid major. When ♡J is played from dummy, East knows that his partner's lead is not fourth highest. Applying the rule of eleven there should be only four cards higher than

(repeated for convenience)

Dealer South. Love All.

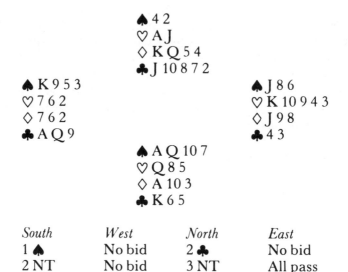

```
                    ♠ 4 2
                    ♡ A J
                    ◇ K Q 5 4
                    ♣ J 10 8 7 2
♠ K 9 5 3                              ♠ J 8 6
♡ 7 6 2                                ♡ K 10 9 4 3
◇ 7 6 2                                ◇ J 9 8
♣ A Q 9                                ♣ 4 3
                    ♠ A Q 10 7
                    ♡ Q 8 5
                    ◇ A 10 3
                    ♣ K 6 5
```

South	West	North	East
1 ♠	No bid	2 ♣	No bid
2 NT	No bid	3 NT	All pass

the seven divided between the hands of North, East and South. East can see five. If he plays ♡ K and returns ♡ 4 dummy will win and lead ♣ J, losing to West's ♣ Q. West returns his last heart but has no more when he regains the lead with ♣ A.

Again, East should not play ♡ K, but ♡ 10 to encourage West. When in with ♣ Q West plays another heart, dislodging ♡ A, and when in again with ♣ A leads his last heart and East's ♡ K fells ♡ Q.

The defence make three hearts and two clubs. The principle in each case was this. If an opponent holds two stoppers in a suit that you are trying to establish, it is to your advantage to compel him to use one stopper on the first round. The situation is equally applicable to declarer's play. Suppose South is playing No-Trumps and needs to establish diamonds in dummy, which has one side entry

◊ K Q 9 8 4 3

◊ 7 5 ◊ A J 10

◊ 6 2

South leads ◊ 6 to ◊ Q and East ducks. South now needs two entries to dummy, one to clear the suit and one to cash the winners. If he has only one side entry it cannot be done. But suppose South plays ◊ 8 on the first lead, East is compelled to win, using up one stopper. Now it is possible for South, with one diamond left, to set up dummy's suit without employing the side entry.

If the opening lead is a high card, third player should indicate, by employing one of the standard signals described earlier, whether he wishes the suit to be continued, or not. Here are three examples, all against suit contracts

(a) ◊ 8 6 3

◊ A led ◊ 7 4 2

Follow with ◊ 2, for you have no reason to believe a continuation will be wise.

(b) ◊ Q 6 4

◊ A led ◊ 7 3

Play ◊ 7. Assuming partner has ◊ K you will trump the third round.

(c) ◊ 7 6 2

◊ K led ◊ J 8 3

Assuming lead is from K Q and not A K, play ◊ 8 to encourage. If in (c) you held ◊ 8 4 3 you would play ◊ 3 to suggest a switch. If partner obstinately continued with ◊ Q, South having played low on the ◊ K, would win with both ◊ A and ◊ J.

While it is usually pointless to play a high card on partner's high card it may be necessary to do so to avoid blocking the suit.

Dealer North. Love All.

```
                    ♠ J 9 7
                    ♡ K J
                    ◊ 7 5 3 2
                    ♣ A K Q 4
♠ 6 2                               ♠ 5 3
♡ 9 6 4                             ♡ A 8 7 5 2
◊ K Q J 10                          ◊ A 6
♣ 10 8 5 2                          ♣ 9 7 6 3
                    ♠ A K Q 10 8 4
                    ♡ Q 10 3
                    ◊ 9 8 4
                    ♣ J
```

South	West	North	East
		1 NT	No bid
		(12–14)	
3 ♠	No bid	4 ♠	All pass

West led ◊ K and East followed with ◊ 6. West continued with ◊ Q, taken by East's ◊ A. With no more diamonds the defence could take only one more trick (♡ A). East should have overtaken ◊ K with ◊ A and returned ◊ 6. West wins with ◊ 10 and cashes ◊ Q on which East discards ♡ 8, a high card to ask for that suit to be led (see Signals) Even if West had not held ◊ J 10 in addition to ◊ K Q East could ruff the third round. A similar situation arose on this hand where South was declarer in Three No-Trumps.

Dealer South. Game All.

```
              ♠ K J 9
              ♡ 7 6 3
              ◊ K 2
              ♣ K J 9 8 7
♠ 3 2                           ♠ 8 7 6 5 4
♡ Q J 10 9 4                    ♡ K 2
◊ Q 10 3                        ◊ 9 6 5 4
♣ A 6 5                         ♣ 3 2
              ♠ A Q 10
              ♡ A 8 5
              ◊ A J 8 7
              ♣ Q 10 4
```

West led ♡ Q and East followed with ♡ 2. South played low, holding up his ace. West continued with ♡ J and East's ♡ K was allowed to win. East could not continue with hearts and South was able ⁺o establish his clubs while still holding ♡ A. Again, East was at fault. He should play ♡ K on ♡ Q and return ♡ 2. West establishes his suit and later gets in with ♣ A. If partner leads a queen and you hold doubleton king or ace (i.e. K x or A x) or if partner leads a king and you hold A x it is almost invariably correct to overtake. The lead of the honour card promises possession of the honour below and is likely to be from a sequence, especially defending against No-Trumps.

4. Second Hand Play

A common precept is "second player plays low". This is logical, for if you are second in hand your partner is fourth and he is in a better position to judge whether or not he can win the trick.

To play high in second position is often both pointless and costly. For example

(i)   ◊ K 5 4
        ◊ Q 3 2   ◊ A 10 9 7
                                       ◊ J 8 6

(ii)   ◊ A 7 5
        ◊ J 6 4   ◊ Q 9 8 2
                                       ◊ K 10 3

In (i) South, needing to take a trick in diamonds leads
◊ 6. If West plays ◊ Q, dummy's ◊ K is taken by ◊ A
but South's ◊ J is a winner. If West plays low and ◊ K
loses to ◊ A, South will later lose his ◊ J to ◊ Q.
In (ii) South leads ◊ 3. If West plays ◊ J, thinking he will
force out ◊ A, he will succeed, but his partner's ◊ Q will
not make as South holds ◊ K 10. Again West should play
low for surely East can beat ◊ 7 if it is played.

But "second player plays low" must not be accepted
blindly. If you urgently need to win a trick you must play
high, or when you may put your winning card in jeopardy by
playing low. For example

                               ♠ Q J 6 3
        ♠ K 2   ♠ 10 8 7
                               ♠ A 9 5 4

South leads ♠ 4 from hand. It is correct to put up ♠ K.
Failure to do so will result in ♠ K falling to ♠ A.
    There are four main situations where it may be necessary
for second player to play high.

(a) *Covering an Honour with an Honour*
It is a widely held belief that it is always correct to cover an
honour with an honour just as if it was a local bye-law.
Many guiding principles are thrust down the throats of
luckless beginners as being rules. No reason is given for
them. It is most important that no guiding principles are
recommended without a sound reason being given.

It is only correct to cover an honour with an honour if there is a reasonable hope of establishing a trick either for yourself or your partner by so doing. Take this simple example

♣ Q 3

♣ 10 4 2   ♣ K 6 5

♣ A J 9 8 7

Playing either in a suit or no-trump contract ♣ Q is led from dummy. If East plays low, so also does South. When ♣ Q wins, ♣ 3 is led and if East plays low again South with ♣ J wins, and follows with ♣ A to make all five tricks. But if East covers ♣ Q with ♣ K, taken with ♣ A, South will also make ♣ J but the third round will be taken by West with ♣ 10.

The point is that East, by covering ♣ Q with ♣ K stood a chance of setting up a trick for his partner on a later round. His partner might not have had ♣ 10 in which case East's king died in vain. But he would not have done any better by playing low.

Alter the diagram a little, only showing the hands of North and East.

♣ Q 3

♣ K 7 6 5

Now there is less to be gained by covering ♣ Q with ♣ K. True, partner might hold ♣ 10 x x, but if you do not cover your king cannot be caught as North has only two cards.

This example is more obvious

♠ K J 10 9

♠ Q 4 3

Declarer leads ♠ J from dummy. It cannot possibly gain to cover. Partner can hardly hold ♠ A. What is more likely is that declarer holds A x x x and is trying to locate ♠ Q. If you play low he may, of course, play low himself and you will not make a trick. But it is quite possible that when you do not cover he may conclude that you do not hold the queen and put up his ♠ A, and finesse towards ♠ K 10 9. Needless to say, you must try and anticipate the possibility of ♠ J being led and decide in advance that you are not going to cover. If you fiddle about there will be no doubt who had the queen.

Here is a further example

♠ J 9 6 4 3

♠ K 2

South, who opened the bidding with one spade, was raised to four spades by North. Having won the opening lead South crosses to dummy and leads ♠ J. Do you cover? What can you hope to gain? It is quite possible that declarer will successfully finesse and you will lose your king, but what can partner hold that will ever become a trick if you cover? He cannot hold ♠ 10 x x for South would only have a three card suit. But it is possible for South to hold five or six spades headed by A Q and if you play low (without hesitation) he may play ♠ A, hoping to fell ♠ K in West's hand.

Moreover you might lose heavily by covering. Suppose South holds ♠ A 10 9 x x or ♠ Q 10 9 x x; in one case you crash your partner's singleton ♠ Q and the other his singleton ♠ A.

It is wrong to cover an honour the first time if you can equally well cover the second

♦ Q J 9 4

♦ 10 7 3   ♦ K 6 5

♦ A 8 2

Declarer leads ♦ Q from the table. Suppose you cover with ♦ K, losing to ♦ A. In a sense you have done some good insofar as West's ♦ 10 might win the third round. But

South may next lead ◊ 2 and when West plays ◊ 7, finesse
◊ 9. He then plays ◊ J, capturing West's ◊ 10. East should
play low on ◊ Q. If ◊ J is led East covers with ◊ K and if
West holds ◊ 10 x x he should make it. If ◊ 4 is led to the
second round, East plays low, for if West has ◊ 10 South
will need to play ◊ A to win.

In this case by playing low first round you have the
option of covering, or not covering, on the second round.
But if you hold a doubleton (K x) you no longer have an
option so it is probably best to cover the first time.

                    ◊ J 10 6 5
    ◊ K 7 4   ◊ Q 9 3
                    ◊ A 8 2

Declarer leads ◊ J from the table. If you cover with ◊ Q
South wins with ◊ A and leads ◊ 8 towards dummy,
making a further trick with ◊ 10. Defenders win one trick.
But if East plays low on ◊ J and South plays low West wins
with ◊ K. East now holds ◊ Q 9 over ◊ 10 6 5 and the
defence wil take two tricks.

The situation may be more difficult if the card is led from
the closed hand

                    ♠ A 7 6
    ♠ K 5 3

South leads ♠ Q. It is best not to cover. It is probable that
South holds ♠ J as well and you retain your option whether
to cover next time. If South held ♠ Q J 9 8, covering the lead
would expose your partner to a finesse against his ♠ 10.

But if dummy has only two cards you do not cover

♠ A 3

♠ K 6 5

South leads ♠ Q. Unless you suspect South of playing a cunning game leading an unsupported queen you must not cover as your ♠ K cannot be captured. Nor do you cover where it is obvious that you cannot gain.

◇ A J 10 9 7 6

◇ K 4 3 2

Playing No-Trumps South leads ◇ Q. How can you possibly gain by covering? If South has only two diamonds he cannot capture your ◇ K.

Here are two further situations where the decision whether or not to cover is not so clear cut

(i)   ♣ A Q J 5

     ♣ K 6 3

                ♣ 10 led

(ii)   ♠ A J 3

     ♠ K 5 4

                ♠ 10 led

In (i) it is correct to cover in the hope that South holds ♣ 10 x and East ♣ 9 x x x, in which case East's ♣ 9 will become a winner. If South has three clubs he will make all the tricks by finessing.

In (ii) it is correct to cover as East may hold ♠ Q 9 x and he will be left with ♠ Q 9 over ♠ J 3. Failure to cover will cost a trick as ♠ 10 will lose to ♠ Q, North playing low, and South will later have a straight finesse against your ♠ K with

♠ A J in dummy.

(b) *Blocking Plays*
Sometimes it may be necessary to play high second in hand to prevent use being made of a long suit, often in dummy. Consider this

Dealer South. Game All.

```
                    ♠ J 10
                    ♡ Q J 2
                    ◇ A Q 10 9 5 2
                    ♣ 7 3
    ♠ Q 8 3                         ♠ 9 7 4 2
    ♡ K 7                           ♡ 9 8 5 3
    ◇ K 6                           ◇ J 4 3
    ♣ K Q J 9 8 2                   ♣ 6 4
                    ♠ A K 6 5
                    ♡ A 10 6 4
                    ◇ 8 7
                    ♣ A 10 5
```

South	West	North	East
1 ♡	2 ♣	2 ◇	No bid
2NT	No bid	3NT	All pass

South opened One Heart in accordance with modern practice of bidding the lower major, holding the values to rebid in No-Trumps. West led ♣ K and continued the suit, South holding up until the third round. South next led ◇ 8, West played low as did dummy and East won with ◇ J. Hoping to put his partner in East returned a spade, but South won with ♠ K and led ◇ 7. West's ◇ K was taken with ◇ A and the contract was easily made. West should have played ◊ K when ◊ 8 was led. South cannot afford to let it hold as West has the rest of the clubs. After winning with ◊ A and playing ◊ Q East will stop the suit with ◊ J. Playing ◊ K is not reckless: if South holds ◊ J he has six sure winners when the finesse succeeds.

Another example

Dealer South. Love All.

```
                    ♠ 7 3 2
                    ♡ A K 10 8 3
                    ◊ 10 5 2
                    ♣ 8 6
    ♠ J 5                               ♠ Q 10 9 8
    ♡ Q 7 2                             ♡ J 9 6
    ◊ Q 8 4                             ◊ 9 7 3
    ♣ K Q J 9 3                         ♣ 7 4 2
                    ♠ A K 6 4
                    ♡ 5 4
                    ◊ A K J 6
                    ♣ A 10 5
```

South	West	North	East
1 ◊	No bid	1 ♡	No bid
2 ♠	No bid	3 ♡	No bid
3NT	All pass		

West leads ♣ K and South holds up ♣ A until the third round. With seven top tricks it is necessary to make use of the hearts. South leads ♡ 5 intending to give up the first trick to East, who will be unable to return a club unless the suit is split 4–4. If West plays low, East will win and whatever he returns the contract will be made with four hearts, two diamonds, two spades and one club. But if West plays ♡ Q on ♡ 5 the suit is blocked. South cannot afford to let West hold the trick and East's jack prevents the suit being enjoyed. Again, playing ♡ Q is not reckless, for if

South held ♡ J he would win all five heart tricks. It is also worth noting that South can only hold two hearts. Firstly, having bid two suits (diamonds and spades) and shown up with three clubs, he can only hold two hearts. Secondly, with three hearts he would be likely to support partner's suit after he rebid to Three Hearts.

Playing high second hand to block the suit may also be necessary in trump contracts. This example is taken from my *Bridge: The Elements of Play*.

Dealer South. Love All.

```
                    ♠ A 6 5
                    ♡ 7 6 5 4
                    ◊ A J 5
                    ♣ J 10 9
    ♠ 10 9 8                        ♠ J 7 3 2
    ♡ –                            ♡ K 9 3 2
    ◊ Q 10 7 6 2                    ◊ 9 8 3
    ♣ A K Q 4 2                     ♣ 8 5
                    ♠ K Q 4
                    ♡ A Q J 10 8
                    ◊ K 4
                    ♣ 7 6 3
```

South	West	North	East
1 ♡	2NT	Dbl.	3 ◊
No bid	No bid	3 ♡	No bid
4 ♡	All pass		

West's Two No-Trumps was the "Unusual No-Trump" Convention indicating a minor two suited hand. West played off ♣ A K Q and switched to ♠ 10, taken in dummy. South next led ♡ 4 and successfully finessed ♡ 10, but West's club discard meant that two more entries were needed in dummy to capture East's ♡ K.

(repeated for convenience)

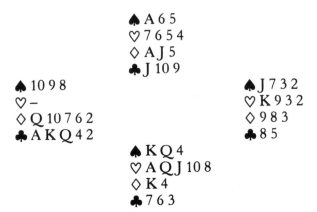

South took his only chance by leading ◊ 4 and finessing ◊ J when West followed low. It was now possible to lead hearts twice through East. But if West had put up ◊ Q on ◊ 4 South's plan would have been countered as the second entry would have been blocked. This play is often missed, even in top level games, but if South held ◊ K x x he could always make three tricks by finessing.

(c) *Protecting Partner's Entry*
Another situation in which it is necessary to play high in second hand is to preserve partner's entry. Suppose partner leads his longest suit in no trumps and declarer has two stoppers. It may be important for the leader's partner to get in early to clear the suit, while his partner still retains an entry. Consider this example

Dealer South. North–South vul.

```
              ♠ K 9 3 2
              ♡ K 3
              ◊ 8 5 2
              ♣ K 4 3 2
♠ J 8 6                        ♠ Q 10 5 4
♡ Q J 10 7 4                   ♡ 9 8 6
◊ Q 6 4                        ◊ A 3
♣ 7 6                          ♣ Q J 10 5
              ♠ A 7
              ♡ A 5 2
              ◊ K J 10 9 7
              ♣ A 9 8
```

South	West	North	East
1NT	No bid	2 ♣	No bid
2 ◊	No bid	3NT	All pass

South opened a strong No-Trump (16–18 points) and North investigated a four card major suit with a conventional Two Clubs. South's Two Diamonds denied holding a four card major suit, so North bid Three No-Trumps.

West led ♡ Q which was allowed to win and continued with ♡ 4 to ♡ K. With six top tricks South needed to establish diamonds and led ◊ 8. East played low, being second in hand, and the finesse lost to ◊ Q. West cleared his suit but never regained the lead. When East won with ◊ A he had no heart to return.

East should have played ◊ A to clear the hearts while his partner held an entry with ◊ Q. It may be necessary to put up an unsupported king.

Dealer South. North-South vul.

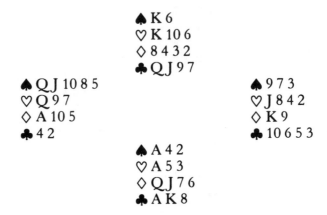

♠ K 6
♥ K 10 6
♦ 8 4 3 2
♣ Q J 9 7

♠ Q J 10 8 5   ♠ 9 7 3
♥ Q 9 7   ♥ J 8 4 2
♦ A 10 5   ♦ K 9
♣ 4 2   ♣ 10 6 5 3

♠ A 4 2
♥ A 5 3
♦ Q J 7 6
♣ A K 8

South opened with a strong No-Trump (16–18) and was raised to Three No-Trumps. West led ♠ Q which held and continued with ♠ 5 to ♠ K. With eight top tricks South needed to make a diamond and led ♦ 2 from the table. East boldly put up ♦ K and returned his last spade. West later gained the lead with ♦ A and was able to cash the remainder of his spades.

The necessity to play high second hand can also arise in a suit contract.

For example

Dealer South. East–West vul.

```
              ♠ K J 7 6 5 4
              ♡ Q 3
              ♢ 5 3
              ♣ 10 8 2
♠ 2                              ♠ 3
♡ K 10 5 4                       ♡ 8 7 6 2
♢ A 9 8                          ♢ K 7 4 2
♣ A K J 9 5                      ♣ Q 7 6 4
              ♠ A Q 10 9 8
              ♡ A J 9
              ♢ Q J 10 6
              ♣ 3
```

South	West	North	East
1 ♠	Dbl.	4 ♠	All pass

West leads ♣ A to which East plays ♣ 7 to encourage a continuation. West follows with ♣ K and South ruffs. South next leads ♠ 8 to ♠ J and plays ♢ 5 from the table. If East plays low, as many would, ♢ 10 loses to ♢ A. West cannot safely lead a heart and can do no better than play a club. South ruffs and leads ♢ Q, taken by East who returns a heart. Too late. South wins with ♡ A, discards ♡ Q on ♢ J and makes his contract.

East should reason on these lines. We have only made one club and our only chance of taking four tricks is with two diamonds and a heart. If West has ♡ K the lead must come through to him and he must have an entry apart from hearts. On his vulnerable double West may well have ♢ A. If he has not, little harm will come from putting up ♢ K. But East must set up West's probable heart trick before South can establish his diamonds.

The next example occurred in a national teams championship final.

Dealer East. Love All.

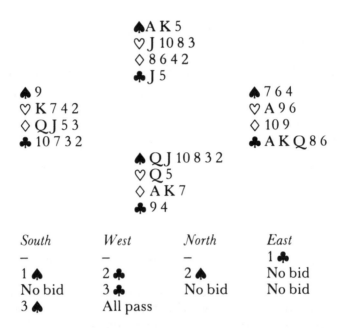

	♠A K 5	
	♡J 10 8 3	
	◇8 6 4 2	
	♣J 5	

♠9		♠7 6 4
♡K 7 4 2		♡A 9 6
◇Q J 5 3		◇10 9
♣10 7 3 2		♣A K Q 8 6

	♠Q J 10 8 3 2	
	♡Q 5	
	◇A K 7	
	♣9 4	

South	West	North	East
–	–	–	1 ♣
1 ♠	2 ♣	2 ♠	No bid
No bid	3 ♣	No bid	No bid
3 ♠	All pass		

West led ♣ 2 and East won the first two tricks with
♣ K Q. He switched to ◇ 10, taken by South with ◇ K,
West playing ◇ 5. Faced with a possible loss of five tricks (2
clubs, 2 hearts and 1 diamond) South sought to establish a
heart for a diamond discard. To the fourth trick he led ♠ 2 to
♠ K and played ♡ 3 from dummy. East played low and ♡ Q
lost to ♡ K. West returned ◇ Q to ◇ A but when South led
♡ 5 to ♡ 10 and ♡ A, East had no more diamonds. He
returned a trump, South won in hand, crossed to the table
with ♠ A drawing the last trump and discarded ◇ 7 on ♡ J.
East should have appreciated the necessity of setting up
West's diamond trick while he had a possible entry and
played ♡ A on the first lead.

(d) *Where it is necessary to win in order to switch*

Under this heading come those situations where there is a danger of declarer being able to discard losers. Another situation arises when your winner is in danger of being ruffed. This hand occurred some years ago in the match between Norway and Denmark in the European Championship.

Dealer South. East-West vul.

```
                    ♠ K
                    ♡ 9 7 4 2
                    ◇ 6 2
                    ♣ K J 10 7 5 2
  ♠ Q 9 4 3 2                      ♠ 8 7 6 5
  ♡ J 10                           ♡ A 3
  ◇ A Q J 8                        ◇ 7 5 4 3
  ♣ 9 8                            ♣ A 6 3
                    ♠ A J 10
                    ♡ K Q 8 6 5
                    ◇ K 10 9
                    ♣ Q 4
```

South	West	North	East
1 ♡	No bid	4 ♡	All pass

West led ♠ 3 taken with ♠ K. Seeing the danger of losing two diamonds plus the aces of clubs and hearts, declarer tried to get into his hand to discard a diamond on ♠ A. He led ♡ 2 but East immediately put up ♡ A and switched to a diamond. He knew that South held ♠ A and if he were allowed to get to his hand with a trump, one of dummy's diamonds might be discarded.

In the next hand it might seem that West was extravagant in putting up an ace to beat a nine, but it was necessary.

Dealer South. East-West vul.

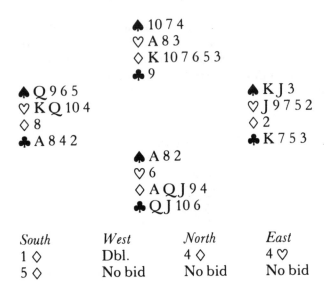

South	West	North	East
1 ◊	Dbl.	4 ◊	4 ♡
5 ◊	No bid	No bid	No bid

West led ♡ K to ♡ A. South entered his hand with ◊ J and led ♣ 6. West won with ♣ A and switched to ♠ 5. He reckoned that East probably held five hearts and therefore the defence would not win a trick in hearts and the only hope lay in spades. If he played low on ♣ 6 and East won with ♣ K and returned a spade, South would win with ♠ A and lead ♣ Q, ruffing if West played ♣ A, or discarding a spade if West played low. In other words South would take what is termed a "ruffing finesse".

The final example is a little more advanced, but it should not prove too difficult to follow.

Dealer North. Love All.

```
                  ♠ Q 10 8 7
                  ♡ K 4 2
                  ◇ A Q 8
                  ♣ Q 10 4
♠ 9 5                             ♠ 3 2
♡ Q J 10 9                        ♡ 8 7 5 3
◇ 9 5 4                           ◇ K J 10 2
♣ 9 7 6 5                         ♣ J 8 3
                  ♠ A K J 6 4
                  ♡ A 6
                  ◇ 7 6 3
                  ♣ A K 2
```

South	West	North	East
–	–	1NT	No bid
		(12–14)	
3 ♠	No bid	4 ♠	No bid
4NT	No bid	5 ◇	No bid
6 ♠	No bid	No bid	No bid

West leads ♡ Q and it seems that the contract depends upon the diamond finesse. Rather than gamble on the position of ◇ K, South plans to force East to lead into dummy's ◇ A Q. It would be equally helpful if East were to lead a suit which could be trumped in either declarer's hand or that of dummy. But clearly East is not going to be so co-operative if he can avoid it. Therefore South must remove all the safe exits. That is to say, East, at the appropriate moment, must not be able to lead a card that does not help South. So he wins with ♡ A and draws trumps. He next plays three rounds of clubs, cashes ♡ K and ruffs ♡ 2 in hand. Now the stage is set and all that is needed is to steer the lead into East's hand. South leads ◇ 3 and this is where West, although second player, must not play low. If he plays ◇ 4 or ◇ 5, ◇ 8 will be put on and East will have to win and he is caught. Either he must lead into

(*repeated for convenience*)

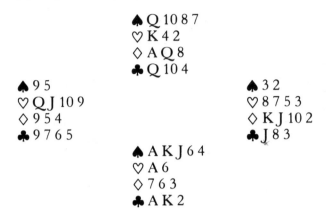

♠ Q 10 8 7
♡ K 4 2
◊ A Q 8
♣ Q 10 4

♠ 9 5
♡ Q J 10 9
◊ 9 5 4
♣ 9 7 6 5

♠ 3 2
♡ 8 7 5 3
◊ K J 10 2
♣ J 8 3

♠ A K J 6 4
♡ A 6
◊ 7 6 3
♣ A K 2

◊ A Q or play a card that South can trump in one hand and discard a diamond from the other. To foil this scheme West must play ◊ 9. South may still play ◊ 8 hoping East has no low card and will have to overtake, but here East can play ◊ 2 and leave his partner with the lead to play through ◊ A Q.

There are other situations where it may be necessary to play high second hand to defend against similar stratagems by declarer. But these are more complicated and not within the scope of this book.

5. Fourth Hand Play

The fourth player has only a limited choice. He can either win the trick or lose it. If he is unable to win it will usually be correct to play the lowest card. The only problem that can arise is where the fourth player is in a position to take the trick but it may not be right to do so. The most common situation in this category is the hold up. Holding the ace of a long suit in dummy it is generally right to hold up the ace until declarer has no more. The example was given in the chapter on Signals (p. 26)

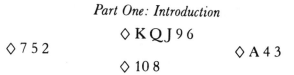

◇ K Q J 9 6

◇ 7 5 2   ◇ A 4 3

◇ 10 8

South leads ◇ 10, West plays ◇ 2 and East ◇ 3. South
leads ◇ 8, West plays ◇ 5 and East plays ◇ A. As West
played his diamonds upwards he should have three and
therefore South holds two.

It is also correct to hold up with a king, for example

◇ A Q J 7 6

◇ 9 4 2   ◇ K 5 3

◇ 10 8

South leads ◇ 10 and finesses, playing dummy's ◇ 6.
East should play low. South is likely to repeat his finesse
and East wins with ◇ K. Dummy's suit is dead unless there
is a side entry.

Another situation in which it is wise not to take the trick
is where you give declarer a guess.

♠ K Q 10 8

♠ J 9 2   ♠ A 4 3

♠ 7 6 5

South leads ♠ 5, West plays ♠ 2 and dummy ♠ K. East
should play low. If he takes with ♠ A, South will
subsequently play from his hand and finesse against ♠ J,
winning with ♠ 10. But if East allows ♠ K to hold, South
will have a problem when he next leads the suit from his
hand and West plays low. Is ♠ A with West or with East?

In the section on Third Hand Play the principle was
stated that it was an advantage to force out one of two
stoppers on the first round. An example was given where
the spade suit was

♠ 6 4 3

♠ 8 5   ♠ K Q 10 9 2

♠ A J 7

East overcalled in spades and South became declarer in No-Trumps. West led ♠ 8 and it was explained that if East played ♠ 9, South was compelled to part with one of his two stoppers. In fourth position it may be necessary to hold up with two stoppers. Consider this situation.

Dealer South. Game All.

♠ 10 9 5
♡ A 7 2
◇ K J 10 9 6
♣ 10 8

♠ K 8 4   ♠ 7 6 3 2
♡ J 10 9 8   ♡ 6 3
◇ 8 3 2   ◇ A Q 7
♣ Q 9 2   ♣ J 6 4 3

♠ A Q J
♡ K Q 5 4
◇ 5 4
♣ A K 7 5

South	*West*	*North*	*East*
1 ♣	No bid	1 ◇	No bid
3NT	No bid	No bid	No bid

South decided to jump to Three No-Trumps with his 19 points and not bid his hearts. West led ♡ J taken in hand with ♡ Q and ◇ 5 was led to ◇ 9. East won with ◇ Q and returned ♡ 6 to ♡ K. It was now possible to establish the diamonds while ♡ A remained as an entry. By winning the first round of diamonds with ◇ Q East has parted with one of his two stoppers. If he allows ◇ 9 to win, South returns to his hand and finesses ◇ 10, losing to ◇ Q. He is now short of an entry. To clear diamonds he needs to get to the table using ♡ A, but has no other means of access.

PART TWO

The Middle Game

6. Further Play by Third Hand*

We have so far considered the initial play by first hand (opening lead) and by third, second and fourth players. Now it is time to consider the action of third player after he was won the first trick.

(a) *No-Trump Contracts*
Assuming partner has led from his longest suit it will in most cases be correct to return the suit. The main objective must be to establish winners and this will obviously be delayed if you switch to something else.

Having decided to return the lead, the next problem is which card to play. In the majority of cases it is right to return the highest. Thus

```
                 ♡ 7 5
♡ K J 9 6 2                    ♡ A 4 3
                 ♡ Q 10 8
```

West leads ♡ 6. East wins with ♡ A and returns ♡ 4. It might appear immaterial whether East returns ♡ 4 or ♡ 3 as they are both of the same value, but it is important for

*(See also Attacking Entries, p. 96).

West to know. If ♡ 3 is returned it is likely to be East's last heart.

With four or more cards in partner's suit return the original fourth best. Not the lowest (if more than four) but the original fourth best. There are two good reasons for this. Firstly it may avoid the suit being blocked, where you have more cards in the suit than your partner. Secondly, it is possible for your partner to apply the rule of eleven.
Examples

(i)   ♡ 6 3

   ♡ K J 9 5   ♡ A 8 7 4

               ♡ Q 10 2

(ii)   ♡ 6 3

   ♡ K J 9 5   ♡ A 8 7

               ♡ Q 10 4 2

(i) Defending against a No-Trump contract West leads ♡ 5 to ♡ A, South playing ♡ 2. East returns ♡ 4, covered by South with ♡ 10 and taken by West with ♡ J. With ♡ 3 and ♡ 2 visible, ♡ 4 from East must be either his best or his fourth highest. If the former East must have held ♡ A 4 leaving South with ♡ Q 10 8 7 2 which would not be consistent with the likely bidding. Therefore it must be the fourth highest and West can safely lead ♡ K to fell ♡ Q.

(ii) Here West leads ♡ 5 which East takes with ♡ A and returns ♡ 8, South following with ♡ 2 and ♡ 10. West wins the second with ♡ J, but reading East for only three cards on his return of ♡ 8, South is marked with ♡ Q 4 and it will be necessary to get East in again to return his last heart through ♡ Q 4 to ♡ K 9.

On this hand the return of the fourth highest proved helpful with the rule of eleven. It also avoided the suit being blocked.

Dealer South. East-West vul.

```
              ♠ J 10 5
              ♡ Q
              ◇ A J 8 3
              ♣ J 9 7 5 2
♠ K Q 8                      ♠ 6 4 3 2
♡ J 9 7 3                    ♡ A 10 6 5 4
◇ 10 6 5 2                   ◇ 7 4
♣ 8 3                        ♣ A 10
              ♠ A 9 7
              ♡ K 8 2
              ◇ K Q 9
              ♣ K Q 6 4
```

South	West	North	East
1 ♣	No bid	1 ◇	No bid
2NT	No bid	3NT	All pass

West led ♡ 3, taken by East with ♡ A and ♡ 5 returned, South playing ♡ 8 and West ♡ 9. If East's return of ♡ 5 was fourth highest, as seemed likely, South could only hold one heart higher than the five. On the rule of eleven $(11 - 5 = 6)$ there were six cards higher than the five between the hands of North, West and South. West had ♡ J 9 7, North ♡ Q and South had produced ♡ 8. Therefore he held one card above the five. West led ♡ J, forcing out ♡ K. East got in with ♣ A and cashed ♡ 10 6. If West had returned ♡ 7 after winning with ♡ 9 he would have been left with ♡ J and the suit would have been blocked.

If, after winning the opening lead, you decide to switch to another suit you must be confident that there is more hope of making tricks in your suit than your partner's. On this hand the switch was clearly justified.

Dealer South. North-South vul.

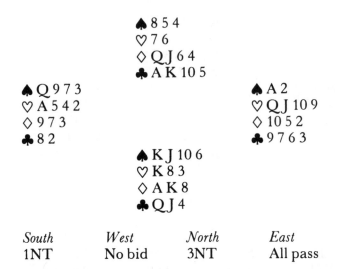

	♠ 8 5 4	
	♡ 7 6	
	◊ Q J 6 4	
	♣ A K 10 5	

♠ Q 9 7 3		♠ A 2
♡ A 5 4 2		♡ Q J 10 9
◊ 9 7 3		◊ 10 5 2
♣ 8 2		♣ 9 7 6 3

	♠ K J 10 6	
	♡ K 8 3	
	◊ A K 8	
	♣ Q J 4	

South	*West*	*North*	*East*
1NT	No bid	3NT	All pass

West led ♠ 3 and East won with ♠ A. The lead had been clearly from a four card suit which meant that South held four and there would be little purpose in returning the lead. Holding a solid sequence in hearts, East returned ♡ Q and the defence won the first five tricks.

If it is apparent that partner cannot hold an entry card to enjoy his suit there is no useful purpose to be served in persevering with it. This is well illustrated on the following hand.

Dealer North. East-West vul.

```
                    ♠ A K J 8
                    ♡ 8 5
                    ◊ 7 6
                    ♣ A Q J 10 6
   ♠ 10 4                              ♠ 7 6 5 2
   ♡ 10 4 3                            ♡ K Q 7 2
   ◊ K 9 8 4 3                         ◊ Q J 5
   ♣ 5 4 2                             ♣ K 3
                    ♠ Q 9 3
                    ♡ A J 9 6
                    ◊ A 10 2
                    ♣ 9 8 7
```

South	West	North	East
		1 ♣	No bid
1 ♡	No bid	1 ♠	No bid
2NT	No bid	3NT	All pass

West led ◊ 4, East played ◊ J and South ◊ 2. East
returned ◊ Q which held and continued with ◊ 5 to
South's ◊ A. South next led ♣ 9 and lost the finesse, but
East had no more diamonds and West had no means of
getting in so the contract was made with an overtrick.

East's play lacked imagination. He could see fifteen high
card points in dummy and held eleven. His partner probably
held ◊ K (three), a total of twenty-nine, leaving eleven, and
South must surely hold these for his second bid of Two No-
Trumps. It might just be possible for West to hold ♡ J if
South had stretched a little and bid Two No-Trumps with
ten points. It should therefore have been evident to East
that his partner had no high cards apart from ◊ K and to
plug away with the suit was pointless. Having won two
tricks with ◊ Q J East should have sought a means of
setting up two more tricks while he had control of the clubs
(♣ K). His best chance would be to lead ♡ 2. South, with
♡ A J 9 6 would be likely to play ♡ 9 as being the best

(continued for convenience)

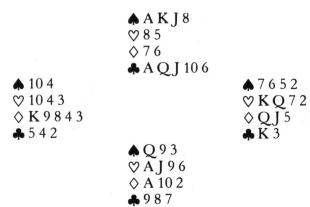

```
              ♠ A K J 8
              ♡ 8 5
              ◊ 7 6
              ♣ A Q J 10 6
♠ 10 4                          ♠ 7 6 5 2
♡ 10 4 3                        ♡ K Q 7 2
◊ K 9 8 4 3                     ◊ Q J 5
♣ 5 4 2                         ♣ K 3
              ♠ Q 9 3
              ♡ A J 9 6
              ◊ A 10 2
              ♣ 9 8 7
```

percentage chance. Playing ♡ 9 gains if East has ♡ 10 while the play of ♡ J (successful as it happens) only gains if East has ♡ K Q.

Assuming South plays ♡ 9 West wins with ♡ 10 and returns the suit to ♡ Q and ♡ A. East regains the lead with ♣ K and defeats the contract with ♡ K. It is correct for East to lead ♡ 2 rather than ♡ K as West might hold ♡ J x and the suit will be blocked.

If your partner has not led his longest suit and it is not a suit bid by you, there is little purpose in returning it, unless you have length and hope to establish it. On this hand the lead was clearly not fourth highest, but East had to select the right card when he switched.

Dealer South. Game All.

```
                  ♠ Q J 10
                  ♡ 10 5 3
                  ◇ J 9 5
                  ♣ K J 10 9
    ♠ 9 8 7                       ♠ A 4 3 2
    ♡ A 4 2                       ♡ 9 8 7
    ◇ 8 7 4                       ◇ A Q 10 2
    ♣ 8 7 6 2                     ♣ 4 3
                  ♠ K 6 5
                  ♡ K Q J 6
                  ◇ K 6 3
                  ♣ A Q 5
```

South	West	North	East
1NT	No bid	2NT	No bid
(16–18)			
3NT	No bid	No bid	No bid

West led ♠ 9 and East won with ♠ A. West's lead was clearly top of nothing and the prospects of establishing the fourth spade were poor. Diamonds looked more promising and East led ◇ Q, South winning with ◇ K. With only seven top tricks South needed to establish hearts. West took ♡ K with ♡ A, returning ◇ 8, and East made three tricks with ◇ A 10 2. Had East returned a low diamond, South would play low and win with ◇ J.

The principle when leading round to weakness in dummy is this. If you hold the two cards immediately above and below dummy's highest, together with an outside honour, lead the card to beat dummy. Here East held ◇ Q 10 over ◇ J, together with ◇ A, so when ◇ Q lost to ◇ K, East held ◇ A 10 over ◇ J 9 and, providing West could get in, would make two tricks plus ◇ 2 if the suit divided well.

If partner leads your bid suit and you take the first trick, whether or not you continue the suit depends on your prospects of establishing it and the number of entries you hold. It may also depend on the number of tricks you can see the opponents will make once they get the lead.

Dealer North. Love All.

```
                    ♠ J
                    ♡ 7 2
                    ◇ A K Q 10 6 4
                    ♣ A Q 7 3
   ♠ 9 4 3                            ♠ A Q 10 8 7
   ♡ Q 9 8 5 3                        ♡ A K 6
   ◇ J 5                              ◇ 7 3 2
   ♣ 10 9 4                           ♣ 8 2
                    ♠ K 6 5 2
                    ♡ J 10 4
                    ◇ 9 8
                    ♣ K J 6 5
```

South	West	North	East
South	*West*	*North*	*East*
–	–	1 ◇	1 ♠
1NT	No bid	3NT	All pass

West led ♠ 9, East won with ♠ A and returned ♠ Q to clear his suit, hoping to get in with ♡ A. Had he looked at dummy he would have realized that lucky situation was not likely to arise for quite a long time. South was sure to take ♠ Q with ♠ K, having called No-Trumps over spades, and there were six tricks in diamonds and at least two clubs, since if South did not hold ♣ K, the finesse would be right.

East should have appreciated that the only chance for the defence was to switch to hearts. Take ♠ A and lead ♡ A. That would produce six tricks in all. Admittedly West could have led a heart at trick one, but his partner bid spades and there was no sound reason not to lead one.

A similar position arose on this hand.

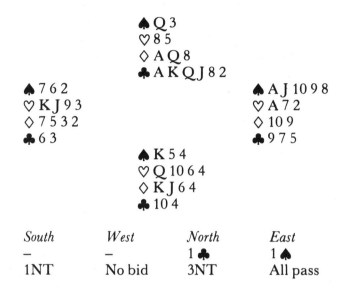

♠ Q 3
♡ 8 5
◇ A Q 8
♣ A K Q J 8 2

♠ 7 6 2
♡ K J 9 3
◇ 7 5 3 2
♣ 6 3

♠ A J 10 9 8
♡ A 7 2
◇ 10 9
♣ 9 7 5

♠ K 5 4
♡ Q 10 6 4
◇ K J 6 4
♣ 10 4

South	*West*	*North*	*East*
–	–	1 ♣	1 ♠
1NT	No bid	3NT	All pass

West leads ♠ 7 and ♠ 3 is played from dummy. It is tempting to play ♠ 8 as East, to clear the suit and hope to get in later with ♡ A. But a glance at dummy will show that the contract is home and dry once South is allowed to win the first trick. East must abandon spades and look for tricks in hearts. He should lead ♡ 2, South plays low and West wins with ♡ 9. The return of ♡ 3 is taken by East with ♡ A and the next lead of ♡ 7 finds West with ♡ K J over South's Q 10.

(b) *Suit Contracts*
Defending against a suit contract the position is less clear cut and much may depend on judgment. Against No-Trumps it is logical to return partner's lead as the main objective is to establish winners in his hand. But in a trump contract it is unlikely that you will take more than three tricks (more likely two) in a suit. Later rounds will be ruffed. Having won the first round, whether you return the suit or not, depends on what you consider your partner

holds. If you think the lead was a singleton it will usually be correct to return the suit for him to trump. If you consider that your partner has led a low card from an honour it will often be correct to return the lead to win tricks quickly. In such a case the highest card is returned unless holding four or more, in which event the original fourth highest is played to give a count.

For example, assuming spades are trumps

$$\lozenge 10\,7\,6$$

$$\lozenge K J 8 3 \qquad\qquad\qquad \lozenge A 9 5 2$$

$$\lozenge Q 4$$

West leads $\lozenge$ 3. East wins with $\lozenge$ A and returns $\lozenge$ 2 which is either his best or fourth highest. When $\lozenge$ Q appears from South the return is probably fourth highest. However, as was stated earlier, a certain amount of judgment is necessary as it may be better to utilise your entry for a more constructive purpose. Consider this hand

Dealer South. Love All.

```
              ♠ Q 7 6
              ♡ J 9 5 3
              ◇ 10 6
              ♣ K Q 10 4
♠ K 4                              ♠ 10 2
♡ K 10 6                          ♡ 8 7 4 2
◇ K J 9 7 5                       ◇ A 8 4 2
♣ 7 6 5                           ♣ 9 3 2
              ♠ A J 9 8 5 3
              ♡ A Q
              ◇ Q 3
              ♣ A J 8
```

South	West	North	East
1 ♠	No bid	2 ♠	No bid
4 ♠	No bid	No bid	No bid

North might have responded Two Clubs or One No-Trump in which case South could reasonably jump to Three Spades and been raised to Four Spades. West led ◇ 7, taken by East who returned ◇ 2 to ◇ Q, ◇ K and ◇ 10. West was now in a difficult position. He could see a third trick with ♠ K and a possible fourth with ♡ K. But as South probably held ♣ A, any losing heart might be discarded. It seemed best to try and set up a heart trick before ♠ K was forced out and to this end he led ♡ 6 but to no avail. There was in fact no hope for the defence at that point. Had East returned a heart at trick two, South tries the finesse which loses and later loses to ♠ K for down one. Before returning ◇ 2 at the second trick East should have stopped to consider from whence the tricks were coming. Assuming West held ◇ K the suit could not be continued as dummy had no more. East was never going to be on lead again and should therefore have made a more constructive effort.

(*repeated for convenience*)

```
            ♠ Q 7 6
            ♡ J 9 5 3
            ◇ 10 6
            ♣ K Q 10 4
♠ K 4                       ♠ 10 2
♡ K 10 6                    ♡ 8 7 4 2
◇ K J 9 7 5                 ◇ A 8 4 2
♣ 7 6 5                     ♣ 9 3 2
            ♠ A J 9 8 5 3
            ♡ A Q
            ◇ Q 3
            ♣ A J 8
```

Suppose we alter South's hand to

(i)   ♠ A K J 9 8 5   ♡ K 10   ◇ Q 3   ♣ A J 8 leaving
      West with
      ♠ 4 3   ♡ A Q 6   ◇ K J 9 7 5   ♣ 7 6 5 or

(ii) ♠ A K J 9 8 5   ♡ A Q   ◇ Q 3   ♣ J 8 5 leaving
      West with
      ♠ 4 3   ♡ K 10 6   ◇ K J 9 7 5   ♣ A 7 6

In each case it is quite likely that the final contract will be
Four Spades and in each case the return of a diamond puts
West in an impossible position, whereas a heart return
beats the contract.

It may be necessary to switch to attack an entry in dummy. The rule of eleven helped to find the right return on this hand.

Dealer South. Love All.

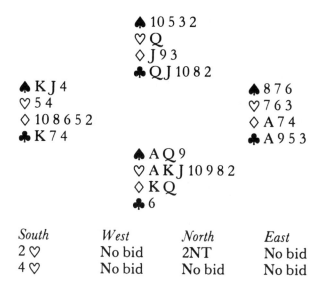

South	West	North	East
2 ♡	No bid	2NT	No bid
4 ♡	No bid	No bid	No bid

South opened with an Acol Two Bid indicating eight or more playing tricks and a powerful suit. North gave a negative reply with Two No-Trumps but South jumped to game as it required practically nothing in partner's hand to produce ten tricks.

West led ◇ 5, taken by East with ◇ A, South playing ◇ Q. The lead appeared to be fourth highest so that there were six diamonds higher than the five, divided between North, East and South. Dummy had two (J 9), East two (A 7) and South had played ◇ Q, leaving him one more. This was likely to be ◇ K, in which case if East returned a diamond, South would win, cross to dummy with ♡ Q and discard a loser on ◇ J. East returned a trump at trick two and removed the entry before ◇ J could be established.

Another occasion where it is necessary to switch is where the return of partner's suit is likely to establish a trick for declarer and enable him to discard a loser. Having decided to switch and also the suit to return, it is important to select the right card as in this hand.

Dealer South. North-South vul.

```
                    ♠ Q 9 5
                    ♡ K 10 7 6
                    ◊ K Q 10
                    ♣ 9 6 2
     ♠ 10 8 4 2                        ♠ A K 6 3
     ♡ 8 5                             ♡ 3 2
     ◊ J 7 5 3                         ◊ 9 6 4
     ♣ K 5 4                           ♣ Q 10 8 3
                    ♠ J 7
                    ♡ A Q J 9 4
                    ◊ A 8 2
                    ♣ A J 7
```

South	West	North	East
1 ♡	No bid	3 ♡	No bid
4 ♡	No bid	No bid	No bid

West led ♠ 2, taken with ♠ K. As the lead appeared to be from a four card suit, South held two so it would be a mistake to cash ♠ A. This would set up ♠ Q on which South could discard a loser. Aware of the necessity to establish an extra trick East led ♣ 3, South played ♣ 7, hoping East held ♣ 10 which would force West to play ♣ K, leaving South with ♣ A J over ♣ Q 10. East should have returned ♣ 10. South cannot afford to play low and if he plays ♣ A he loses to both ♣ K and ♣ Q. The only card left is ♣ J. This loses to ♣ K and the return of ♣ 5 finds East with ♣ Q 8 over ♣ 9 6.

The return of ♣ 10 is in accordance with the principle stated earlier that holding the cards immediately above and below dummy's highest, together with an outside honour, it is right to lead the card to beat the table.

While it is usually right to return partner's singleton lead for him to trump, it may be important to prepare the ground for another trick later. This hand illustrates the point.

Dealer East. North-South vul.

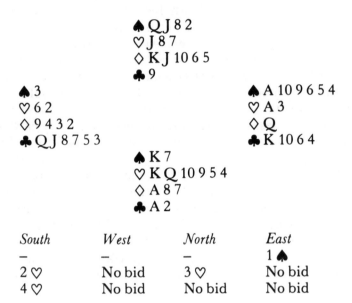

♠ Q J 8 2
♡ J 8 7
◇ K J 10 6 5
♣ 9

♠ 3   ♠ A 10 9 6 5 4
♡ 6 2   ♡ A 3
◇ 9 4 3 2   ◇ Q
♣ Q J 8 7 5 3   ♣ K 10 6 4

♠ K 7
♡ K Q 10 9 5 4
◇ A 8 7
♣ A 2

South	West	North	East
–	–	–	1 ♠
2 ♡	No bid	3 ♡	No bid
4 ♡	No bid	No bid	No bid

South's hand really justified a strong overcall of Three Hearts, but he considered that a vulnerable two level overcall would imply a good hand. West led ♠ 3 to which dummy played ♠ 2, East ♠ A and South ♠ 7. Clearly West had only one spade for with ♠ K 7 he would lead ♠ K. Had he held ♠ K 7 3 he would lead ♠ 3, but in that case South would be void. East returned a spade, West ruffed and returned ♣ Q. South won and led a trump. East took his ace and played a spade but South ruffed high and the contract was made.

East was in too great a hurry to give his partner a ruff. As he held the ace of trumps he was in control. At trick two he should play ◇ Q. This is won by South who leads a trump, East gets in with ♡ A and now plays a spade. West trumps and returns a diamond which East ruffs.

If you are defending you should approach the situation in the same way as you would as declarer. If you are playing the contract, after dummy goes down you count up your tricks.

If there are not enough you plan how you can make more. Similarly, if you are defending you count up how many tricks you can expect to win and if there are not enough you work out how to get more.

Reverting to the hand above. After the lead of ♠ 3 East can see three tricks for the defence – ♠ A, ♡ A and one ruff. One more needed. West is unlikely to produce any ace or king, but the singleton diamond offers good prospects, especially as East has the ace of trumps and will regain the lead before all the trumps have been drawn.

It may be necessary for the third player to overtake his partner's high card in order to direct the defence. Such was the case on this hand.

Dealer South. Love All.

```
                    ♠ Q 10 9
                    ♡ K 10 5 3
                    ◇ K Q 10 9
                    ♣ J 2
   ♠ J 7 6                              ♠ 5 4 3 2
   ♡ 7                                  ♡ 6 4 2
   ◇ 6 5 4 3 2                          ◇ A
   ♣ K Q 10 9                           ♣ A 8 7 4 3
                    ♠ A K 8
                    ♡ A Q J 9 8
                    ◇ J 8 7
                    ♣ 6 5
```

South	West	North	East
1 ♡	No bid	3 ♡	No bid
4 ♡	No bid	No bid	No bid

West leads ♣ K. Putting yourself in the East seat and counting your tricks on the lines just suggested, you can see two probable winners in clubs and one in diamonds. Three in all and you need four. It is unlikely that West has any high cards in either spades or hearts so you must try for a

(*repeated for convenience*)

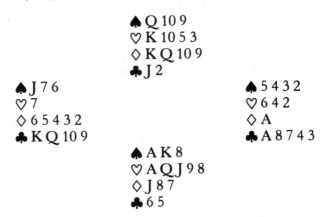

```
                    ♠ Q 10 9
                    ♡ K 10 5 3
                    ◇ K Q 10 9
                    ♣ J 2
♠ J 7 6                                  ♠ 5 4 3 2
♡ 7                                      ♡ 6 4 2
◇ 6 5 4 3 2                              ◇ A
♣ K Q 10 9                               ♣ A 8 7 4 3
                    ♠ A K 8
                    ♡ A Q J 9 8
                    ◇ J 8 7
                    ♣ 6 5
```

diamond ruff. You take partner's ♣ K with ♣ A and lay down ◇ A. Next return a club to partner's ♣ Q (he led ♣ K so must hold ♣ Q) and he will play back a diamond for you to trump.

7. Further Play By Opening Leader

Having considered the action of third player after winning the opening lead it is now time to consider the position of the opening leader. He may still be on lead at trick two or he may have won the return by his partner and be playing to the third trick.

Play to Trick 2.
(a) *No-Trump Contracts*
After winning the first trick it will often be best to continue the suit in order to establish it. This will certainly be the case if the suit is a strong one headed by a sequence with honours, e.g. K Q J x x or Q J 10 x x. The opening lead is likely to win as declarer will probably hold up his stopper. But if the suit is not solid, continuation will depend on partner's play to the opening lead

               ◇ 6 4
◇ K Q 10 9 2

West leads ◇ K to which East follows with ◇ 3 and South
◇ 5. West must not continue the suit as South probably
holds ◇ A J. Had East held ◇ J he should play it on ◇ K.
The lead must be from a near sequence and it is mandatory
for partner to play ◇ J if he has it to clarify the position.
Similarly if West leads a queen, East should play the ten if
he has it. The lead is probably from Q J 9 and others, and
the ten is an important card.

It is also wise to switch if it is necessary to have the suit
returned to you through declarer e.g.

               ◇ 7 4
◇ A K J 8 6   ◇ 9 5 2
               ◇ Q 10 3

You lead ◇ A and East plays ◇ 2. As South, who called
No-Trumps, is likely to hold ◇ Q x x, a continuation with
◇ K will give away a trick. On the other hand if partner can
get in and return a diamond you will take five tricks and
therefore a switch at trick two is advisable.

Another situation when it is necessary to switch is where
the opponent will win the next trick if you continue your
suit and is known to have a long and solid suit to play. A
good example of this is after an opening bid of Three No-
Trumps, showing a long and solid minor suit with little or
nothing outside. This hand illustrates the point

Dealer South. Love All.

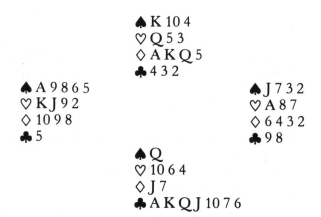

♠ K 10 4
♡ Q 5 3
◇ A K Q 5
♣ 4 3 2

♠ A 9 8 6 5
♡ K J 9 2
◇ 10 9 8
♣ 5

♠ J 7 3 2
♡ A 8 7
◇ 6 4 3 2
♣ 9 8

♠ Q
♡ 10 6 4
◇ J 7
♣ A K Q J 10 7 6

South opens Three No-Trumps and all pass. If West makes his "normal" lead of ♠ 6 (fourth highest) South will make the first twelve tricks. But, as explained at the end of the chapter on Opening Leads, the correct action is to play an ace if possible and decide your next move after viewing dummy. After winning the ♠ A the only chance is to switch to hearts. East is known to hold ♡ A as South's opening bid promises little or nothing apart from a long solid minor suit. West must switch to ♡ J. If ♡ Q is played from dummy East wins with ♡ A and returns ♡ 8 and West, holding ♡ K 9 2 over South's ♡ 10 6, takes three more tricks. A switch to ♡ 2 will not succeed as South will play low from the table, hoping for ♡ J to be on his left and East will have to play ♡ A.

It is rather similar to the principle explained earlier that when leading round to dummy you lead a card to beat the table, if holding the cards immediately above and below dummy's highest plus an outside honour. Here you are leading round to the hidden hand, but if it holds ♡ 10 x x and you hold ♡ K J 9 x you do have the cards immediately above and below the ten.

(b) *Suit Contracts*

Having won the opening lead, whether or not to continue the suit in a trump contract will depend on various factors, what partner has played to the trick and what dummy holds. If partner has played his lowest card it is unwise to continue unless your suit is solid. For example, defending against a spade contract you lead ◊ A and this is the position

◊ Q J 7 6

◊ A K 10 9   ◊ 8 5 4 2

◊ 3

On ◊ A partners plays ◊ 2 and South ◊ 3. Partner has indicated he has no interest in diamonds and suggests you switch to another suit. If you disregard his warning and put down ◊ K, it will be trumped and ◊ Q J in dummy will be tricks. This point was explained in the earlier chapter on Signals. If the position were this

◊ Q J 7 6

◊ A K 10 9   ◊ 8 2

◊ 5 4 3

East would play ◊ 8 on the first round. Reading this as an encouraging card West could cash ◊ K and continue with a third round for East to ruff.

In the chapter on Signals it was pointed out that if the queen were played on the ace it implied possession of the knave and a low card should be led to trick two. Example

Dealer South. East–West vul.

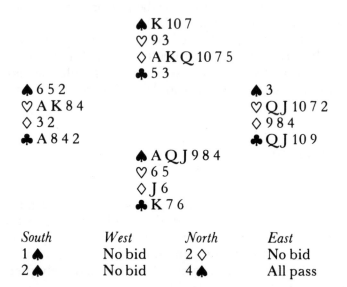

South	West	North	East
1 ♠	No bid	2 ◇	No bid
2 ♠	No bid	4 ♠	All pass

West leads ♡ A and East follows with ♡ Q. West must now lead a low heart for East to win and return ♣ Q. East can see that the only chance of defeating the game is to take two hearts and two clubs. It is essential to win the second trick in order to lead ♣ Q through South and by playing ♡ Q he relies on his partner playing a low card to his ♡ 10.

In the next hand it was necessary to switch in order to establish a trick before a long suit in dummy could be employed for discards.

Dealer South. North–South vul.

```
              ♠ Q 10 6
              ♡ K 7 5
              ◇ K Q J 9 4
              ♣ Q 4
♠ A K 7 3                      ♠ J 9 5 2
♡ A 4                          ♡ 3
◇ 7 5                          ◇ 10 6 3 2
♣ J 10 6 5 3                   ♣ K 9 7 2
              ♠ 8 4
              ♡ Q J 10 9 8 6 2
              ◇ A 8
              ♣ A 8
```

South	West	North	East
1 ♡	Dbl.	Redbl.	1 ♠
3 ♡	No bid	4 ♡	All pass

West led ♠ A on which East played ♠ 2 and South ♠ 4. It would be wrong to continue with ♠ K as this would establish dummy's ♠ Q, apart from the risk of South ruffing. If West could make his ♠ A K and ♡ A there would need to be a fourth trick, and to trick two West led ♣ J covered by ♣ Q, ♣ K and ♣ A. South, faced with four losers, played three rounds of diamonds, discarding ♣ 8. He had to hope that West held three diamonds or that he might have to ruff with ♡ A. But his hopes did not materialise and the contract was one down due to the timely switch at trick two.

The defence on the next hand is more difficult

Dealer West. East–West vul.

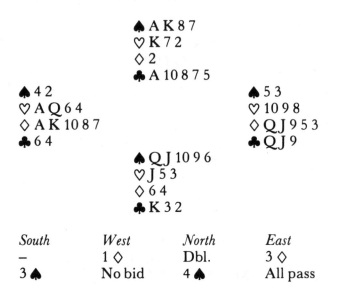

♠ A K 8 7
♡ K 7 2
◊ 2
♣ A 10 8 7 5

♠ 4 2   ♠ 5 3
♡ A Q 6 4   ♡ 10 9 8
◊ A K 10 8 7   ◊ Q J 9 5 3
♣ 6 4   ♣ Q J 9

♠ Q J 10 9 6
♡ J 5 3
◊ 6 4
♣ K 3 2

South	West	North	East
–	1 ◊	Dbl.	3 ◊
3 ♠	No bid	4 ♠	All pass

West leads ◊ A, covered by ◊ 2, ◊ 3 and ◊ 4. There are
no more tricks to be won in diamonds and probably none in
spades. Unless partner has two club tricks it will be
necessary to make two tricks in hearts. It has to be assumed
that East has one club trick. If the suit is solid there is no
hope, so it is a question of selecting the right card for the
switch. It must be ♡ Q. This is taken with ♡ K and trumps
are drawn. East gets in with a club and returns a heart
through declarer's ♡ J for two heart tricks. A low heart at
trick two would not do, as this could be run round to
South's ♡ J.

If it is apparent that you need to switch after the first
trick because a continuation of your initial suit is either
pointless or dangerous, it may not always be clear which
suit you should attack. In the hands cited above it was fairly
clear that you needed to set up tricks quickly and there was
little choice about which suit to attack. But it is not always
so straightforward.

A common precept is to play through strength. This has

a certain amount of logic insofar as it may compel declarer to play a high card second in hand if he has no high cards himself and wants to win the trick. But like so many of these so called "rules" which are laid down with no reason being given, they must not be followed blindly and without thought. It is better to advise leading through short strength and to avoid leading through a suit in dummy that is missing more than one of the top three honours.

Consider these examples

(i)

$\heartsuit$ A J 10 7

$\diamondsuit$ 8 6 2 $\diamondsuit$ Q 5 3

$\diamondsuit$ K 9 4

(ii)

$\diamondsuit$ A Q 7

$\diamondsuit$ 10 9 2 $\diamondsuit$ K J 8 5

$\diamondsuit$ 6 4 3

(iii)

$\diamondsuit$ A K 6

$\diamondsuit$ 8 7 5 3 $\diamondsuit$ Q 9 4

$\diamondsuit$ J 10 2

In (i) to lead a diamond "through strength" will be fatal. You will merely succeed in trapping your partner's queen, which he might well have made had you left the suit alone. Declarer would probably have finessed. In (ii) and (iii) the lead of a diamond is safe as it is unlikely that partner can have an honour than can be trapped.

Play to Trick 3
(a) *No-Trump Contracts*
We have now to consider the position where partner wins the opening lead and returns the suit and we are having to decide what to play to the third trick.

If the opening lead was a suit bid by partner, it will almost certainly be best to carry on and establish it. If partner had no confidence in his suit and saw the necessity to switch he would have returned a different suit e.g.

♠ 6 4

♠ Q 7 2   ♠ A 10 9 5 3

♠ K J 8

South is declarer in No-Trumps, East having bid spades. West leads ♠ 2 correctly from three headed by an honour. East wins with ♠ A and returns ♠ 5 and West takes ♠ J with ♠ Q. He should return ♠ 7 to clear the suit.

If the original lead was your own best suit and partner returns it, whether or not you carry on with it must depend upon its strength, the prospects of establishing it and eventually getting in to cash winners.

We saw earlier that the sight of a long solid suit in dummy might necessitate a switch by third player at trick 2. A similar position may arise where the opening leader can see that to persevere with his suit cannot meet with success.

Dealer North. Love All.

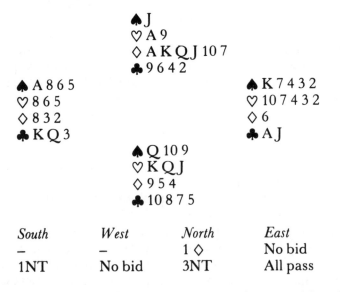

```
                    ♠ J
                    ♡ A 9
                    ◇ A K Q J 10 7
                    ♣ 9 6 4 2
    ♠ A 8 6 5                          ♠ K 7 4 3 2
    ♡ 8 6 5                            ♡ 10 7 4 3 2
    ◇ 8 3 2                            ◇ 6
    ♣ K Q 3                            ♣ A J
                    ♠ Q 10 9
                    ♡ K Q J
                    ◇ 9 5 4
                    ♣ 10 8 7 5
```

South	West	North	East
–	–	1 ◇	No bid
1NT	No bid	3NT	All pass

North's Three No-Trumps was a reasonable shot.

Providing that his partner was not defeated at the start, chances of making nine tricks were good. West leads ♠ 5, East wins with ♠ K and correctly returns ♠ 3, his original fourth highest. South follows to the first two tricks with ♠ 9 and ♠ 10. West wins with ♠ A. He can see seven sure winners in dummy. South is known to hold ♠ Q, or East would have played it rather than ♠ K at trick one. That totals eight tricks and if South has ♣ A he has nine certain winners. Therefore West must assume partner holds ♣ A. Moreover he must lead ♣ 3, not ♣ K, as East may hold ace and one other club. The defence take two spades and three clubs. Of course the same result would have been achieved had East switched to ♣ A at trick two, but this would not have been sound. South could have held ♠ Q 9 8 and West ♠ A 10 6 5. Now the defence take the first five tricks on a spade return.

A sound principle in defence is this. If partner needs to hold a certain card in order to defeat a contract, and the possession of that card leaves opponent with a reasonable holding for his bid, then assume partner has the vital card.

In the hand above the only hope is that East holds ♣ A. That still leaves South with ♠ Q and ♡ K Q, enough for his response of One No-Trump. In fact he held ♡ J and could have had ♣ J also giving him 9 high card points and still leave room for East to hold ♣ A.

(b) *Suit Contracts*
If your partner returns your lead, defending against a suit contract, your play to the third trick will depend on what you see in dummy and what you consider your partner holds. If it seems probable that your partner had a doubleton you continue for him to ruff.

(i)   ♡ Q J 7 6
        ♡ K 9 5 3   ♡ A 2
                                       ♡ 10 8 4

(ii)   ♡ 8 6 3
    ♡ K J 7 2   ♡ A 9 4
                           ♡ Q 10 5

(iii)   ♡ 8 6 5
    ♡ K J 9 3   ♡ A 10 7 2
                           ♡ Q 4

Defending against a spade contract you decide to lead your fourth highest heart.

In (i) ♡ 6 is played from dummy, East wins with ♡ A and returns ♡ 2, South following with ♡ 4 and ♡ 8. East's ♡ 2 is either his fourth best or his highest. Dummy's holding and the cards played by South point to East having ♡ A 2 only. Therefore you win and return the suit for him to ruff.

In (ii) East wins with the ♡ A and returns ♡ 9, South following with ♡ 5 and ♡ 10. It appears that East has three cards in the suit; therefore win with ♡ J and cash ♡ K.

In (iii) East wins with ♡ A and returns ♡ 2, South following with ♡ 4 and ♡ Q. Indications are that South has only two hearts and East's ♡ 2 is fourth highest. Win with ♡ K and play ♡ J. This will be trumped by South but that will weaken his trump holding and in the absence of any better attack is probably the best defence.

If your partner returns a different suit you should ask yourself why he did not return yours. If dummy's holding makes it unlikely that your partner had a singleton, his switch will either be because there is no future in playing back your suit, or there is a need to set up tricks quickly. If he returns a low card he is likely to hold an honour in the suit and is prepared for you to return it. If he returns a high card (e.g. 9 or 8) it is improbable that he has an honour and, seeing no advantage in returning your suit, is "getting off play" as safely as possible, probably playing up to weakness in dummy. It is possible that he is playing a singleton or doubleton and some clue in this respect can usually be found from dummy. Should he return a trump his object will be to prevent dummy ruffing and you should co-operate by returning a trump if you have the lead at trick three.

8. Ducking

When discussing the action by the original leader after his partner has returned his suit in a No Trumps contract, it was stated that the decision as to whether to clear the suit depended upon its strength and upon entries.

With no sure entry outside it may be best not to win the return, in order to keep communications open with partner. Consider this hand

Dealer South. Game All.

```
                        ♠ 6 2
                        ♡ Q J 2
                        ◇ K 10 4
                        ♣ K J 10 9 4
       ♠ K 10 7 5 4                        ♠ A 8 3
       ♡ K 4                               ♡ 10 9 8 7 6
       ◇ 5 3 2                             ◇ A 8 6
       ♣ 7 5 2                             ♣ 8 6
                        ♠ Q J 9
                        ♡ A 5 3
                        ◇ Q J 9 7
                        ♣ A Q 3
```

South	West	North	East
South	*West*	*North*	*East*
1NT	No bid	3NT	All pass

West led ♠ 5, taken by East with ♠ A, South playing ♠ 9. East returned ♠ 8, covered by ♠ J and won with ♠ K. West cleared his suit, hoping to get in with ♡ K. South played off five winning clubs, discarding ♡ 5 3 from his hand and next played ◇ K. East won with ◇ A but South won the rest of the tricks. West should have played low on the second spade lead. If he gets in with ♡ K, well and good, but if his

(repeated for convenience)

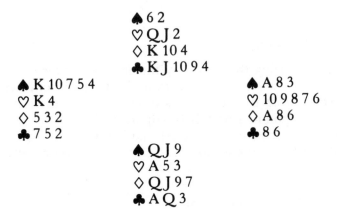

♠ 6 2
♡ Q J 2
◇ K 10 4
♣ K J 10 9 4

♠ K 10 7 5 4
♡ K 4
◇ 5 3 2
♣ 7 5 2

♠ A 8 3
♡ 10 9 8 7 6
◇ A 8 6
♣ 8 6

♠ Q J 9
♡ A 5 3
◇ Q J 9 7
♣ A Q 3

partner gets in and is able to return his last spade, West will take three tricks. With North–South holding about 26 high card points and West holding 6, East is marked with about 8. He has produced 4 (♠ A) but may still have an ace (as he did) or he might hold ♣ Q and win if South finesses.

Here is a second example

Dealer South. Love All.

♠ K J 10
♡ 8 7 5
◇ A Q 10 8 7
♣ J 8

♠ 8 4 2
♡ 10 4 2
◇ 6 5
♣ A 10 7 6 4

♠ 9 7 6 5
♡ Q J 6
◇ K 3 2
♣ K 3 2

♠ A Q 3
♡ A K 9 3
◇ J 9 4
♣ Q 9 5

South	West	North	East
1 ♡	No bid	2 ◇	No bid
2NT	No bid	3 ♡	No bid
3NT	No bid	No bid	No bid

North's Three Hearts was forcing, offering South the option of bidding Four Hearts, holding five, or Three No-Trumps with four.

West leads ♣ 6 and South correctly plays ♣ 8 from the table to ensure winning a trick. East wins with ♣ K and returns ♣ 3, his highest. West must duck and allow ♣ J to win. He must rely on his partner getting in and being able to return a club. This is likely as ♣ 2 has not appeared. South played ♣ 5 and ♣ 9 on the first two tricks. South enters his hand with ♡ K and leads ◇ J. The finesse loses to East who returns ♣ 2 and the contract is one down.

Ducking in defence is not confined to no trump contracts as is shown on this hand.

Dealer South. Love All.

```
                 ♠ 9 7 5
                 ♡ 3 2
                 ◇ A K 8 3
                 ♣ K J 7 4
  ♠ J 10 3                      ♠ 6 2
  ♡ A Q 8 6                     ♡ K 9 7 4
  ◇ Q 10 7 6                    ◇ J 9 5
  ♣ 8 6                         ♣ A 9 5 3
                 ♠ A K Q 8 4
                 ♡ J 10 5
                 ◇ 4 2
                 ♣ Q 10 2
```

South	West	North	East
1 ♠	No bid	2 ♣	No bid
2 ♠	No bid	3 ♠	No bid
4 ♠	No bid	No bid	No bid

(*repeated for convenience*)

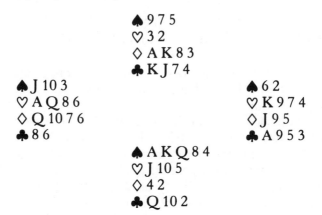

♠ 9 7 5
♡ 3 2
◇ A K 8 3
♣ K J 7 4

♠ J 10 3
♡ A Q 8 6
◇ Q 10 7 6
♣ 8 6

♠ 6 2
♡ K 9 7 4
◇ J 9 5
♣ A 9 5 3

♠ A K Q 8 4
♡ J 10 5
◇ 4 2
♣ Q 10 2

South's final bid was hardly justified as his opening One Spade was minimum. Maybe he liked his club fit. Anyway, West led ◇ 6 taken with ◇ K. There might appear to be ten tricks in the shape of five spades, two diamonds and three clubs, but if trumps are drawn before playing clubs the defence can take three heart tricks. Appreciating this South tried for a heart ruff in dummy. West won ♡ Q and switched to ♣ 8. Had East won with ♣ A South would have got home. But East ducked, having decided that ♣ 8 was the upper half of a doubleton. Now, when South played his second heart, ace and another club gave West a ruff to defeat the contract by one.

9. Attacking Entries

When the opponents are known to hold a long suit that is likely to become established, the defence may be able to prevent the suit being utilised by attacking entries. This more frequently occurs when the long suit is in dummy and therefore visible. There are various methods of attacking the entry.

(a) *Forcing the Dummy*

Whilst it is often wrong to allow dummy to ruff it may nevertheless deprive the hand of a necessary entry. This hand occurred in a duplicate pairs tournament where the importance of making extra tricks is great.

Dealer South. Love All.

```
                    ♠ 9 6
                    ♡ Q 8 6
                    ◇ A K 7 6 3
                    ♣ 9 5 3
♠ Q 10 4 2                         ♠ A K J 5
♡ 10 7                            ♡ 9 4 3
◇ J 9 8                          ◇ Q 10 4
♣ A J 8 4                        ♣ 10 7 6
                    ♠ 8 7 3
                    ♡ A K J 5 2
                    ◇ 5 2
                    ♣ K Q 2
```

South	West	North	East
1 ♡	No bid	2 ◇	No bid
2 ♡	No bid	No bid	No bid

This would not be a very interesting hand at rubber bridge as there are eight fairly obvious tricks. But in the tournament several pairs made ten tricks. West led ♠ 2 taken by East who returned either a club or a trump to stop a ruff in dummy. The result was the same. South got in and cashed ♡ A K, followed by ◇ A K. He next ruffed a low diamond in hand with ♡ J. When each opponent followed he crossed to the table, drawing the last trump, and cashed two winning diamonds. He made five tricks in trumps, four in diamonds and one club. Had East continued spades, forcing dummy to ruff, South would have been unable to enjoy the diamonds as he could not draw all the outstanding trumps and finish in dummy.

The next hand is similar

Dealer South. East–West vul.

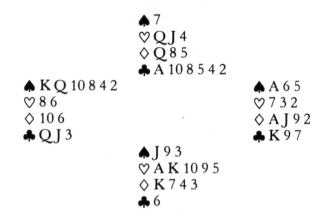

```
                    ♠ 7
                    ♡ Q J 4
                    ◇ Q 8 5
                    ♣ A 10 8 5 4 2
♠ K Q 10 8 4 2                        ♠ A 6 5
♡ 8 6                                 ♡ 7 3 2
◇ 10 6                                ◇ A J 9 2
♣ Q J 3                               ♣ K 9 7
                    ♠ J 9 3
                    ♡ A K 10 9 5
                    ◇ K 7 4 3
                    ♣ 6
```

South opened One Heart and West overcalled in spades. After a contested auction South became declarer in Four Hearts doubled and West led ♠ K which held. He switched to ◇ 10 on which dummy played ◇ 5, East ◇ 2 and South ◇ K. South could see nine tricks if he ruffed two spades on the table, but he saw a chance of making his doubled contract if the clubs split 3–3 and trumps were 3–2. He led ♣ 6 to ♣ A, ruffed ♣ 2 with ♡ 9. He crossed to the table with ♡ J and ruffed ♣ 4 with ♡ K. When each opponent followed dummy's clubs were good. He played ♡ A followed by ♡ 5 to ♡ Q, drawing the outstanding trumps and made ten tricks.

Again, the defence should have seen the danger of the long club suit becoming set up. The only entry was in trumps, so by continuing spades and forcing dummy the game would have been saved. East should overtake ♠ K and return the suit as he can see he has three trumps which will be enough if dummy can be reduced to two.

In the next hand the defence needs to time the play carefully.

Dealer South. Love All.

```
                ♠ 7 4
                ♡ 8 4
                ◊ A Q J 9 3
                ♣ K Q J 4
♠ 9 5                           ♠ K 8 3
♡ A K 7 5                       ♡ Q J 9 2
◊ 7 2                           ◊ 10 6 5
♣ 8 6 5 3 2                     ♣ A 10 7
                ♠ A Q J 10 6 2
                ♡ 10 6 3
                ◊ K 8 4
                ♣ 9
```

South	West	North	East
1 ♠	No bid	2 ◊	No bid
2 ♠	No bid	3 ♣	No bid
3 ♠	No bid	4 ♠	All pass

West leads ♡ A (ace from ace–king). Putting yourself in the East seat how should you plan the defence? You reckon to make two hearts and ♣ A. There is no real hope in diamonds, so that leaves your king of spades. South must surely hold the remaining spade honours on the bidding and your king is due to be finessed. But dummy has only two spades and to catch your king South must be able to lead twice from the table. If dummy can be reduced to only one spade your king is safe. If you encourage with ♡ 9 West will cash ♡ K and may continue with a third round forcing dummy to ruff. South leads ♠ 7 and finesses ♠ 10 which wins and cashes ♠ A. Well, you have saved your king but not the contract. South next plays diamonds and you have to follow three times. On the fourth diamond South discards his single club and you can ruff with ♠ K but it will not help.

The correct defence is to play ♡ Q on ♡ A. This, you will remember, promises possession of ♡ J, and partner should

(*repeated for convenience*)

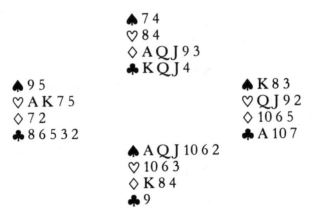

```
                    ♠ 7 4
                    ♡ 8 4
                    ◇ A Q J 9 3
                    ♣ K Q J 4
♠ 9 5                                    ♠ K 8 3
♡ A K 7 5                                ♡ Q J 9 2
◇ 7 2                                    ◇ 10 6 5
♣ 8 6 5 3 2                              ♣ A 10 7
                    ♠ A Q J 10 6 2
                    ♡ 10 6 3
                    ◇ K 8 4
                    ♣ 9
```

lead a low heart at trick two. You win with ♡ J, cash ♣ A, and next play a third heart forcing dummy to ruff.

(b) *Entry Killing Play (Merrimac Coup)*

This is rather a high-sounding play but it is not complicated. It involves leading a high, usually unsupported, honour to kill an entry that would be needed to reach a long suit. Here is an example.

Dealer North. East-West vul.

```
                    ♠ A 3
                    ♡ 6 4 3
                    ◇ K Q J 10 9 5
                    ♣ 9 8
♠ J 9 7 5                                ♠ K 6 2
♡ 10 9 8 7                               ♡ A 5 2
◇ 6                                      ◇ A 8 2
♣ Q 7 5 4                                ♣ J 10 6 3
                    ♠ Q 10 8 4
                    ♡ K Q J
                    ◇ 7 4 3
                    ♣ A K 3
```

South	West	North	East
–	–	1 ◇	No bid
1 ♠	No bid	2 ◇	No bid
3NT	No bid	No bid	No bid

West makes the natural lead of ♡ 10 and East wins with ♡ A. Before automatically returning the suit he should look at dummy and consider prospects. To make the contract South is likely to need the diamonds and East holds ◇ A. If this card is held up South will need an entry to the table and there is only one, ♠ A. If this is removed before the diamonds are established South will be deprived of many of his tricks. The certain way of forcing out ♠ A is to play ♠ K; a low spade is not good enough as South can play ♠ Q.

(c) *Shut Out Play*
A third method of attacking entries is by setting up a tenace over dummy. This will occur where dummy has no immediate entry, such as an ace, but an honour combination that will provide an entry. By forcing this combination to be used prematurely its value as an entry will be destroyed. Consider this hand.

Dealer South. Game All.

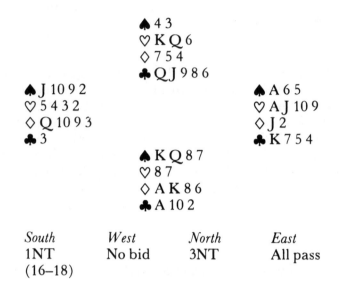

South	West	North	East
South	*West*	*North*	*East*
1NT	No bid	3NT	All pass
(16–18)			

North raised to Three No-Trumps on the strength of his five card club suit. West leads ♠ J and East wins with ♠ A. There is little point in returning the suit as South must surely hold ♠ K Q, having regard to the fact that he has no honours in hearts. Dummy's clubs will be needed and these cannot be fully employed while East holds the well guarded king. If West were to return a spade South would win and play ♣ A and ♣ 10 forcing out ♣ K and would eventually make four clubs, one heart, two spades and two diamonds. But if East returns ♡ J, forcing out ♡ Q, he retains ♡ A 10 9 over ♡ K 6 and dummy no longer has an entry.

10. Forcing Declarer

It is usually bad play for declarer to lead cards from dummy and ruff in his own hand, for in so doing he is merely weakening his trumps. So it follows that it is often good policy for the defenders to attack with a strong suit and compel declarer to use his trumps. Consider this simple position

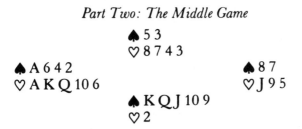

```
              ♠ 5 3
              ♡ 8 7 4 3
♠ A 6 4 2                    ♠ 8 7
♡ A K Q 10 6                 ♡ J 9 5
              ♠ K Q J 10 9
              ♡ 2
```

Spades are trumps and West leads top hearts. South ruffs the second. From an original trump holding of five (South) against four (West) the position is now four each. South leads ♠ K, West wins with ♠ A and plays another heart which South ruffs. West has now three spades against South's two.

A similar position defeated South on this hand

Dealer South. North–South vul.

```
                  ♠ 6 3 2
                  ♡ 9 4 3
                  ◇ K J
                  ♣ A K 10 9 8
♠ A 8 5 4                           ♠ 7
♡ A K Q 10 8                        ♡ 7 6 2
◇ 9 3                               ◇ 10 8 7 5 4 2
♣ 4 2                               ♣ 7 5 3
                  ♠ K Q J 10 9
                  ♡ J 5
                  ◇ A Q 6
                  ♣ Q J 6
```

South	West	North	East
1 ♠	2 ♡	3 ♣	No bid
3 ♠	No bid	4 ♠	All pass

West led ♡ A and continued with ♡ K and ♡ Q, South ruffing the third. South led ♠ K which was allowed to win as was also ♠ Q, East discarding a diamond. West won the next lead of ♠ J at which point West held ♠ 8 and South

(repeated for convenience)

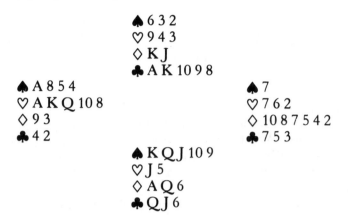

<pre>
                    ♠ 6 3 2
                    ♡ 9 4 3
                    ◊ K J
                    ♣ A K 10 9 8
♠ A 8 5 4   ♠ 7
♡ A K Q 10 8   ♡ 7 6 2
◊ 9 3   ◊ 10 8 7 5 4 2
♣ 4 2   ♣ 7 5 3
                    ♠ K Q J 10 9
                    ♡ J 5
                    ◊ A Q 6
                    ♣ Q J 6
</pre>

♠ 10. A further heart lead forced South to use his last trump and West was now in control. It was important for West to wait until the third round of trumps was played to use his ace as dummy had no more trumps and could not therefore protect declarer against a renewed attack with hearts. Nor would it have helped declarer to abandon trumps after two rounds as West would have ruffed diamonds or clubs on the third lead.

On this next hand the defence forced both dummy and declarer to defeat a game contract.

Dealer South. Love All.

```
                    ♠ 10 8 3 2
                    ♡ 9 8 7 6
                    ◇ A J 7
                    ♣ K Q
   ♠ K Q J 9 4                      ♠ A 7
   ♡ A 5 4 2                        ♡ 3
   ◇ 6 2                            ◇ 8 4 3
   ♣ 8 6                            ♣ 10 9 7 5 4 3 2
                    ♠ 6 5
                    ♡ K Q J 10
                    ◇ K Q 10 9 5
                    ♣ A J
```

South	West	North	East
1 ◇	1 ♠	2 ◇	No bid
2 ♡	No bid	4 ♡	All pass

North has a slightly difficult bid over One Spade. Modern players might use a "sputnik" double which shows at least four hearts and is more akin to a take out double than penalties. But this convention was not available when the hand arose and in any case we are more concerned with the defence. West led ♠ K and East overtook with ♠ A and returned ♠ 7 to ♠ J. West next led ♠ 4 which East ruffed with ♡ 3, forcing South to overruff with ♡ 10 and reducing his trumps to three.

South next led ♡ K and ♡ Q, East discarding clubs. West held up his ♡ A. South could not afford to switch to diamonds as West would ruff the third and still make ♡ A, so South continued with ♡ J which West took. At this point the trump position was ♡ 9 in dummy, East and South void, and West with ♡ 5. When West led ♠ Q South could not ruff and the next lead of ♠ 9 forced dummy to use his last trump, leaving West's ♡ 5 a winner for two down.

PART THREE

Planning the Defence

We have so far considered the early play in defence, starting with the opening lead and the tactics to be adopted for the first two or three tricks. It is now time to consider the general planning of the hand on a broader basis.

11. Assuming Partner has the Vital Cards

Earlier (p. 86) the principle was given that if a contract could only be defeated if partner held one or more vital cards you were justified in assuming such a position providing it left the opponent with a reasonable holding for his bid. The example quoted involved leading a low club from K Q 3 on the assumption that partner held the ace. A similar assumption needed to be made on this hand where a rather ambitious game contract was reached.

Dealer South. Love All

```
                    ♠ Q J 10 9 7
                    ♡ A 9 5
                    ◇ Q 8 6
                    ♣ 7 6
 ♠ K 6 2                              ♠ 8 5 3
 ♡ J 10 8 7                           ♡ 6 3 2
 ◇ K 3 2                              ◇ J 10 4
 ♣ A 9 3                              ♣ K J 10 2
                    ♠ A 4
                    ♡ K Q 4
                    ◇ A 9 7 5
                    ♣ Q 8 5 4
```

South	West	North	East
1 ◇	No bid	1 ♠	No bid
1NT	No bid	2 ♣	No bid
2 ◇	No bid	3NT	All pass

North–South were playing a weak No-Trump (12–14) so that the rebid by South would show 15–16 high card points. North employed the Crowhurst convention with Two Clubs. This enquired about the range and distribution of South's rebid of One No-Trump. South rebid Two Diamonds to indicate the lower range (15 as opposed to 16* points) and indicating a doubleton spade. With three he would bid Two Spades. North bid game on the strength of his five card suit. West led ♡ J, won in hand with ♡ Q and South played ♠ A and ♠ 4. West won and continued hearts to ♡ K. With eight tricks in sight South next led ◇ 5. West won with ◇ K and noted East's ◇ 4 (his lowest) which discounted any hope of finding him with ◇ A. Therefore West could see that declarer had four spades, three hearts and two diamonds, probably three. The defence needed three tricks to defeat the contract and this would only be possible if East held ♣ K J 10.

---

* Using Crowhurst it is possible to make the rebid of 1NT more fluid (12-16 points).

South had so far shown up with ♠ A = 4, ♡ K Q = 5, and probably ◇ A = 4, total 13. If he held ♣ K J he would have had 17 points and rebid Two No-Trumps over One Spade. With only ♣ K he would have 16 points and shown a maximum No-Trump rebid with Two No-Trumps Therefore West led ♣ 3, East won with ♣ K and returned ♣ J and the defence took three tricks. Admittedly there was no guarantee that East held ♣ 10, but this had to be assumed.

In the next hand partner needed to hold either one of two cards, the possession of which would still be consistent with the bidding.

Dealer South. Love All.

```
              ♠ Q 9
              ♡ Q 8 4
              ◇ K 9 8 5 2
              ♣ K 9 4
♠ J 7 6 5                      ♠ 10 4 3 2
♡ J 10 9 6                     ♡ 7 3 2
◇ A 7 4                        ◇ Q 6
♣ 8 3                          ♣ A Q J 5
              ♠ A K 8
              ♡ A K 5
              ◇ J 10 3
              ♣ 10 7 6 2
```

South	West	North	East
1 ♣	No bid	1 ◇	No bid
1NT	No bid	3NT	All pass

(repeated for convenience)
Dealer South. Love All.

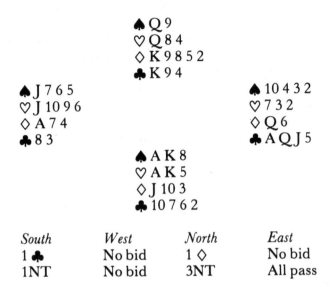

```
                    ♠ Q 9
                    ♡ Q 8 4
                    ◇ K 9 8 5 2
                    ♣ K 9 4
♠ J 7 6 5                              ♠ 10 4 3 2
♡ J 10 9 6                             ♡ 7 3 2
◇ A 7 4                                ◇ Q 6
♣ 8 3                                  ♣ A Q J 5
                    ♠ A K 8
                    ♡ A K 5
                    ◇ J 10 3
                    ♣ 10 7 6 2
```

South	*West*	*North*	*East*
1 ♣	No bid	1 ◇	No bid
1NT	No bid	3NT	All pass

South's rebid showed 15–16 points. West leads ♡ J on which dummy plays ♡ 4. East ♡ 2 and South ♡ K. South next leads ◇ J, West and North play low and East wins with ◇ Q. How should East plan the defence? There is not much future in returning a heart as South is likely to hold ♡ A K. Even if West had led from ♡ A J 10, dummy's ♡ Q would win a trick.

Clubs offer the best chance and it is tempting to return ♣ Q, but this will not be good enough as South is likely to hold four which may well be headed by the ten. South's lead of ◇ J rather suggests that West holds ◇ A, for with ◇ A J 10 South might have laid down ◇ A first in case ◇ Q was single. Therefore, if East when in with ◇ Q, returns ♣ 5 this will leave him with ♣ A Q J over ♣ K 4 and a club lead from West will yield three tricks. That leaves South with ♠ A K = 7, ♡ A K = 7, ◇ J = 1, a total of 15, consistent with his rebid.

Suppose South did hold ◇ A, the return of ♣ 5 will still succeed providing West holds ♠ A. Assuming South holds

$\Diamond$ A and loses the finesse to $\Diamond$ Q, he has four diamonds, three hearts and one club ($\clubsuit$ 9), a total of eight tricks.

If he has $\spadesuit$ A the contract cannot be defeated but if he holds $\spadesuit$ K, even $\spadesuit$ K J, he will have 15–16 points. ($\heartsuit$ A K, $\Diamond$ A J, $\spadesuit$ K or K J) and West can hold $\spadesuit$ A.

The next example features a suit contract

Dealer North. East-West vul.

```
                    ♠ 10 9 8 4
                    ♡ A K
                    ◇ Q 6 3
                    ♣ A K Q J
   ♠ A 6                            ♠ 5 2
   ♡ Q J 10 9 8                     ♡ 7 5 3 2
   ◇ K J 9 4                        ◇ A 8 7
   ♣ 8 5                            ♣ 9 6 3 2
                    ♠ K Q J 7 3
                    ♡ 6 4
                    ◇ 10 5 2
                    ♣ 10 7 4
```

South	West	North	East
–	–	1 $\clubsuit$	No bid
1 $\spadesuit$	No bid	4 $\spadesuit$	All pass

West leads $\heartsuit$ Q. Dummy wins and leads $\spadesuit$ 10, East plays $\spadesuit$ 2, South $\spadesuit$ 3 and West wins with $\spadesuit$ A. Clearly the only chance is to make three tricks in diamonds which presumes East to hold $\Diamond$ A. This still leaves South with a spade suit headed by K Q J (6 points). So West leads $\Diamond$ J, covered by $\Diamond$ Q and $\Diamond$ A, and $\Diamond$ 8 is returned, West holding $\Diamond$ K 9 over $\Diamond$ 10 5.

This hand occurred in a bridge congress in Tunbridge Wells, Kent, in 1955.

Dealer East. North-South vul.

```
              ♠ Q J 9 7 5
              ♡ J 3
              ◇ K 6
              ♣ 7 5 4 3
♠ 4                              ♠ 8
♡ K Q 8 7 4 2                    ♡ 10 6 5
◇ 9 8                            ◇ Q J 10 7 5 4 3
♣ A J 6 2                        ♣ K 9
              ♠ A K 10 6 3 2
              ♡ A 9
              ◇ A 2
              ♣ Q 10 8
```

South	*West*	*North*	*East*
–	–	–	3 ◇
3 ♠	No bid	4 ♠	All pass

South is rather strong for a competitive bid over Three Diamonds but North evidently knew his partner's style. West led ◇ 9, taken with ◇ A, and trumps were drawn in one round. After cashing ◇ K declarer played ♡ A and ♡ 9 to which East followed with ♡ 5 and ♡ 6, indicating an odd number, clearly three. West was now on play needing three tricks to defeat the contract and the only chance lay in clubs. It was essential to lead a low club and this presumed possession of ♣ K by East. With no high honours in either spades or hearts and only queen high in diamonds, East could ♣ K and not be too strong for his pre-emptive opening bid.

On the next hand partner needed to have one of two possible cards and the problem was how to select the right suit to play.

Dealer West. North-South vul.

```
                 ♠ Q 10 6 2
                 ♡ 2
                 ◇ A K Q 8 7 6
                 ♣ 4 3
♠ A 4                              ♠ 7 3
♡ K J 9 7 6 4                      ♡ Q 10 8
◇ 3                               ◇ 9 5 4 2
♣ A Q 10 5                         ♣ K J 8 2
                 ♠ K J 9 8 5
                 ♡ A 5 3
                 ◇ J 10
                 ♣ 9 7 6
```

South	West	North	East
–	1 ♡	2 ◇	2 ♡
2 ♠	4 ♡	4 ♠	All pass

West led ◇ 3 taken with ◇ A, East playing ◇ 2.* West won the first round of trumps and now had to decide wherein lay partner's entry. On the raise to Two Hearts it could well be that East held ♡ A, but this was not certain. If he did not hold ♡ A he must surely hold ♣ K. West, therefore, led ♣ A. When East encouraged with ♣ 8 West continued with ♣ 5 to ♣ K and ruffed the diamond return. Had East discouraged in clubs with ♣ 2 West would have switched to a heart hoping East held ♡ A.

On the next hand it needed a bold underlead to defeat a game contract that was bid sacrificially.

---

* ◇ 2 might be read as a suit preference signal. Holding ♡ A East could play ◇ 9. See page 144.

Dealer South. North-South vul.

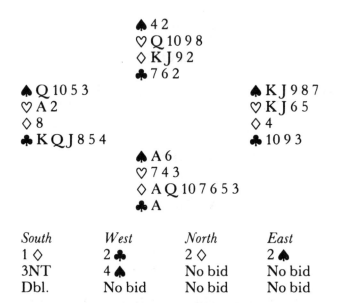

♠ 4 2
♡ Q 10 9 8
◊ K J 9 2
♣ 7 6 2

♠ Q 10 5 3   ♠ K J 9 8 7
♡ A 2   ♡ K J 6 5
◊ 8   ◊ 4
♣ K Q J 8 5 4   ♣ 10 9 3

♠ A 6
♡ 7 4 3
◊ A Q 10 7 6 5 3
♣ A

South	West	North	East
1 ◊	2 ♣	2 ◊	2 ♠
3NT	4 ♠	No bid	No bid
Dbl.	No bid	No bid	No bid

South was almost strong enough for an Acol Two Diamond opening, showing eight playing tricks, but may have preferred a more solid suit. After the raise to Two Diamonds South called Three No-Trumps as it seemed probable that the diamonds would provide seven tricks and the risk of losing many hearts was not great. Placing South with a powerful diamond suit West was not sure of defeating Three No-Trumps and bid Four Spades to save the game.

South led ♣ A to which North played ♣ 2. With three tricks in sight a club ruff was required. On the raise to Two Diamonds North was likely to hold ◊ K so South led ◊ 3 at trick two. North won and returned a club.

In the next hand, apart from the hope that partner holds the right cards, the switch to another suit involved a novel point

Dealer North. East–West vul.

```
                    ♠ J 10 9 8
                    ♡ K Q 7 5
                    ◇ –
                    ♣ K Q J 10 9
  ♠ K 3                              ♠ 4 2
  ♡ 10 4                             ♡ A J 2
  ◇ A 10 7 6 4 2                     ◇ Q J 9 8 5 3
  ♣ 5 4 2                            ♣ A 7
                    ♠ A Q 7 6 5
                    ♡ 9 8 6 3
                    ◇ K
                    ♣ 8 6 3
```

South	*West*	*North*	*East*
–	–	1 ♣	1 ◇
1 ♠	4 ◇	4 ♠	All pass

Although Five Diamonds may only go one down, vulnerability being adverse a possible defeat by two tricks, probably doubled, would cost 500.

West leads ◇ A, ruffed in dummy, East playing ◇ Q indicating possession of ◇ J. It might also suggest values in hearts for reasons that will be explained in a later chapter. South next leads ♠ J from the table and finesses, losing to West.

To defeat the contract it is necessary to make two tricks in hearts plus a club. This presupposes East has ♣ A together with some heart holding as good as A J x. The two heart tricks must be set up before the clubs are established and therefore West must switch to hearts when in with ♠ K. Normally with two cards in a suit the higher card is led but if West leads ♡ 10, covered by ♡ Q and ♡ A, East cannot safely return the suit. If he plays ♡ 2, ♡ 9 will win, and the return of ♡ J will be no more successful. The answer is to lead ♡ 4, covered by ♡ Q and ♡ A. Now East can return ♡ 2 and West's ♡ 10 will force out ♡ K and establish ♡ J. This is an unusual position and illustrates the principle that it is correct to lead the lower card of a doubleton if you are prepared for the suit to be returned. You are in fact leading the suit constructively with a view to establishing tricks rather than showing the possession of a doubleton and hoping to make a ruff.

12. Trump Promotion

This has been defined as the creation of trump tricks through forcing the premature use of trump cards of the opposition. For example

♠ J 9 7 4

♠ Q 2   ♠ 5 3

♠ A K 10 8 6

Spades are trumps and East leads a suit of which both South and West are void. If South ruffs low he is over-trumped. If he ruffs with ♠ A or ♠ K West will make ♠ Q. If South had been able to lead trumps himself ♠ A K would have captured ♠ Q and West would not win a trick.

On this hand the defence were on the right track but made a small error which allowed a game contract to be made.

Dealer South. Love All.

                    ♠ K J 10 7
                    ♡ J 9 5 2
                    ◇ Q J 7
                    ♣ Q J
♠ Q 9 8 6 5 2   ♠ A 3
♡ Q 8   ♡ 10 7
◇ A 5   ◇ K 9 8 6 4 2
♣ 9 6 3   ♣ 10 5 2
                    ♠ 4
                    ♡ A K 6 4 3
                    ◇ 10 3
                    ♣ A K 8 7 4

South	West	North	East
1 ♡	1 ♠	3 ♡	No bid
4 ♡	No bid	No bid	No bid

West led ◇ A and East encouraged with ◇ 9. West continued with ◇ 5 to ◇ K and East returned the suit for his partner to ruff. This he did, but South discarded ♠ 4 and the defenders took no more tricks. East should have cashed ♠ A before leading the third diamond, and West would have made the setting trick with ♡ Q. It was likely that South held a singleton spade as West had overcalled with One Spade on a queen high suit and therefore was likely to hold six.

It is not always an honour card that is promoted. On this hand the defenders took advantage of a careless play by declarer to promote a seven.

Dealer South. Love All.

```
              ♠ A 9 7 5
              ♡ Q J 8 6
              ◇ Q 7 5
              ♣ 9 8
 ♠ 10 8 4 2                    ♠ K J 3
 ♡ 9 2                         ♡ A K 7 5 4
 ◇ J 9 8 2                     ◇ 10 6 3
 ♣ 7 4 2                       ♣ A K
              ♠ Q 6
              ♡ 10 3
              ◇ A K 4
              ♣ Q J 10 6 5 3
```

South	West	North	East
1 ♣	No bid	1 ♡	No bid
2 ♣	No bid	No bid	No bid

West led ♠ 2, ♠ 5 was played from dummy and East won with ♠ K. East next led ♡ A K, West petering high-low, and a third heart was ruffed by South with ♣ 10. South led ♣ 3 on which West played ♣ 4, dummy ♣ 8 and East ♣ K. A further heart was ruffed by South with ♣ J and the next lead of ♣ 5 was covered by ♣ 2, ♣ 9 and ♣ A. West's play of ♣ 4 followed by ♣ 2 was a "three trump echo", indicating the possession of a third trump, so East played another heart. At this point the trump position was

```
              ♣ –
 ♣ 7                      ♣ –
              ♣ Q 6
```

It can be seen that when East led his last heart South had to lose a trump trick. If he ruffed with ♣ 6 he would be over-ruffed with ♣ 7. If he ruffed with ♣ Q, ♣ 7 would be a winner.

Declarer should have played ♠ A at trick one.

It is usually wrong to concede a ruff and discard. That is to say to lead a card that declarer can ruff in either hand and discard from the other. But sometimes it can be clearly seen that there is no useful discard. Such was the case on this hand

Dealer East. East–West vul.

```
            ♠ A Q 4
            ♡ 9 7 6 4
            ◊ A K Q 4
            ♣ 4 3
♠ 10 8 7 2               ♠ 6 5 3
♡ Q 5                   ♡ A
◊ 10 9 6 2              ◊ 8 7 3
♣ 9 6 2                ♣ A K J 10 8 5
            ♠ K J 9
            ♡ K J 10 8 3 2
            ◊ J 5
            ♣ Q 7
```

South	West	North	East
–	–	–	1 ♣
1 ♡	No bid	4 ♡	All pass

West leads ♣ 9 and East wins with ♣ K and cashes ♣ A, South's ♣ Q falling. East can see three tricks for the defence but there is little hope of a trick in either spades or diamonds. Even if West held ♠ K the finesse would be right. Therefore the fourth trick must come from trumps. East continues with a third club in order to remove the last club from West. This concedes a ruff and discard but it is evident that no discard can be of help to declarer. The club is ruffed in dummy and ♡ 4 led. East wins with ♡ A and plays a fourth club which promotes West's ♡ Q. All that was needed was for West to hold either ♡ Q x or ♡ J x x.

Refusal to Over Ruff

An extra trump trick may often be gained by refusal to over ruff. Consider this simple example

$$♡ 8 5 2$$

♡ A J   ♡ 3

$$♡ K Q 10 9 7 6 4$$

Hearts are trumps and East leads a suit of which both South and West are void. If South ruffs with ♡ Q and West over-ruffs with ♡ A it can be seen that ♡ J will fall on ♡ K. But if West discards he will retain ♡ A J over ♡ K 10 and make two tricks. The following hand illustrates the position

Dealer South. North–South vul.

```
              ♠ 8 7 6 5
              ♡ 6 4 3
              ◊ K 9 7 4
              ♣ A 6
♠ K 10 4                        ♠ –
♡ 2                             ◊ A K Q J 10 7 5
◊ Q J 6 5 3                     ◊ 10 8
♣ 9 8 4 2                       ♣ Q J 10 7
              ♠ A Q J 9 3 2
              ♡ 9 8
              ◊ A 2
              ♣ K 5 3
```

South	West	North	East
1 ♠	No bid	2 ♠	4 ♡
4 ♠	No bid	No bid	No bid

South was correct to bid Four Spades over Four Hearts. For one thing, he had a good chance of making Four Spades. For another, he was uncertain whether he could defeat Four Hearts. West led ♡ 2 to ♡ 10. East next led ♡ A and continued with ♡ K. South ruffed with ♠ Q and West over-ruffed with ♠ K, returning a club. South was now able to draw ♠ 10 4 with ♠ A J and make the contract, trumping his losing club on the table. Had West discarded on ♡ K and not over-ruffed ♠ Q with ♠ K he would have held ♠ K 10 4 over ♠ A J 9 and made two tricks.

The next example is less easy to recognise.

Dealer South. Love All.

```
                    ♠ A 7
                    ♡ K 7 6
                    ◊ J 6 3 2
                    ♣ A 8 4 2
   ♠ J 8 5 3                        ♠ Q
   ♡ 10 8 3                         ♡ 9 5 4 2
   ◊ 10 9                           ◊ A K Q 8
   ♣ K 9 7 5                        ♣ Q 10 6 3
                    ♠ K 10 9 6 4 2
                    ♡ A Q J
                    ◊ 7 5 4
                    ♣ J
```

South	West	North	East
1 ♠	No bid	2NT	No bid
3 ♠	No bid	No bid	No bid

(*repeated for convenience*)

```
                    ♠ A 7
                    ♡ K 7 6
                    ◊ J 6 3 2
                    ♣ A 8 4 2
♠ J 8 5 3                              ♠ Q
♡ 10 8 3                               ♡ 9 5 4 2
◊ 10 9                                 ◊ A K Q 8
♣ K 9 7 5                              ♣ Q 10 6 3
                    ♠ K 10 9 6 4 2
                    ♡ A Q J
                    ◊ 7 5 4
                    ♣ J
```

South	West	North	East
1 ♠	No bid	2NT	No bid
3 ♠	No bid	No bid	No bid

West leads ◊ 10 and East takes the diamond continuation and plays ◊ A and ◊ K. South ruffs the fourth diamond with ♠ 9 or ♠ 10 and it is tempting for West to over-ruff with ♠ J. But if he does South will be able to draw his trumps with ♠ A, ♠ K and ♠ 10 (or ♠ 9) to make nine tricks. West should discard. The trump position will now be

```
                    ♠ A 7
♠ J 8 5 3                              ♠ Q
                    ♠ K 10 6 4 2
```

When ♠ 2 is led to ♠ A and ♠ Q falls from East, West is left with ♠ J 8 5 over ♠ K 10 6 and will make an extra trick. The possibility of East holding a singleton honour is quite good. The bidding indicated that South opened on a light hand as he signed off with Three Spades over Two No-Trumps. He probably has a six card suit, but if it had been as good as ♠ K Q 10 9 x x he might well have bid Four Spades and not Three Spades over Two No-Trumps. A sound principle is this: if you have one certain trump trick and a possibility of a second, don't over-ruff.

Uppercut

An uppercut occurs when one defender employs a trump for ruffing, forcing a higher trump from declarer or dummy and in so doing establishes a trump trick for his partner. For example

$$♡7654$$
$$♡Q3 \qquad\qquad ♡J2$$
$$♡AK1098$$

Hearts are trumps and West leads a card of a suit in which both East and South are void. East ruffs with ♡J forcing out ♡K. Had East ruffed with ♡2, South would over-ruff with ♡8 and by leading ♡A and ♡K draw the trumps without loss.

There are various situations where an uppercut can occur. Sometimes it may involve conceding a ruff and discard and sometimes it may require more than one ruff. It is not always an honour that is promoted. Indeed it may be a card as low as the six.

The examples that follow illustrate the various features of the uppercut.

Dealer North. North–South vul.

```
              ♠ A Q 4 3 2
              ♡ J 2
              ◇ 6 5 4
              ♣ A Q 10
♠ K 10                          ♠ J 8 6 5
♡ A 9 7                         ♡ 10 6
◇ A K 10 7 3 2                  ◇ 9 8
♣ 8 5                           ♣ 9 7 6 3 2
              ♠ 9 7
              ♡ K Q 8 5 4 3
              ◇ Q J
              ♣ K J 4
```

South	West	North	East
–	–	1 ♠	No bid
2 ♡	3 ◇	No bid	No bid
3 ♡	No bid	4 ♡	All pass

West leads ◇ A and East encourages with ◇ 9. West continues with ◇ K, East completing a peter with ◇ 8. West can see one sure trick with ♡ A but there is little hope of another as ♠ K is badly placed. If East holds ♣ K (unlikely) it will probably make anyway. West leads a low diamond and East ruffs with ♡ 10, forcing out ♡ Q. South leads ♡ 3 covered by ♡ 7, ♡ J and ♡ 6 but is left with ♡ K 8 under West's ♡ A 9 and must lose two tricks.

Dealer North. Love All.

```
                    ♠ K Q 10 3
                    ♡ Q 9
                    ◊ J 9 8
                    ♣ K Q 9 4
♠ A 9 8                                    ♠ 7 6 5 4
♡ J 10 2                                   ♡ 8 3
◊ A K Q 6 3 2                              ◊ 7 4
♣ 3                                        ♣ J 10 8 7 6
                    ♠ J 2
                    ♡ A K 7 6 5 4
                    ◊ 10 5
                    ♣ A 5 2
```

South	West	North	East
–	–	1 ♣	No bid
1 ♡	3 ◊	No bid	No bid
3 ♡	No bid	4 ♡	All pass

West leads ◊ A K, East playing high–low with ◊ 7 4. West can see one more trick with ♠ A but on the bidding South is likely to hold ♣ A. In any case if East has it he must surely make it. Again the best chance is to promote a trump, so West leads a low diamond to ensure East ruffs. To lead ◊ Q should be all right as there should be a good suit on the Three Diamond overcall, but it is always sound policy to make life easy for partner. East ruffs with ♡ 8 forcing out ♡ K and this serves to promote a trick for West. It is almost invariably correct for a defender, holding useless trumps to ruff with his highest. The last example in this category is

Dealer South. East–West vul.

```
                  ♠ A 4
                  ♡ 8 6 5
                  ◇ A K 10 7
                  ♣ K J 9 7
  ♠ 10 8 3                       ♠ J 2
  ♡ K Q J 9 3                    ♡ A 4
  ◇ 6 5                          ◇ J 9 8 4 2
  ♣ Q 10 6                       ♣ 8 4 3 2
                  ♠ K Q 9 7 6 5
                  ♡ 10 7 2
                  ◇ Q 3
                  ♣ A 5
```

South	West	North	East
South	*West*	*North*	*East*
1 ♠	No bid	2 ♣	No bid
2 ♠	No bid	3 ◇	No bid
3 ♠	No bid	4 ♠	All pass

After South's rebid of Two Spades North might reasonably bid Four Spades but he decided to bid Three Diamonds. When his partner could only reiterate his spades he raised to game.

West led ♡ K and East correctly overtook with ♡ A to unblock and the defence won the first three tricks. As South must surely hold ♣ A to justify his opening bid the only chance of a fourth trick lay in a trump promotion. West led a fourth heart, East ruffing with ♠ J, forcing out ♠ Q and West later made ♠ 10.

It was stated earlier that it is often wrong to lead a card that could be ruffed either in dummy or in declarer's hand. But when it is evident that there is no hope of a trick apart from trumps it may be justified to concede a ruff and discard.

Dealer South. Love All.

```
                  ♠ 7 3
                  ♡ K Q 8 5
                  ◇ A K Q 3 2
                  ♣ 5 4
♠ A 8 5 2                          ♠ 9 4
♡ 6 3                             ♡ J 9 7 4
◇ 7                              ◇ J 8 6 5
♣ A K Q 8 6 3                     ♣ 10 9 7
                  ♠ K Q J 10 6
                  ♡ A 10 2
                  ◇ 10 9 4
                  ♣ J 2
```

South	West	North	East
1 ♠	3 ♣	3 ◇	No bid
3 ♠	No bid	4 ♠	All pass

After North's bid of Three Diamonds over Three Clubs South could only rebid his suit. North, with an opening bid in his own right, raised to Four Spades, hoping his partner held a six card suit.

West led ♣ A K, East following with ♣ 7 and ♣ 9. West could see little hope as South must hold ♡ A for the opening bid. But if partner held a fair sized trump there was a chance. West led a third club, giving a ruff and discard. This could not matter, but it was essential to remove East's last club. South won in dummy and led ♠ 7 to ♠ 10 and ♠ A.

West now led a fourth club which East ruffed with ♠ 9, forcing out ♠ J, leaving West with ♠ 8 5 2 over ♠ K Q 6. Promoting ♠ 8 defeated the contract.

Dealer South. East–West vul.

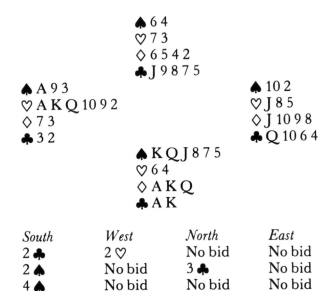

South	West	North	East
2 ♣	2 ♡	No bid	No bid
2 ♠	No bid	3 ♣	No bid
4 ♠	No bid	No bid	No bid

After cashing ♡ A K it is clear to West that the only hope of defeating the contract is to make two trumps. East can hold nothing in high cards but might have a decent sized trump. So West continues with a third heart, giving a ruff and useless discard. South wins in dummy and leads ♠ 6 to ♠ J and ♠ A. A fourth heart is ruffed by East with ♠ 10, forcing out ♠ Q and promoting ♠ 9.

A little perseverence might be required before a trump is promoted.

Dealer West. Love All.

```
              ♠ K 4 3 2
              ♡ 5
              ◇ 7 4 3
              ♣ K J 9 6 3
♠ J 7                           ♠ Q 10 8 6
♡ A 8 6                         ♡ 9 7 2
◇ K J 9 6 5                     ◇ A Q
♣ Q 8 2                         ♣ 10 7 5 4
              ♠ A 9 5
              ♡ K Q J 10 4 3
              ◇ 10 8 2
              ♣ A
```

South	West	North	East
–	1 ◇	No bid	1 ♠
3 ♡	No bid	No bid	No bid

South's Three Hearts bid was strong but not forcing. It would indicate about seven playing tricks and would contain a good six card suit. West led ◇ 6, taken by East with ◇ A, and ◇ Q was returned, overtaken with ◇ K, and ◇ J cashed. As partner could hardly hold many more high cards, West led a low diamond, ruffed with ♡ 9 and over-ruffed with ♡ 10. The trump position then became

```
                    ♡ 5
♡ A 8 6                           ♡ 7 2
                    ♡ K Q J 4 3
```

South leads ♡ K to ♡ A. West leads another low diamond, ruffed by East with ♡ 7, forcing out ♡ J and promoting ♡ 8.

On the next hand a lowly six was promoted.

Dealer South. East-West vul.

```
                    ♠ 7
                    ♡ 10 8 5 4
                    ◇ K 9 2
                    ♣ A K J 9 4
♠ A 6 5                              ♠ 9 8 4
♡ A K Q 7 3                          ♡ 6 2
◇ Q 10 7 3                           ◇ 8 6 4
♣ 3                                  ♣ 8 7 6 5 2
                    ♠ K Q J 10 3 2
                    ♡ J 9
                    ◇ A J 5
                    ♣ Q 10
```

South	West	North	East
1 ♠	2 ♡	3 ♣	No bid
3 ♠	No bid	3NT	No bid
4 ♠	No bid	No bid	No bid

North had a problem after Three Spades. Hoping partner held a heart honour he bid Three No-Trumps but South wisely took it back to Four Spades. West led ♡ A K and followed with ♡ 3 to ♠ 8 and ♠ 10. South led ♠ K to ♠ A and a further heart was ruffed with ♠ 9 and over-ruffed with ♠ J. This left South with ♠ Q and West made the setting trick with ♠ 6.

Careful timing was needed to defeat a part score on this hand from a pairs tournament.

Dealer South. Game All.

```
                    ♠ 5 4
                    ♡ A K 8 7 5
                    ◇ Q 10 7 6
                    ♣ J 2
   ♠ J 3 2                        ♠ 10 9
   ♡ 4 3                          ♡ Q J 6 2
   ◇ A K 3 2                      ◇ 8 4
   ♣ A 9 5 4                      ♣ K 10 8 7 6
                    ♠ A K Q 8 7 6
                    ♡ 10 9
                    ◇ J 9 5
                    ♣ Q 3
```

South	West	North	East
1 ♠	No bid	2 ♡	No bid
2 ♠	No bid	No bid	No bid

West led ◇ A and ◇ K, East following with ◇ 8 and ◇ 4.
West next led ◇ 2 and East ruffed with ♠ 9. He returned
♣ 7 to ♣ A and ◇ 3 was returned. East ruffed with ♠ 10 but
South discarded ♣ Q and made eight tricks.

After ruffing with ♠ 9 East should have led ♣ K followed
by ♣ 7 to ♣ A. Now, ruffing the fourth diamond with ♠ 10
forces ♠ Q from South, establishing West's ♠ J for the
setting trick. The situation is slightly analogous to the
principle of cashing side tricks when playing on a cross ruff.

It is also similar to the position in the hand on p. 113
where it was essential to cash ♠ A before returning a
diamond to promote partner's queen of trumps.

The final examples of the uppercut combine the principle
outlined earlier regarding refusal to over-ruff.

Dealer North. North-South vul.

```
                   ♠ A 3
                   ♡ A 5 4 3
                   ◊ 10 5 4
                   ♣ A K Q 7
♠ Q 10 9 7 2                        ♠ 8 6 4
♡ K 9 8                             ♡ 7
◊ Q 9                               ◊ A K J 8 3
♣ 10 9 4                            ♣ J 6 5 3
                   ♠ K J 5
                   ♡ Q J 10 6 2
                   ◊ 7 6 2
                   ♣ 8 2
```

South	West	North	East
–	–	1 ♣	1 ◊
1 ♡	No bid	3 ♡	No bid
4 ♡	No bid	No bid	No bid

West led ◊ Q and continued with ◊ 9 to ◊ J. East cashed
◊ A, West discarding ♠ 2. With little hope of a spade trick
on West's discouraging discard, the best chance lay in
promoting a trump. East led ◊ K and South ruffed with
♡ Q. Had West covered with ♡ K, losing to ♡ A, his
♡ 9 8 would have been drawn with ♡ J 10. But West
correctly did not over-ruff and subsequently made a trump
trick to defeat the contract.

Dealer North. Love All.

```
                    ♠ K Q J 4
                    ♡ K
                    ◊ A K Q 6 5
                    ♣ 10 9 3
♠ 10 9                              ♠ A 8 7 6 5
♡ A 8 2                             ♡ 9 7 3
◊ 10 7 2                            ◊ J 3
♣ K J 7 6 2                         ♣ A 8 4
                    ♠ 3 2
                    ♡ Q J 10 6 5 4
                    ◊ 9 8 4
                    ♣ Q 5
```

South	West	North	East
–	–	1 ◊	No bid
1 ♡	No bid	1 ♠	No bid
2 ♡	No bid	2NT	No bid
3 ♡	No bid	No bid	No bid

North had a problem over Two Hearts. With 18 high card points he was entitled to bid again and Two No-Trumps was probably restrained, but with no club stopper and singleton ♡ K the hand needed to be devalued. A possible alternative to Two No-Trumps would be Three Clubs, fourth suit forcing, to find out more of partner's hand but this would only bring forth Three Hearts.

West led ♣ 6 taken with ♣ A and ♣ 8 was returned to ♣ Q and ♣ K. South ruffed ♣ J and led ♡ 4 to ♡ K which won. To return to hand the ♠ K was led, taken with ♠ A and ♠ 6 was returned to ♠ 9 and ♠ J. A third spade was ruffed in hand with ♡ 10 and West did not over-ruff, discarding a club. South next led ♡ Q which West won with ♡ A and led a club. East ruffed with ♡ 9, forcing out ♡ J and leaving West with ♡ 8 as a winner.

13. Active and Passive Defence

If you are defending a contract, say Four Spades, there are two ways of going about it. One is to set out to win four tricks (active defence) and the other is to wait for declarer to lose four tricks (passive defence). The occasions when an active form of defence is needed is where there is evidence of a long suit that may provide discards of losers. Referring back to the first chapter about opening leads it was recommended that an attacking lead was advisable if the bidding suggested the presence of a long suit. If the contract were a small slam in a suit the need for an attacking lead was great. It was important to establish a winner that could be cashed if declarer had to lose the lead before making his twelve tricks. After the opening lead has been made and the dummy hand exposed the need to switch the attack may be evident, whether the final contract is in a suit or no trumps. Examples of this were given in earlier chapters. A passive type of defence is correct where the bidding suggests that there is little to spare. Against a small slam contract in no trumps it is unwise to lead away from unsupported honours as it is unlikely that partner holds any high cards. You should endeavour to select the lead that is least likely to help the other side and hope that two tricks come your way.

After dummy has been revealed the decision to play a passive type of defence is influenced largely by the absence of a long suit. If the supporting hand has little if anything to spare, declarer is likely to have a difficult task to make the contract and any help he may get from the defence may provide him with the trick he needs. A common error with beginners and average players is to keep switching suits. If the initial lead does not meet with immediate success they try another. If this does not succeed they try another. In so doing they are likely to give away unnecessary tricks. Only switch if it is obvious that time is not on your side.

This hand occurred in a county tournament.

Dealer South. Love All.

```
                    ♠ A 9 4 2
                    ♡ K Q 4
                    ◇ J 9 3
                    ♣ 10 6 4
    ♠ 10 3                          ♠ 7 6 5
    ♡ A J 3                         ♡ 10 9 8
    ◇ A 10 6 2                      ◇ Q 8 7 4
    ♣ 9 8 7 3                       ♣ K Q 5
                    ♠ K Q J 8
                    ♡ 7 6 5 2
                    ◇ K 5
                    ♣ A J 2
```

South	West	North	East
1 ♠	No bid	3 ♠	No bid
4 ♠	No bid	No bid	No bid

West led ♣ 9 covered by ♣ 4, ♣ Q and ♣ A. South drew trumps with ♠ K Q J, West discarding ♣ 3. South next led ♣ 2 to ♣ 10 and ♣ K. At this point East returned ◇ 4, South played low and West won with ◇ A, returning ◇ 2 which East ducked, and South won with ◇ K. With ♡ A favourably placed the contract was made. East presented South with his vital trick when he led back a diamond. Had he played a club South would eventually have been forced to lead a diamond from the table and hope to make the king. How was East to know? Dummy had a balanced ten points. No long suit and no ruffing value. Unless South had a lot to spare the contract was likely to be difficult, possibly depending upon some assistance from the opposition.

On this hand, despite a combined count of twenty six high card points, game in No-Trumps proved to be impossible against a solid passive defence.

Dealer South. North-South vul.

```
                    ♠ J 3 2
                    ♡ A Q 10 8 2
                    ◇ 10 2
                    ♣ Q 3 2
        ♠ 8 7 6                        ♠ A 10 9 4
        ♡ 9 5 3                        ♡ K 7 6
        ◇ K J 6 5                      ◇ 9 8 3
        ♣ 10 7 6                       ♣ K 9 5
                    ♠ K Q 5
                    ♡ J 4
                    ◇ A Q 7 4
                    ♣ A J 8 4
```

South	West	North	East
1 ◇	No bid	1 ♡	No bid
2NT	No bid	3NT	All pass

Ruling out a diamond lead after South's opening bid West led ♠ 8, an unbid major. Dummy played ♠ 2 and East ♠ 4. The lead was clearly not fourth best (rule of eleven) and East wished to retain ♠ A over ♠ J. South won with ♠ Q and led ♡ J on which West played ♡ 3, dummy ♡ 2 and East ♡ 6. South continued with ♡ 4, covered by ♡ 5, ♡ 10 and taken with ♡ K. As West played hearts upwards (♡ 3 and later ♡ 5) he was marked with an odd number (three) so East knew South had only two originally.

East returned ◇ 9. This would suggest no honours in the suit. He could not afford to play a spade as this would provide an entry to dummy. South played ◇ 4 and West won with ◇ J, leading back ♠ 7. When ♠ 3 was played from the table East played ♠ 9 and South won with ♠ K. There was now no way to get to dummy. South tried ♣ 4 to ♣ Q but East won with ♣ K. After cashing ♠ A 10 he returned a diamond and the contract ended two down.

Careful defence was needed to defeat a part score on this hand.

Dealer South. Love All.

```
                    ♠ J 8 4 2
                    ♡ J 5
                    ◇ 10 6 3
                    ♣ Q 8 6 3
  ♠ K 3                              ♠ A 7 6
  ♡ 9 8 7 6                          ♡ K 10 3 2
  ◇ 7 5 4 2                          ◇ A 9 8
  ♣ K 9 2                            ♣ A 10 7
                    ♠ Q 10 9 5
                    ♡ A Q 4
                    ◇ K Q J
                    ♣ J 5 4
```

South	West	North	East
1 ♠	No bid	No bid	Dbl.
No bid	2 ♡	2 ♠	All pass

West led ♡ 9 and South won with ♡ Q. There appeared to be eight tricks if a club trick could be made. South led ♠ 5, won by West who returned a heart to ♡ A. South ruffed a heart in dummy and led ♠ J. East won and returned his last trump, West discarding a diamond. South forced out ◇ A but the suit was returned and eventually South had to open up the clubs. He tried ♣ 4 to ♣ Q and ♣ A but was left with ♣ J 5 under West's ♣ K 9. Had the defence either led a club or discarded one the contract would probably have been made.

Discarding

Many contracts are made through careless discards by the defence. It is all too easy when holding a worthless hand to lose interest and feel that it will make no difference what you throw. Two guiding principles which may be helpful are these

1. Do not discard from a four card suit if dummy also has four of that suit, e.g.

♠ A K 6 4

♠ J 10 8   ♠ 7 5 3 2

♠ Q 9

Assume the contract is No-Trumps and South plays a suit to which East cannot follow. It may seem harmless to discard a spade but it will be fatal. South leads ♠ Q and ♠ 9, cashing ♠ A. If East has parted with ♠ 2 dummy's last spade is a winner.

2. Do not discard from a suit where declarer has a two way finesse, e.g.

◊ K J 10 9

◊ 6 3 2

East may well consider his diamonds are of no value, but if he discards them he may disclose the position of ◊ Q, South holding ◊ A. Neglect of this principle allowed an under-pointed game to slip through.

Dealer South. Game All.

♠ A J 10 4
♡ 6 5 2
◊ K J 3
♣ A 6 4

♠ Q 8 3 2   ♠ K 9 5
♡ J 10 9   ♡ K Q 8 7
◊ 7 6 5   ◊ Q 9 8 4
♣ 5 3 2   ♣ K 7

♠ 7 6
♡ A 4 3
◊ A 10 2
♣ Q J 10 9 8

South	*West*	*North*	*East*
No bid	No bid	1 ♠	No bid
2NT	No bid	3NT	All pass

North had little justification for bidding Three No-Trumps but he was keen not to miss a vulnerable game. West led ♡ J, East encouraged with ♡ 8 and South played low. South won the third round of hearts and led ♣ Q, the finesse losing to East, who cashed ♡ K and passively returned ♣ 7. On East's winning heart South discarded ♠ 6, West ♠ 2 and dummy ♠ 4. South then played off his three winning clubs and West, imbued with the idea that he must keep cover for his queen of spades, discarded ◇ 5 and ◇ 6. Dummy discarded ♠ 10 and ◇ J and East ◇ 4, ♠ 5 and ♠ 9. South led ◇ 2 to ◇ K and returned ◇ 3, successfully finessing ◇ 10.

Admittedly, each defender was in difficulties having to find discards. West should have known his partner held ♠ K. If South had it he had nine sure tricks. South must hold ◇ A because East would have cashed it for the setting trick when in with ♣ K. Therefore if South held ♠ K, ♡ A, ◇ A and ♣ A J he would have had fourteen points and would have opened the bidding. So West should have held on to his three little diamonds and left ♠ Q single. East, needing to find three discards, should throw ♠ 5 and ◇ 8 4. This is likely to leave declarer with the impression that ◇ Q is with West and cause him to finesse unsuccessfully. The value of counting declarer's points will be explained in a later chapter.

When there is a long suit and discards will need to be found it is important to indicate early which suit you can protect so that you and your partner do not discard from the same suit. The discard of a high card is the normal signal to show strength in a suit.

On this hand West was saved an awkward guess by his partner's helpful discard.

Dealer South. Love All.

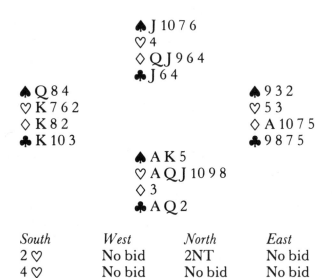

South	West	North	East
2 ♡	No bid	2NT	No bid
4 ♡	No bid	No bid	No bid

South, having opened with an Acol Two Bid, thought it would place too much strain on partner to raise to game if he merely rebid Three Hearts.

Holding defensive values West made a passive lead of ♡ 2. South won with ♡ 8 and played ♡ A and ♡ Q. West won and returned his last trump. South next played ♠ A, ♠ K and ♠ 5 putting West on lead, with only diamonds and clubs left. Had he led a club, dummy's ♣ J would have won and ♠ J would be the tenth trick. But East had discarded ◊ 7 early and this enabled West to lead a diamond safely and the defence took one trick in each suit.

14. Counting Declarer's Points

One of the factors that go towards planning a successful defence is the ability to place the unseen cards. The most obvious example of knowing the cards held by partner is the information given by an opening lead, particularly an honour card that is the top of a sequence.

But much information can be gained by counting the points known to be held by declarer when he has made a limit bid, e.g. No-Trumps. Take a simple example. South having opened with a weak No-Trump (12–14 points) is declarer in Three No-Trumps. You lead a heart and dummy's ♡ K takes the trick.

Declarer plays off some high cards totalling nine points. He is known to hold ♡ A as partner did not play it on the king, so this brings the total to thirteen. Therefore any queen or higher honour that is not visible either in your hand or dummy must be with your partner. Otherwise declarer would be in excess of his points for the opening bid.

Similarly, declarer opens a strong No Trump (16–18) and his partner raises to Three No-Trump and puts down nine high card points. Opponents therefore have between 25–27 points between them. If you hold a blank hand with no honour cards do not be too disheartened, and above all do not look bored and start moaning about the abysmal cards you always hold. Your partner must have 13 or 14 points and it is up to you to play as carefully as possible so as not to expose all his honour cards to finesses.

In the same way, if in similar circumstances you hold 14 points you must realise that your partner holds nothing and it will be up to you to win all the tricks of your side.

On this hand poor play by declarer helped the defence to find the right line.

Dealer South. Love All.

```
                    ♠ A K J 5
                    ♡ 9 6
                    ◇ J 8 7
                    ♣ 10 6 5 4
  ♠ 7 6 2                            ♠ Q 10 3
  ♡ Q J 5 4                          ♡ 10 8 3 2
  ◇ K 6 5 2                          ◇ A Q 3
  ♣ 7 2                              ♣ Q 9 3
                    ♠ 9 8 4
                    ♡ A K 7
                    ◇ 10 9 4
                    ♣ A K J 8
```

South	West	North	East
1 ♣	No bid	1 ♠	No bid
1NT	No bid	2NT	No bid
3NT	No bid	No bid	No bid

Playing a weak opening No-Trump, South's rebid showed 15–16 points. North was just entitled to raise to Two No-Trumps but South should pass having the minimum for his rebid.

West led ♡ 4 on which dummy played ♡ 6, East ♡ 8 and South ♡ 7. East returned ♡ 2, South won with ♡ A and played ♣ A. He next crossed to dummy with ♠ A and led ♣ 5 and successfully finessed ♣ J, all following. He continued with ♠ 8 and finessed ♠ J, losing to East. East counted South for ♣ A K J (8 points) and it was clear he held ♡ A K (7 points). He could not hold ◇ K as that would bring his total to 18 and his rebid would have been Two No-Trumps. East accordingly switched to ◇ A and ◇ Q and the contract was two down.

South's play was poor. He should win the first trick for fear of a diamond switch. Furthermore he should win with ♡ K which would be consistent with a holding such as ♡ K Q x, leaving West with ♡ A J x x. In this event he might hold ◇ K for a total of 16 points, consistent with his final bid of Three No-Trumps. East might then return a heart when in with ♠ Q. Finally, taking ♡ 2 with ♡ A was silly as it marked him with ♡ A K. West would not lead ♡ 4 from ♡ K Q J 4.

A count of declarer's points enabled the defence to put a vulnerable contract of One No-Trump two down for an excellent score in a duplicate pairs tournament.

Dealer South. Game All.

```
                    ♠ J 7 6 2
                    ♡ 9 6 4
                    ◇ K 3
                    ♣ 7 6 4 2
♠ Q 8 5                             ♠ A K 9 4
♡ A Q 7 5                           ♡ J 8 2
◇ Q J 2                             ◇ 10 9 5 4
♣ J 10 5                            ♣ K 3
                    ♠ 10 3
                    ♡ K 10 3
                    ◇ A 8 7 6
                    ♣ A Q 9 8
```

South	West	North	East
1NT	No bid	No bid	No bid

South was one of those intrepid players, whose boldness outweighs their wisdom, in playing a weak No-Trump vulnerable. West led ♡ 5 covered by ♡ 4, ♡ J and ♡ K. South led ◇ 6 to ◇ K and returned ♣ 2, successfully finessing ♣ Q. He cashed ♣ A and led a third round, losing to ♣ J, East discarding ♡ 2. South had so far shown up with ♡ K (3 points) ♣ A Q (6 points) and presumably held ◇ A (4 points) as East did not take ◇ K, a total of 13 points, on a 12–14 No Trump bid. West therefore reasoned that East must hold ♠ A K and so led ♠ 5. East won with ♠ K; he also could count and knew South would have fifteen points if he

(repeated for convenience)

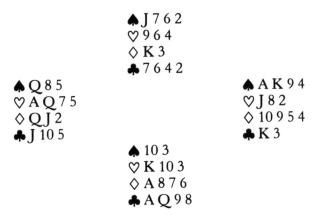

```
                    ♠ J 7 6 2
                    ♡ 9 6 4
                    ◇ K 3
                    ♣ 7 6 4 2
    ♠ Q 8 5                        ♠ A K 9 4
    ♡ A Q 7 5                      ♡ J 8 2
    ◇ Q J 2                        ◇ 10 9 5 4
    ♣ J 10 5                       ♣ K 3
                    ♠ 10 3
                    ♡ K 10 3
                    ◇ A 8 7 6
                    ♣ A Q 9 8
```

held ♠ Q. So East returned ♠ 4 covered by ♠ 10, ♠ Q and ♠ 6. East now held ♠ A 9 over dummy's ♠ J 7 and the defence took four tricks in spades, three in hearts and one in clubs, defeating the contract by two for the excellent score of 200.

15. Counting Distribution

It is also important to try and count the distribution of declarer's hand. Some inferences may be obtained from the bidding. For example

South	West	North	East
1 ♡	No bid	2 ◇	No bid
2NT	No bid	3 ♡	No bid
3NT	No bid	No bid	No bid

North's Three Hearts indicated three card support and offered an option between Four Hearts and Three No-Trumps. When South rebid Three No-Trumps he would have a four card suit.

Another example

South	West	North	East
1 ♡	No bid	2 ◇	No bid
2 ♠	No bid	2NT	No bid
3 ♠	No bid	4 ♠	All pass

When South rebid Two Spades on the second round he indicated that he held more hearts than spades and a good hand. At that point he could be 5–4 (i.e. five hearts and four spades). When he rebid Three Spades he must hold five spades and as hearts were the longer suit he must hold at least six hearts and five spades.

Counting the distribution from the cards played is less easy. It is often regarded as being the prerogative of the expert just as counting the hand is declarer's. In fact it is not so difficult. It is very important to be able to do so when you find yourself in a difficult position towards the end of a hand. It is generally impressed upon beginners that it is wrong to give a ruff and discard, but as we saw in the chapter on trump promotion there were times when the ruff and discard was harmless. So before you panic and lead a suit that gives declarer his vital extra trick try and count up his hand. Here are two examples.

Dealer South. Game All.

```
                    ♠ 10 9 7 3
                    ♡ A 5
                    ◇ K 9 6 4
                    ♣ K J 8
♠ Q 8 4                                  ♠ 5
♡ K Q J 8                                ♡ 10 9 7 6 4 3
◇ J 7 5                                  ◇ Q 8
♣ 7 6 2                                  ♣ 10 9 4 3
                    ♠ A K J 6 2
                    ♡ 2
                    ◇ A 10 3 2
                    ♣ A Q 5
```

South	West	North	East
1 ♠	No bid	3 ♠	No bid
4 ♣	No bid	4 ♡	No bid
6 ♠	No bid	No bid	No bid

West led ♡ K, taken with ♡ A and ♠ A K were played off but declarer was disappointed when East discarded a heart. With a loser in trumps some way had to be found of avoiding a loser in diamonds, and this might be achieved if the opponents could be lured into leading the suit. South crossed to dummy with ♣ K and led ♡ 5, ruffing in hand. He next cashed ♣ A Q, all following, and led a spade. West won with ♠ Q and East discarded his fourth club, a helpful move.

West knew that a heart would give declarer the chance to ruff in one hand and discard from the other so rather than do that he led ◇ 5 hoping for the best. Dummy played ◇ 4, East ◇ Q and South ◇ A. South next led ◇ 10 and finessed against West for ◇ J and made the slam. Before making that panic lead of a diamond West should have tried to build a picture of declarer's hand.

He was known to hold five spades because East discarded on the second round. So mentally you record ♠ A K J x x.

South ruffed dummy's low heart so you can add ♡ x. That is six cards accounted for. South played three rounds of clubs and when East helpfully discarded his fourth club on the trump lead it was known that South held ♣ A Q x. That is nine cards so he must have four diamonds. If these are headed by A Q there is nothing to be done. But if East has ◇ Q x you will take a trick between you *providing you do not open up the suit*. Therefore lead a heart as a ruff and discard cannot help the declarer.

Another example.

Dealer North. Love All.

```
                 ♠ K J 8 5
                 ♡ 8 4
                 ◇ K 8 5
                 ♣ A J 8 2
   ♠ 9 7 3                      ♠ 10
   ♡ K 10 5 3 2                 ♡ Q J 9 7 6
   ◇ Q J 10                     ◇ 9 6 3 2
   ♣ 10 4                       ♣ Q 5 3
                 ♠ A Q 6 4 2
                 ♡ A
                 ◇ A 7 4
                 ♣ K 9 7 6
```

South	West	North	East
–	–	1 ♣	No bid
2 ♠	No bid	3 ♠	No bid
4 ♣	No bid	4 ♠	No bid
4NT	No bid	5 ◇	No bid
6 ♠	No bid	No bid	No bid

West leads ◇ Q. The trumps are solid and there is no losing heart. But there is a losing diamond which seems to indicate that the slam may depend on the club finesse. Rather than gamble on the finesse some effort should be made to induce opponents to play clubs.

(*repeated for convenience*)

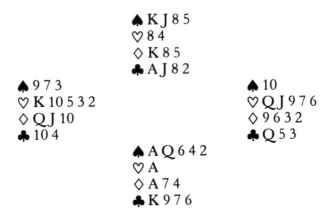

South wins with ◇ A and draws trumps in three rounds, East discarding ♡ 7 6. After cashing ♡ A dummy is entered with ◇ K, East following with ◇ 2, completing a peter having played ◇ 3 on the first round. South next ruffs ♡ 8 in hand and exits with a diamond, putting West on lead with ◇ J. It is tempting now to lead ♣ 10 as a heart would concede a ruff and discard. But ♣ 10 would be covered by ♣ J, ♣ Q and ♣ K and South would be spared the anxiety of the club finesse.

Again, before making the panic lead of ♣ 10 West should try and reconstruct South's hand. He started with five spades as East followed once only. He had one heart as he ruffed the second. He also held three diamonds as East indicated a four card holding, playing ◇ 3 on the first round and ◇ 2 on the second. That leaves South with four clubs. If West leads a heart giving a ruff and discard, South will have to rely on the club finesse and is likely to finesse ♣ J and lose, as he does not hold ♣ 10.

16. Suit Preference Signals

This most important conventional signal to ensure co-operation between the two defending partners was originated by Hy Lavinthal of Trenton, New Jersey, U.S.A. as far back as 1934. The convention was later popularized by Walter E. McKenney, secretary of the American Contract Bridge League and in Europe the signal is often referred to as "McKenney".

It comprises the play, lead or discard of an unnecessarily high or low card, directing partner to play either the higher ranking or lower ranking of the two possible remaining suits. Some examples may serve to illustrate the various situations where the signal can be applied.

(a) *Returning the Lead*
Dealer South. Love All.

```
            ♠ J 7 2
            ♡ Q J 4
            ◇ 5 4 3
            ♣ K Q J 2
♠ 9 6 5                      ♠ 8 3
♡ 10 8 6                     ♡ A 7 5 3
◇ Q 10 9 8 6 2               ◇ J 7
♣ 3                          ♣ A 10 9 5 4
            ♠ A K Q 10 4
            ♡ K 9 2
            ◇ A K
            ♣ 8 7 6
```

South	West	North	East
1 ♠	No bid	2 ♠	No bid
4 ♠	No bid	No bid	No bid

North–South were playing five card major suits so that North knew South held five spades. West led ♣ 3 covered by ♣ J and ♣ A. East could reasonably assume that the lead was a singleton and that West would ruff a club return. After that, if West returned a heart East would win and lead back another club for West to ruff. The suit preference signal is the answer.

(*repeated for convenience*)

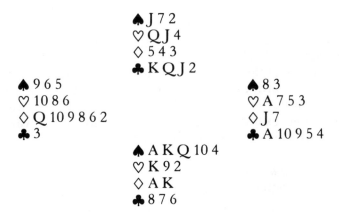

Having ruffed the club West is bound to switch as he has no clubs. As it is unlikely that a trump lead will be effective it leaves two possible suits for West to play. These are hearts and diamonds. Hearts is the higher ranking suit so East returns ♣ 10, his highest available club to suggest the return of the higher of the suits in dummy, hearts as opposed to diamonds. Had East held ◊ A he would return ♣ 4, his lowest, to request return of the lower ranking suit.

Dealer East. Love All.

```
                    ♠ K J 8 3
                    ♡ A K 6 3
                    ◊ J 9 6 4
                    ♣ 3
♠ 7 6 4 2                            ♠ A 10 9
♡ 10 7 2                             ♡ 4
◊ 3                                 ◊ A 10 8 7 2
♣ Q 10 9 7 2                        ♣ K J 8 6
                    ♠ Q 5
                    ♡ Q J 9 8 5
                    ◊ K Q 5
                    ♣ A 5 4
```

South	West	North	East
–	–	–	1 ◊
1 ♡	No bid	4 ♡	All pass

West leads ◊ 3 and East wins with ◊ A. South following with ◊ 5 thereby making it easy for East to read the lead as a singleton. West would not lead ◊ 3 from ◊ K Q 3. In order to guide West into returning a spade, East leads back ◊ 10, a high diamond requesting the return of the higher of the remaining suits. West cannot lead a diamond and hearts, being trumps, are excluded. That leaves a choice of two suits, spades and clubs. The return of ◊ 10 (high) asks for the higher ranking suit (spades).

Good defence defeated a doubled contract by two tricks on this hand.

Dealer North. Game All.

```
                    ♠ 8
                    ♡ Q 10 8 4
                    ◊ J 7 6 4
                    ♣ J 6 3 2
♠ Q 9 3                              ♠ J 10
♡ K J 9 5 3                          ♡ –
◊ A Q 5 2                            ◊ K 10 9 8 3
♣ 4                                  ♣ A Q 10 9 8 5
                    ♠ A K 7 6 5 4 2
                    ♡ A 7 6 2
                    ◊ –
                    ♣ K 7
```

South	West	North	East
–	–	No bid	1 ♣
4 ♠	Dble	All pass	

South might have doubled the opening bid but this would have led to a contract of Four Hearts with an adverse 5–0 trump split.

(*repeated for convenience*)

Dealer North. Game All.

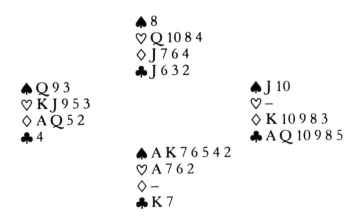

West led ♣4 taken by East with ♣A and ♣10 was returned asking for the higher suit (hearts). West duly led back a low heart and East ruffed. Another club promoted West's ♠Q and the defence still had to make a heart trick for a total of five tricks. Final example

Dealer East. North–South vul.

```
                    ♠ A 8 4
                    ♡ 4
                    ◊ K Q 8 7 5
                    ♣ Q J 7 3
    ♠ 3 2                              ♠ 7 6 5
    ♡ A Q J 10 8 7                     ♡ K 6 3
    ◊ J 10 9 3                         ◊ 4 2
    ♣ 2                                ♣ A 9 6 5 4
                    ♠ K Q J 10 9
                    ♡ 9 5 2
                    ◊ A 6
                    ♣ K 10 8
```

South	West	North	East
–	–	–	No bid
1 ♠	2 ♡	3 ♢	3 ♡
3 ♠	No bid	4 ♠	All pass

West leads ♣ 2, almost certainly a singleton and East wins, returning ♣ 9 (highest available). West ruffs and leads ♡ 7, won by East, and a second club ruff defeats the contract.

(b) *Following Suit*

The play of an unnecessarily high or low card when following suit to the opening lead can be used as a suit preference signal, providing only that no more simple interpretation can make sense.

For example

$$\diamondsuit\ 7\ 5\ 2$$

♢ A

Against a spade contract West leads ♢ A and East follows with ♢ 3. This simply means that East has no interest in diamonds. He has no potential winner, he cannot ruff, and suggests a switch. It does not suggest a switch to any particular suit. The suit preference signal is liable to abuse. Players treat every card played as a McKenney. If a card is capable of bearing a simple meaning of encouragement or discouragement that should be the interpretation. Only if it is clear that the player on lead is certain to switch at the following trick should the card played to the lead be interpreted as a suit preference signal.

In the two examples that follow there should be no confusion.

Dealer North. East–West vul.

```
                    ♠ 9
                    ♡ 7 6
                    ◇ A K Q 9 7 5
                    ♣ Q 9 4 3
♠ Q 7 4 3 2                             ♠ A J 8 6
♡ J 10 9 8 4                            ♡ Q 5 3 2
◇ 2                                     ◇ J 10 4 3
♣ A 5                                   ♣ 6
                    ♠ K 10 5
                    ♡ A K
                    ◇ 8 6
                    ♣ K J 10 8 7 2
```

South	West	North	East
–	–	1 ◇	No bid
2 ♣	No bid	3 ♣	No bid
5 ♣	No bid	No bid	No bid

South considered Three No-Trumps, which would be made on a heart lead, but not on a spade. West led ◇ 2 and East, reading this as a singleton, played ◇ J, an unnecessarily high card, to indicate wherein lay his entry. West won the first round of trumps and duly led a spade as East's ◇ J asked for the higher of the two suits (spades and hearts). There it was clear that West, if and when he got in, would be unable to play another diamond.

Dealer South. Game All.

```
                    ♠ J 8 7 6 5
                    ♡ J 9
                    ◇ K 2
                    ♣ K 10 8 6
  ♠ Q 4 3 2                          ♠ A K
  ♡ 6 4 3                            ♡ 2
  ◇ 10 9 6 5 3                       ◇ Q J 8 7 4
  ♣ A                                ♣ 9 7 5 4 2
                    ♠ 10 9
                    ♡ A K Q 10 8 7 5
                    ◇ A
                    ♣ Q J 3
```

South	*West*	*North*	*East*
2 ♡	No bid	2NT	No bid
3 ♡	No bid	4 ♡	All pass

West leads ♣ A. It is not usually good play to lead an unsupported ace and with ♣ K in dummy it appears to be a singleton. Therefore East follows with ♣ 9, his highest club, to direct a switch to spades (higher suit). Again, this cannot be an encouraging card as West will be unable to lead the suit again.

(c) *Leading*

Sometimes the initial lead can be read as a signal. This usually occurs where the leader's partner is void and consequently will have to play back a different suit. The successful defence on this hand from a duplicate pairs tournament was due largely to the inference drawn by the player with the opening lead.

Dealer North. Love All.

```
              ♠ 7
              ♡ J 8 7
              ◊ A K 10 7 3
              ♣ Q J 9 5
♠ 6 4 3                        ♠ K J 9 8 5
♡ A 6 5                        ♡ K 10 4
◊ Q 9 8 6 2                    ◊ —
♣ A 3                          ♣ K 10 7 6 2
              ♠ A Q 10 2
              ♡ Q 9 3 2
              ◊ J 5 4
              ♣ 8 4
```

South	*West*	*North*	*East*
–	–	1 ◊	Dbl.
Redbl.	1NT	No bid	No bid
2 ◊	Dbl.	No bid	No bid
2 ♡	Dbl.	All pass	

South would have done better to double West's One No-Trump. With nine points and his partner having opened, his side held the balance of strength and would expect to win the balance of tricks. However, we are not so much concerned with the bidding as the defence against the doubled contract of Two Hearts. With diamonds bid and supported East was likely to be short and, hoping he was void, West led ◊ 2. East ruffed and correctly interpreted the lead of the very low diamond as suggesting a club return. The contract ended up two down.

The next example was also based on the expectation of partner being void in the suit led, but in this case the situation was easier to recognize owing to a conventional double.

Dealer South. North–South vul.

```
              ♠ 7
              ♡ 8 5
              ◇ Q 9 6 5
              ♣ A Q J 7 6 2
♠ K Q J 10 6 2                    ♠ 9 8 4 3
♡ –                              ♡ 10 7 6 2
◇ A J 2                          ◇ 10 8 7 4 3
♣ 10 9 8 3                       ♣ –
              ♠ A 5
              ♡ A K Q J 9 4 3
              ◇ K
              ♣ K 5 4
```

South	West	North	East
2 ♡	3 ♠	4 ♣	4 ♠
4NT	No bid	5 ◇	No bid
6 ♡	No bid	No bid	Dbl.
No bid	No bid	No bid	

East's double was a "Lightner" double, a convention introduced by the late Theodore A. Lightner, a member of the Culbertson team some fifty years ago. The double implied that the contract might be defeated if West made an "unusual" lead. In other words neither a spade, the suit bid by the defenders, nor a trump. It probably requested a club lead, the suit bid by dummy, East being void. As the opponents had stopped in a little slam, they expected to lose a trick, but not a first round ruff. There was therefore a fair expectation of another defensive winner.

Anticipating that his partner would ruff the opening club lead it was necessary to ensure that the right suit was returned. If partner tried a spade, hoping that the spade bid included an ace the result would be fatal. West led ♣ 3, his lowest available club. East duly ruffed and returned a diamond, the lower suit as opposed to spades, and a second club ruff defeated the slam by two tricks. East–West have a cheap sacrifice in Six Spades, but defeating the slam is more satisfactory.

(d) *No-Trumps*

The suit preference signal can also be used in No-Trumps. It might seem that the choice is wider as there is no trump suit to exclude, but in most cases the position is clear.

Dealer South. Love All.

```
                    ♠ K J 6
                    ♡ 10 7 4
                    ◊ A Q 10 7 4 2
                    ♣ 6
    ♠ A 2                              ♠ 9 8 5 4 3
    ♡ K J 9 6 5 3                      ♡ Q 2
    ◊ 8 3                              ◊ K 5
    ♣ 7 4 3                            ♣ J 10 9 5
                    ♠ Q 10 7
                    ♡ A 8
                    ◊ J 9 6
                    ♣ A K Q 8 2
```

South	*West*	*North*	*East*
1 ♣	1 ♡	2 ◊	No bid
2NT	No bid	3NT	All pass

East might have doubled Three No-Trumps to demand a lead of his partner's suit. As it was West led ♡ 6 and ♡ Q won. East returned ♡ 2, won by South, West playing low. South next led ◊ J and the finesse lost to East who had no heart to return and had to guess how to get his partner in. Not unnaturally he led ♣ J to the weak suit on the table and nine tricks were made.

West should have played ♡ K or ♡ J on the second trick. This unnecessarily high card would indicate that his entry lay in the higher of the two possible suits. Diamonds could obviously be excluded, leaving spades (higher suit) and clubs (lower suit)

Dealer South. North–South vul.

```
                ♠ 7 4 3
                ♡ K J 9
                ◊ A J 10 9 6
                ♣ 6 3
♠ Q 10 8 6 2                      ♠ A K
♡ A 7 4                          ♡ 6 5 3 2
◊ 7 4 2                          ◊ 5 3
♣ 7 2                            ♣ 10 9 8 5 4
                ♠ J 9 5
                ♡ Q 10 8
                ◊ K Q 8
                ♣ A K Q J
```

South	West	North	East
1 ♣	No bid	1 ◊	No bid
2NT	No bid	3NT	All pass

West leads ♠ 6, East wins with ♠ A and follows with ♠ K. Normal practice is to win with the lower of equal cards so East's play would indicate that ♠ A K were alone. That being so East will be unable to play a third spade and will have to switch. Using the suit preference signal West puts ♠ 10 on ♠ K, a high card to indicate an entry in hearts, the higher suit.

This hand occurred in the annual University match between Oxford and Cambridge.

Dealer North. Love All.

```
                    ♠ Q 7
                    ♡ 6 3
                    ◇ A K Q J 7 2
                    ♣ K 10 8
♠ 9 8 5 3 2                           ♠ A K J
♡ J 9 8                               ♡ 10 7 5 4
◇ 10 3                                ◇ 9 6 5
♣ A 9 5                               ♣ Q 6 2
                    ♠ 10 6 4
                    ♡ A K Q 2
                    ◇ 8 4
                    ♣ J 7 4 3
```

South	*West*	*North*	*East*
–	–	1 ◇	No bid
1 ♡	No bid	3 ◇	No bid
3NT	No bid	No bid	No bid

West led ♠ 3, ♠ Q was played from dummy and taken by ♠ K. East cashed ♠ A, West playing ♠ 2, and continued with ♠ J, West playing ♠ 5. These low spades indicated a club entry and East played ♣ 2. West won and cashed two more spades. Had West held ♡ A and not ♣ A he would play ♠ 9 on the third round.

The suit preference signal can also supply the valuable clue by the card selected to clear a suit.

Dealer South. Game All.

```
                    ♠ 10 7
                    ♡ K 6
                    ◊ J 6 3 2
                    ♣ A Q J 3 2
♠ K J 8 4 2                          ♠ Q 6 5
♡ A 8 4                              ♡ 10 7 3 2
◊ 5 4                                ◊ 10 9 8 7
♣ 9 7 6                              ♣ K 4
                    ♠ A 9 3
                    ♡ Q J 9 5
                    ◊ A K Q
                    ♣ 10 8 5
```

South	*West*	*North*	*East*
1NT	No bid	3NT	All pass

West leads ♠ 4 to ♠ Q which wins. East returns ♠ 6 and South holds up his ace and West wins with ♠ J. At this point any spade that West leads will have the same effect in that it will draw out the ace. Therefore West, by selecting his card carefully, can convey to his partner wherein lies his entry. In this case he leads ♠ K for the higher suit (hearts). Had he held ◊ A he would lead ♠ 2 to clear the suit.

Here is another example

Dealer South. North–South vul.

```
                    ♠ Q 10 7 6
                    ♡ 4 3 2
                    ◇ J 4
                    ♣ A 10 8 6
    ♠ K J 2                        ♠ 9 8 4
    ♡ A 8                          ♡ J 9 7 6 5
    ◇ Q 9 7 5 3                    ◇ K 10 2
    ♣ 5 3 2                        ♣ K 9
                    ♠ A 5 3
                    ♡ K Q 10
                    ◇ A 8 6
                    ♣ Q J 7 4
```

South	West	North	East
1NT	No bid	2♣	No bid
(16–18)			
2 ◇	No bid	2NT	All pass

North is borderline for his bid but considered that game in spades might be possible if South held a maximum and four spades.

West led ◇ 5 covered by ◇ J, ◇ K and ◇ 6. East returned ◇ 10, South played ◇ 8 and West overtook with ◇ Q. West next led ◇ 9 to indicate that he wanted a spade returned when East got in. Despite holding ♡ A it was important to set up the spade winner before ♡ A was knocked out. South won the third round with ◇ A and led ♣ Q, losing to ♣ K. East returned ♠ 9 and the contract was two down. On a heart return South will be able to go only one down if he guesses the heart position.

17. Deception

Contracts can often be defeated by misleading the declarer. Contracts can likewise be made by misleading the defenders. In this field the declarer has an advantage in that he has no partner to deceive. In defence, on the other hand, you have to appreciate that your partner may also be misled and this may lead to loss of mutual confidence. To give a common example it may occasionally be sound tactics to lead the two from a five card suit against No-Trumps, creating the impression that you have only four in the suit. Similarly, leading from, say, ◊ 10 8 6 4 2 you start with ◊ 4 and on the next round play ◊ 6, concealing ◊ 2, so that it may appear to be a four card suit.

Playing the card you are known to hold
This cardinal principle of defence can best be shown from the declarer's angle.

♣ A J 9 7 5 3
♣ 10 6 2   ♣ K Q
♣ 8 4

Assume the contract is in No-Trumps and South needs to make five tricks in clubs. He starts with ♣ 8 on which West plays ♣ 2, dummy ♣ 3, East ♣ Q. South wins East's return and leads ♣ 4 on which West plays ♣ 6. What should declarer play from dummy? He should play ♣ A as the only hope is to find East with ♣ K Q alone. Suppose he finesses ♣ J and it holds and East discards. The suit cannot be run as West still has ♣ K 10. The point is that once ♣ 8 brought ♣ Q from East ♣ 10 was marked in West's hand. Therefore West must play ♣ 10 on the second lead of the suit as this is a card he is known to possess. The probabilities are that South will now finesse ♣ J, losing to ♣ K as West's play is perfectly consistent with an original holding of ♣ K 10 2.

Here are further examples

♠ A 9 6 2
♠ 8 7 4   ♠ Q 10 3
♠ K J 5

South leads ♠ 2 from the table and East follows with ♠ 3

and South wins with ♠ J. South next plays ♠ K and East must follow with ♠ Q, the card he is known to hold. Now, when South plays ♠ 5 and West ♠ 8 there is the problem whether to play ♠ 9 or ♠ A from the table. If East's ♠ Q is a true card, the finesse of ♠ 9 is correct. Had East played ♠ 10 on ♠ K on the second round there would be no problem, for ♠ Q would be marked with East and would be certain to fall.

◇ A K J 8 5

◇ Q 9 4　　　　　　　　　　　　　◇ 10 6 2

◇ 7 3

South leads ◇ 7, playing in either a suit or No-Trump contract. West plays ◇ 4 and ◇ J wins. South next leads ◇ A from dummy and West should play ◇ Q as he is known to hold that card. This may create the impression that West holds ◇ Q 4 and East ◇ 10 9 6 2. If he continues with ◇ K he may be setting up a trick for East.

♡ A Q 6 4

♡ K J 10 3　　　　　　　　　　　　♡ 9 7 5

♡ 8 2

Playing in a spade contract South leads ♡ 8, West plays ♡ 3 and dummy's ♡ Q wins. When ♡ A is next played West should follow with ♡ K, otherwise South will be able to ruff the next heart low, knowing that West will follow suit holding ♡ K.

False Cards

A player is said to false card when he plays a card other than his lowest with intent to deceive the declarer. There must be intent to deceive the declarer. Thus, if third player plays a high card this is in no sense a false card. He is merely attempting to win the trick or force out a high card from declarer. Nor is the play of the higher of two cards as the start of a high–low signal for, again, there is no intent to

deceive. Here is a simple example

♠ A J 10 9

♠ 7 5 4   ♠ K Q 6

♠ 8 3 2

South leads ♠ 2 and finesses ♠ 9, East winning with ♠ K. This is a false card because standard practice is to follow suit with the lower of equal value cards. Therefore, winning with ♠ K denies possession of ♠ Q.

A common and rather pointless false card is this

♡ K 10 9 3

♡ 8 5   ♡ Q J

♡ A 7 6 4 2

South leads ♡ A and it is a common practice for East to play ♡ Q, hoping to induce a finesse against West. It is not especially clever as declarer is likely to finesse anyway as representing the best percentage play. But the point to remember is that you must vary the play. If you make a habit of playing the queen the time will inevitably arise when you are dealt the singleton knave. Now, when you follow with the knave the declarer, if he has been noting your methods, will finesse with confidence for he will know that had you held the queen and knave you would have played the queen.

There are some fairly standard situations where a false card is likely to gain

(a)   ◇ K J 8 6 4

◇ Q 7 5   ◇ 10 3

◇ A 9 2

South leads ◇ A and East plays ◇ 10. This may mislead South into placing East with ◇ Q 10 alone and play ◇ K on the next round, and West's ◇ Q is rescued.

(b)   ♠ K J 8 6 5

   ♠ 10 7 2   ♠ Q 4

                   ♠ A 9 3

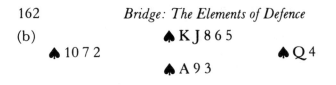

South leads ♠ A covered by ♠ 2, ♠ 5, ♠ 4 and follows with ♠ 3. It cannot hurt for West to follow with ♠ 10 to induce a finesse of ♠ J.

(c)   ♣ K J 9 8 5 4

   ♣ 7 6 2   ♣ Q 10

                   ♣ A 3

Playing in No-Trumps, South leads ♣ A, West follows with ♣ 2 and dummy with ♣ 4, East playing ♣ Q. When South next leads ♣ 3 and West follows with ♣ 6 it is quite probable that South will finesse ♣ 8. The play is quite consistent with West holding ♣ 10 7 6 2 and East ♣ Q. The merit of these false cards is that they may well be true.

A false high–low signal may serve to promote a trump trick as on these hands.

Dealer North. North–South vul.

                 ♠ A Q J 6 4
                 ♡ Q J 10 3
                 ◊ 10 4
                 ♣ K 3

♠ 9 8 7 5   ♠ 3 2
♡ 7   ♡ K 9 5
◊ A K Q 7 6 5   ◊ 8 3 2
♣ J 5   ♣ A 10 9 4 2

                 ♠ K 10
                 ♡ A 8 6 4 2
                 ◊ J 9
                 ♣ Q 8 7 6

South	West	North	East
–	–	1 ♠	No bid
2 ♡	3 ◊	3 ♡	No bid
4 ♡	No bid	No bid	No bid

West leads ◊ A and East can see three tricks (◊ A K and ♣ A). There is little hope in spades and the king of hearts appears to be ill-placed. The clubs are not likely to produce more than one trick. In the hope of promoting a trump trick East plays ◊ 8 on the opening lead and follows with ◊ 2 on the second. West duly continues with ◊ Q and South, fearful lest East should ruff with ♡ 9 thereby forcing out ♡ A, ruffs in dummy with ♡ 10. East follows with a diamond but now holds ♡ K 9 5 over ♡ Q J 3 and must make a trick.

This situation requires a little luck

$$\begin{array}{ccc} & \heartsuit \text{Q } 10\,7\,6 & \\ \heartsuit \text{A K } 4 & & \heartsuit \text{J } 8\,2 \\ & \heartsuit 9\,5\,3 & \end{array}$$

West leads ♡ A and East plays ♡ 8. West continues with ♡ K and East completes his high–low peter with ♡ 2. When West next leads ♡ 4 can declarer be blamed for playing ♡ 10 from dummy and losing to ♡ J? Why play ♡ Q when East was going to ruff?

In this hand West managed to divert declarer from a winning line.

```
                    ♠ J 7 2
                    ♡ A Q
                    ◇ 7 4 3 2
                    ♣ K J 10 2
     ♠ 10 8 3                        ♠ K 6
     ♡ 10 9 8 7                      ♡ K J 6 4 2
     ◇ A 8 5                         ◇ J 10 9 6
     ♣ A 8 7                         ♣ 6 5
                    ♠ A Q 9 5 4
                    ♡ 5 3
                    ◇ K Q
                    ♣ Q 9 4 3
```

South	West	North	East
1 ♠	No bid	2 ♣	No bid
3 ♣	No bid	3 ♠	No bid
4 ♠	No bid	No bid	No bid

West led ♡ 10 and ♡ Q lost to ♡ K; Dummy won the return. Having lost a heart and with two aces missing South could not afford to lose a trump. Missing ♠ 10 the choice lay between leading ♠ J, intending to take a further finesse towards ♠ Q 9, assuming ♠ K to be with East, and leading a low spade to ♠ Q, hoping for ♠ K x to be with East. This appeared to be the better chance and ♠ 2 was played on which East put ♠ 6 and South ♠ Q. West could see that South had adopted a winning line and sought to divert him from it by playing ♠ 8. This succeeded as South crossed to dummy with a club and led ♠ J, hoping to find East with ♠ K x x and West ♠ 10 x in which case East would cover and ♠ A would pin ♠ 10. This did not work out as hoped and West's ♠ 10 set the contract.

The next hand originally occurred in a Par Contest organized by Waddington's before the war. A Par Contest involves a number of prepared hands where points are awarded for bidding, leads, play and defence. On this hand a neat false card persuaded declarer that his finesse had succeeded and consequently dissuaded him from taking another which would succeed.

Dealer South. North–South vul.

```
                    ♠ K J 10
                    ♡ J 10 6
                    ◇ 4 3
                    ♣ K J 10 7 5
  ♠ 9 7 3                              ♠ 8 5 4 2
  ♡ 9 4 2                              ♡ K 8 5 3
  ◇ K Q J 7 6                          ◇ 9 8 5
  ♣ 8 3                                ♣ A Q
                    ♠ A Q 6
                    ♡ A Q 7
                    ◇ A 10 2
                    ♣ 9 6 4 2
```

South	West	North	East
1NT	No bid	3NT	All pass

West leads ◇ K and South holds up until the third round. He has five top tricks and needs four more and naturally attacks clubs. He leads ♣ 9, West plays ♣ 3, North ♣ 5 and East ♣ A. East returns ♡ 3. As West is clearly marked with diamonds it would be foolish to risk the finesse and let West in with ♡ K for his diamonds. So South won with ♡ A and led ♣ 2, confidently finessing ♣ 10 and losing to ♣ Q. East now cashed ♡ K for the setting trick.

Had East won the first club with ♣ Q South would have had only eight tricks and would need to take the heart finesse. Knowing that the heart finesse was right East succeeded in convincing declarer that there was no need to take it.

Finally, a brilliant false card that succeeded in defeating an apparently impregnable slam. It was reported by the American writer, Fred Karpin, and occurred in the U.S. Masters Championship in 1955.

Dealer West. Love All.

```
                 ♠ Q 7 5
                 ♡ 8
                 ◇ A Q 10 9 7
                 ♣ A K 10 6
♠ J                              ♠ 10 6
♡ A J 10 9 7 6 4                 ♡ K 5 2
◇ 6                              ◇ 8 4 3 2
♣ Q J 9 4                        ♣ 8 7 5 2
                 ♠ A K 9 8 4 3 2
                 ♡ Q 3
                 ◇ K J 5
                 ♣ 3
```

South	West	North	East
–	4 ♡	No bid	No bid
4 ♠	No bid	6 ♠	All pass

West led ♡ A and East played ♡ K. West naturally continued with ♡ J and South ruffed with ♠ Q from table to avoid the overruff. When East followed with a low heart South stopped to consider why he should false card with ♡ K. The obvious answer was that East held ♠ J 10 6 and wanted to induce declarer to ruff with ♠ Q and thus promote ♠ J. So South led ♠ 7 and when East followed with ♠ 6 finessed, losing to singleton ♠ J. As Karpin stated, before criticising declarer, East might still have played ♡ K if he held ♠ J 10 6 and in that case declarer would have been a temporary genius instead of a gullible victim.

18. Timing

The time element plays an important part in both Declarer play and defence. For example, playing in a contract of Four Spades there may well be ten potential winners, but it can easily happen that four tricks are lost before ten are won.

Similarly in defence, there may be enough tricks to defeat the contract, but declarer may win the race and make his quota of tricks before the defenders can get theirs. The importance of timing the defence has been frequently stated earlier in this book. Here are three final examples.

Dealer East. East–West vul.

```
              ♠ Q 8
              ♡ Q J 9 6 3
              ◇ Q J 2
              ♣ Q 9 5
♠ 7 2                        ♠ A 6 5
♡ 10 8 7 4                   ♡ A K 2
◇ 10 9 6 4 3                 ◇ K 7 5
♣ A 4                        ♣ K J 8 3
              ♠ K J 10 9 4 3
              ♡ 5
              ◇ A 8
              ♣ 10 7 6 2
```

South	West	North	East
–	–	–	1NT
			(16–18)
2 ♠	No bid	No bid	No bid

West leads ♣ A and East encourages with ♣ 8. West continues with ♣ 4 and East covers ♣ 9 with ♣ J, South having played ♣ 2 and ♣ 6.

West clearly has a doubleton so East can see three tricks

(*repeated for convenience*)

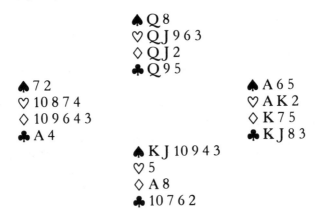

in clubs, one spade and possibly two hearts. But on the overcall South is likely to hold six spades and is marked with four clubs, leaving him with three cards divided between hearts and diamonds. It is therefore probable that he has only one heart in which case the defensive winners are reduced to five. West can ruff the fourth club but he will not have a high enough trump to beat dummy's ♠ Q.

But with careful timing six tricks can be made. At trick three East returns ♣ 3 which West ruffs with ♠ 2. West now returns ♠ 7 and East wins with ♠ A and removes the last trump from the table. South successfully finesses ◇ Q but must still lose to ♠ A, ♣ K and ♡ A.

In the next hand West thought he had got off play with a safe card, but he hadn't.

Dealer East. Love All.

```
                    ♠ 5 3
                    ♡ K 7 4
                    ◇ Q 5 4 3
                    ♣ J 10 9 6
♠ A 4 2                                    ♠ 7
♡ 10 9 2                                   ♡ A Q J 8 5 3
◇ K J 10 7 2                               ◇ 9 8
♣ 4 3                                      ♣ Q 8 7 2
                    ♠ K Q J 10 9 8 6
                    ♡ 6
                    ◇ A 6
                    ♣ A K 5
```

South	West	North	East
–	–	–	1 ♡
4 ♠	No bid	No bid	No bid

West led ♡ 10 which held, and continued with ♡ 9, covered by ♡ K and ♡ A and ruffed by South with ♠ 6. South led ♠ K which won and continued with ♠ Q which West won. West passively returned his last heart, ruffed by South and the last trump was drawn. South now played ◇ A and ◇ 6. West won with ◇ K and could not avoid giving the lead to dummy with either a diamond, or a free finesse in clubs.

After winning with ♠ A West should have led back his last spade and retained his third heart as a safe exit card.

This last example will come as a shock to those who have been brought up on the principle of playing up to weakness and not into strength. But as I have constantly stressed, you cannot play this game by sticking rigidly to "rules". Obviously it is correct in the majority of cases to lead up to weakness for the reasons given earlier in this book. Declarer is compelled to play high from his hand in the second position if he wants to win the trick. But there are exceptions as shown on this hand.

Dealer North. East–West vul.

```
                  ♠ 8 3
                  ♡ K 6 2
                  ◊ A Q 6
                  ♣ A Q J 7 6
   ♠ 7                              ♠ A K 4
   ♡ Q J 10 9 4                     ♡ A 8 7 5 3
   ◊ 10 7 3 2                       ◊ K J 5
   ♣ 8 5 3                          ♣ K 2
                  ♠ Q J 10 9 6 5 2
                  ♡ –
                  ◊ 9 8 4
                  ♣ 10 9 4
```

South	West	North	East
–	–	1 ♣	Dbl.
4 ♠	No bid	No bid	Dbl.
No bid	No bid	No bid	

West leads ♡ Q, dummy plays ♡ K, East ♡ A and South ruffs. South leads ♠ Q and East wins. East can see two tricks in spades and presumably one in clubs. South's heart void was a disappointment but there should be at least one trick in diamonds with ◊ A Q 6 under ◊ K J 5. So the defence might make four or even five tricks. But this is where the time factor emerges. South may easily make ten tricks before the defence gets four. Suppose East returns a heart, South ruffs and leads ♠ J to ♠ A. East plods on with a heart or returns a trump. South, with the last trump drawn, leads ♣ 10 and finesses. East wins but South makes the rest.

When in with the first trump lead East must realize that his partner can have no tricks and that he must defeat the contract virtually on his own. He needs to establish a diamond trick while he has two entries (♠ A and ♣ K) and must lead ◊ 5 into dummy's ◊ A Q 6. He has to hope that partner holds ◊ 10. Even ◊ 9 might do if South held ◊ 10 8 x as he might play ◊ 8. East gets in with ♠ A and leads ◊ K or ◊ J and establishes the fourth trick for the defence while still holding ♣ K.

BRIDGE TIPS BY WORLD MASTERS

'In this book Terence Reese develops and enlarges the famous Bols Bridge Tips. The Reese style is apparent throughout, but the real merit is that twenty-four of the world's best players have put their ideas into print.'

Derek Rimington, *Jersey Evening Post*

'Terence Reese has polished the raw material with the skill of a diamond cutter, adding his own comments on the value of the instruction.'

Jeremy Flint, *The Times*

'*Bridge Tips by World Masters* is a tour de force. There are twenty-four tips from twenty-four experts. All are worthy of study and some are quite outstanding.'

International Popular Bridge Magazine

ACOL IN THE 90s
Terence Reese & David Bird

'No tournament player can afford to miss this book. It is an introduction to the modern state of the art.'

Derek Rimington, *Jersey Evening Post*

'Well presented and clearly written by two first-class authors.'

International Popular Bridge Monthly

'Sets out clearly the general framework of bidding. This book will prove of great value to the experienced tournament player.'

G.C.H. Fox, *Daily Telegraph*

BRIDGE PLAY TECHNIQUE
Pat Cotter & Derek Rimington

'In 34 categories from *Assumption* through *Coups, Safety Plays, Timing* and *Unblocking* this book includes most of the techniques of declarer play and defence. The first few pages are on elementary card combinations but, as the authors point out, this book is not for beginners.

Many of the hands used as examples are famous for employing the designated techniques. The analyses, all sound, are not given in lesson form but as explanations of the techniques.

The book does not claim new ideas but shows techniques dealt with by many authors. Few have glossarized and compiled the material so well.'

Jack Wynns, *American Contract Bridge League Journal*

SQUEEZE PLAY MADE EASY
Terence Reese & Patrick Jourdain

'Dick Lederer used to say that if you played your cards in the right order you wouldn't miss any simple squeeze. Maybe, but you have to understand the order.'

Boris Schapiro, *Sunday Times*

'Nobody can call himself expert who is not also an expert in squeeze play. This book perfectly shows the way.'

Jean Besse, *Journal de Genève*

MODERN BRIDGE CONVENTIONS
William S. Root & Richard Pavlicek

'This fine book, by two great players, conveys in depth many conventions that are popular with the experts. Many of the problems that arise from them are stated and solved for the first time.'

Alan Truscott

'This work by Bill Root and Richard Pavlicek fills a long-standing gap in the field of bridge literature - a thorough and comprehensive treatise on popular bidding conventions. Every bridge enthusiast should have it on his bookshelf.'

Alfred Sheinwold

'Highly recommended.'

Albert Dormer, *The Times*

THE PLAY OF THE HAND
William S. Root

'I strongly recommend this book to anyone who wants to improve his declarer play.'

E.P.C. Cotter, *Financial Times*

'William S. Root is considered by many to be the world's premier bridge teacher.'

Omar Sharif

'It is without doubt destined to become one of the classics on play'

Irish Bridge Journal

THE PLAY OF THE CARDS
Terence Reese & Albert Dormer

'The book covers the whole range of play from opening leads to end plays, and, as we may expect from the authors, the illustrative hands and deals are well chosen.'

George F. Hervey, *The Field*

'*The Play of the Cards* covers the ground from elementary principles to the threshold of expert play.'

Rixi Markus, *Guardian Weekly*

THE EXPERT GAME
Terence Reese

'The best bridge book ever written.'

Pat Cotter, *Country Life*

'If there is a way to bring home to the average player the art and technique of first-class card play then Terence Reese in this book has found it. It is a real effort to show the bridge student the thought processes of the expert player, and one which, in my view, succeeds to an unexpected extent.'

Rixi Markus, *Guardian*

PLAY BRIDGE WITH THE EXPERTS
Derek Rimington

'From every one of the hundred hands in this book there is a lesson to be learnt, be it in bidding or in play or in both, but the most important lesson of all is in the art of thinking the expert way. The occasional lapses, as Josephine Culbertson's and Colonel Beasley's, are no less instructive than the numerous examples of polished technique.'

Victor Mollo, *Irish Bridge Journal*

'Spans the history of contract bridge and is instructive as well as entertaining.'

Albert Dormer, *The Times*

REESE ON PLAY

'One of the great classics...the book covers every aspect of advanced play and lays particular stress on control and communications. An important book for any player who wishes to raise his standard.'

R. A. Priday, *Sunday Telegraph*

'One of the greatest books ever written about play.'

Frank Cayley, *Sydney Morning Herald*

PRECISION BIDDING & PRECISION PLAY
Terence Reese

'Terence Reese, in his usual logical style, has cleared up many sequences and situations which are missing in earlier books on the system and he has added some innovations.'

Rixi Markus, *Guardian*

'By far the best book we have seen on the Precision system.'

Bridge World

'Reese, as always, has written a clear, thorough and authoritative book.'

C. C. Wei

COMPETITIVE BIDDING
Jeremy Flint & Richard Sharp

'It is in the field of competitive bidding that most bridge tournaments are won or lost. In this comprehensive account of modern methods the authors stress the importance of judgement while advancing some provocative new ideas.'

Terence Reese

'A standard work on competitive bidding. It will be of use to every player irrespective of system or standard of play. Competitive doubles, co-operative doubles, sputnik doubles, and lead directing doubles are all put under the spotlight and explained in detail.

A good book for any working partnership.'

Irish Bridge Journal

OPENING LEADS
Robert B. Ewen

'Mr Ewen's book covers the subject of opening leads from every possible angle. The advice given is well presented and backed up with good reasoning. An excellent book, strongly recommended.'

G.C.H.Fox, *Daily Telegraph*

'Original and important...bridges the gap between the average player and the expert.'

Alan Truscott, *New York Times*

PRECISION BIDDING FOR EVERYONE
Charles H. Goren & C. C. Wei

'An up-to-date text book of the system which covers every aspect of basic Precision, liberally illustrated with example deals and quizzes. Ideal for teachers and newcomers to the system.'

R. A. Priday, *Sunday Telegraph*

'The system is played in many styles, but the early form was best.'

Terence Reese, *Evening Standard*

HOW TO READ YOUR OPPONENTS' CARDS
Mike Lawrence

'A workmanlike effort with a straightforward objective: to introduce the reader to some of the experts' secrets. May be new and of value even to the experienced player.'

Bridge World

'A difficult subject well handled. Recommended for above-average readers who are keen to sharpen up their declarer play.'

Bridge Plus

BRIDGE: THE COMPLETE GUIDE TO DEFENSIVE PLAY
Frank Stewart

'Defensive technique is difficult to master so I am pleased to recommend an excellent new book on the subject.'

R.A. Priday, *Sunday Telegraph*

'This is a good book for the serious player.'

Albert Dormer, *The Times*